Off The
SWITZERLAND

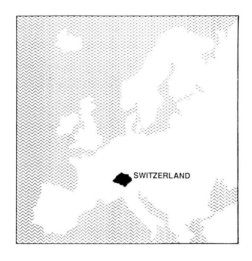

Off the Beaten Track
SWITZERLAND

Kenneth Loveland • John Marshall • Richard Sale

MOORLAND PUBLISHING

Published by:
Moorland Publishing Co Ltd,
Moor Farm Road West, Ashbourne,
Derbyshire, DE6 1HD, England

ISBN 0 86190 497 4 (UK)

The Globe Pequot Press,
6 Business Park Road,
PO Box 833, Old Saybrook,
Connecticut 06475-0833

ISBN 1-56440-300-9 (USA)

First published 1989. Reprinted 1990
Revised 2nd edition 1994
© Moorland Publishing Co Ltd 1994

Front Cover: *Swiss National Tourist Office*

Black and white illustrations have been
supplied by:
ETT, Bellinzona; K. Loveland; Lugano
Tourist Office; J. Marshall; R. Sale;
Swiss Post-Bus Service, Bern; Swiss
National Tourist Office.

Colour illustrations have been supplied
by:
J. Marshall; R. Sale; Swiss National
Tourist Office .

Printed in Hong Kong by:
Wing King Tong Co Ltd

British Library Cataloguing in Publication Data:
A catalogue record for this book is available from the British Library.

Library of Congress Cataloging-in-Publication Data
Loveland, Kenneth
    Off the beaten track. Switzerland/Kenneth Loveland, John Marshall, Richard
Sale. — Rev. 2nd ed.
        p. cm.
    Includes Index.
    ISBN 1-56440-300-9
    1. Switzerland— Guidebooks.   I. Marshall, John. II. Sale, Richard, 1946-
III. Title. IV Title: Switzerland.
DQ16.L68 1994
914.9404'73 —dc20   93-4065
                                                                                  CIP

Contents

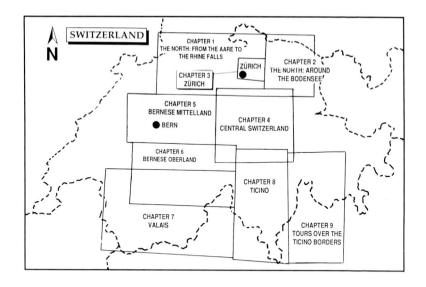

Museums and Other Places of Interest

Wherever possible opening times have been checked, and are as accurate as possible. However, during the main holiday period they may be extended. Conversely, outside the main season, there may be additional restrictions, or shorter hours. Local tourist offices will always be able to advise you.

Generally all churches, and abbeys and monasteries still in use, are open every day, except during services. You should remember that these are places of worship as well as historical monuments, so dress and conduct should be appropriate.

Note on Maps

The maps for each chapter, while comprehensive, are not designed to be used as route maps, but to locate the main towns, villages and places of interest.

Introduction

Western Europe is a continent of great diversity, well visited not just by travellers from other parts of the globe but by the inhabitants of its own member countries. Within the year-round processes of trade and commerce, but more particularly during the holiday season, there is a great surging interchange of nationalities as one country's familiar attractions are left behind for those of another.

It is true that frontiers are blurred by ever quicker travel and communications, and that the sharing of cultures, made possible by an increasingly sophisticated media network, brings us closer in all senses to our neighbours. Yet essential differences do exist, differences which lure us abroad on our annual migrations in search of new horizons, fresh sights, sounds and smells, discovery of unknown landscapes and people.

Countless resorts have evolved for those among us who simply crave sun, sea and the reassuring press of humanity. There are, too, established tourist 'sights' with which a country or region has become associated and to which clings, all too often, a suffocating shroud — the manifestations of mass tourism in the form of crowds and entrance charges, the destruction of authentic atmosphere, cynical exploitation. Whilst this is by no means typical of all well known tourist attractions, it is familiar enough to act as a disincentive for those of more independent spirit who value personal discovery above prescribed experience and who would rather avoid the human conveyor belt of queues, traffic jams and packed accommodation.

It is for such travellers that this guidebook has been written. In its pages, no more than passing mention is made of the famous, the well documented, the already glowingly described — other guidebooks will satisfy the appetite for such orthodox tourist information. Instead, the reader is taken if not to unknown then to relatively unvisited places — literally 'off the beaten track'. Through the specialist

knowledge of the authors, visitors using this guidebook are assured
of gaining insights into the country's heartland whose heritage lies
largely untouched by the tourist industry. Occasionally the reader is
urged simply to take a sideways step from a site of renowned tourist
interest to discover a place perhaps less sensational, certainly less
frequented but often of equivalent fascination.

From wild, scantily populated countryside whose footpaths and
byways are best navigated by careful map reading, to negotiating the
side streets of towns and cities, travelling 'off the beaten track' can be
rather more demanding than following in the footsteps of countless
thousands before you. The way may be less clear, more adventurous
and individualistic, but opportunities do emerge for real discovery
in an age of increasing dissatisfaction with the passive predictability
of conventional holidaymaking. With greater emphasis on exploring
'off the beaten track', the essence of Switzerland is more likely to be
unearthed and its true flavours relished to the full.

Martin Collins
Series Editor

1 • The North: From the Aare to the Rhine Falls

Olten

Towns which stand at crossroads can be at a disadvantage. Everybody passes through en route to somewhere else, and not many stay. Olten is rather like that. Regular visitors to Switzerland will almost inevitably have changed trains there at some time or another. Olten is where the line from Zürich to Bern and on to the resorts of Lac Léman and to Geneva crosses that from Basle to Lucerne, the famous St Gotthard Pass, the Italianate Ticino, thence to Milan and Italy itself. A busy place at which most tourists cast no more than a cursory glance and pass on.

Olten deserves better. It has several features which make it a useful starting point for a tour across north Switzerland, a kind of advance taster of the delights to come. It nestles cosily around the Aare, which is crossed by an old wooden bridge that immediately reminds you of its bigger brother in Lucerne. Walk over it, and you are in the old town, all peace and quiet. The focal point is the Rathaus (town hall), with a fine sixteenth-century tower that dominates the many charming houses in the vicinity, and one of its most striking houses offers a reminder that the Swiss have been at the business of looking after travellers for a long time. The Herberg zum Goldenen Löwen is on the site of an inn which was active five hundred years ago. The present guest house was erected in the eighteenth century.

With only 20,000 inhabitants, Olten is a lively and flourishing town. Because of its pattern of communications, they will tell you it is an ideal place for a rendezvous. Two thirds of the Swiss population can reach it in less than an hour by road or rail. The manufacturing industries on which the town's importance has been built include iron, wire, linen, cotton and shoes, and it is a major centre for the Swiss book publishing trade. But Olten, in common with so many small Swiss towns, has been careful not to buy prosperity at the

Olten

expense of damage to its character. That remains.

Before heading north, you might care to spend a day discovering the Oberaargau (Upper Aargau). Ignore the motorway, and take the road south for **Langenthal** (route 13). This is the capital of the region, with gentle sloping hills, beech forests and wooded ridges in the background. Stop at **Wynau** to see the rapids, and make a detour to the left, north of Langenthal, to see the former monastery of St Urban, which has a famous baroque church.

Back at Olten, follow route 5 north-east to Aarau.

Aarau

There is a pamphlet which tells the reader how to see Aarau in 45 minutes. But who would want to? You need time to savour all it has to offer, time to absorb the atmosphere of a town so steeped in history, where the past has been jealously guarded in the very shadow of a brisk commercial development.

There is the Aarau around the Bahnhofstrasse, a powerful thoroughfare which cries success and prosperity aloud, wide as a Parisian boulevard, fringed with banks, commercial buildings, department stores, and all the paraphernalia of a sophisticated modern city, though, even with its developing environs, it accommodates not much more than 50,000 people. But turn a corner, walk a few yards,

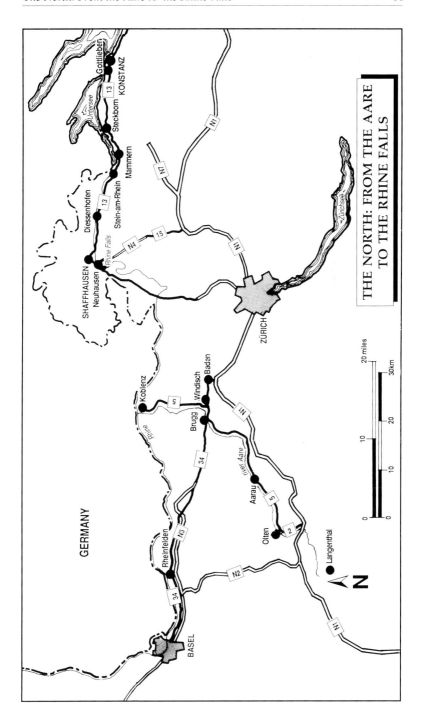

THE NORTH: FROM THE AARE TO THE RHINE FALLS

The picturesque old town of Aarburg, just a few minutes drive south of Olten

and suddenly you have stepped back centuries, to the old town, a place where it is sleepy quiet and easy to believe all they say about Aarau's eventful past.

As you stroll through the narrow streets, be sure to look upwards at regular intervals, and you will discover why they call Aarau the town of the beautiful gables. It has several surprises. The first is to

Old town gate, Aarau

discover that it has two gates, and to find out why, it is necessary to learn a little about the town's origins and early history. The date generally reckoned for the birth of Aarau is 1240. In or about that year Count Hartmann of Kyburg built the town on a rock that was surrounded on three sides by the river Aare. The plan was so concise and symmetrical that its lines can still be traced today, especially if you look down on Aarau from a height. The count built a wall around the town and reckoned he was secure. No doubt he was safe from

Classical houses, Aarau

enemies, but not from fate. Within three decades, the house of the Kyburgs had died out, and in marched the Habsburgs. Aarau became absorbed in their empire, which eventually sprawled across a large area of Europe, imposing both its rule and culture on a curiously assorted collection of peoples and languages.

The town received its charter in 1283 from Rudolf himself, who, more than any other ruler of the line, was responsible for building the Habsburg power. (The charter still exists and the seal can be seen in the town museum, which more than repays a visit.) But what was good enough for the Kybergs was hardly likely to be good enough for the Habsburgs, so they built a second wall, only a few yards away. Which is why you can pass through two town gates within a minute.

Brief though their influence may have been, the Kyburgs are still commemorated by a statue to Count Hartmann between the two

gates. However, it is the watch tower beside them that commands the
attention. It dominates the town from any direction, looking across
the river and seeming to peer cautiously at the last limb of the Jura
mountains in the distance, a reminder of the days when an enemy
might appear in the valley below. Beside the arms of Aarau, it also
bears those of Bern. The Habsburgs, though they kept a tight hold on
much of Europe, were not the longest serving overlords of Aarau.
The Swiss yearning for independence was soon aflame throughout
the cantons, and led to the famous Confederation. Gradually, the
hold of the Habsburgs weakened. The Swiss proved to be ferocious
fighters, and in 1415 the Habsburgs were driven out of the Aargau,
but although Aarau was allowed to keep the rights granted by the
Habsburgs, it was soon clear to the Argovians that Swiss victory
merely meant they had exchanged one landlord for another. For four
hundred years the town was subject to Bern, and had no real influence on Swiss politics until 1798. Though the Argovians shared in the
Swiss military triumphs of the Middle Ages, and always under their
own flag, they did so under the strict command of Bern. So the arms
of Bern are there to this day.

Before passing on to the maze of closely clustered streets of the old
town, spare another glance at the tower. The clock that adorns it is
four hundred years old, still keeps perfect time, and chimes its
reminders every quarter of an hour. No excuse for turning up late for
an appointment in Aarau. It is a municipal duty for someone to climb
up to wind it every day. A sundial tells us that time was important
even before the Swiss started making clocks and watches. But this
one is a curiosity, decorated with fantastic figures depicting the
dance of death. These, however, are not part of Aarau's medieval
history, but were painted in the 1950s by Felix Hoffmann, a local
artist.

A walk around Aarau brings one face to face with two architectural styles that are clearly defined, quite different, but which make
a genial harmony. One is Gothic, the other baroque. This too is a
reflection of Aarau history. Despite the control of Bern, trade and
industry grew and, as they did, many imposing structures appeared
in the sixteenth to eighteenth centuries. The fine town church, the
Rathaus (town hall), confident-looking houses with well proportioned façades and artistically modelled gables all date from this
period and proclaim that money was not too much of a problem to
the burghers, who were steadily becoming more wealthy. The town
brook, now covered over, became a source of energy for saw mills
and other trades. Even into the nineteenth century there were thirty

water wheels turning along it. Factories appeared outside the town, as did the spacious new houses of the merchants. The move to the country outside had begun, and so had Aarau's export trade, at that time mostly textiles.

Inevitably, the control of Bern was no longer tolerable. Eventually, a distinction came Aarau's way which resulted in one of its most striking thoroughfares. After a walk through the old town, the visitor will turn into the Laurenzenvorstadt, and note at once its noble sweep, with its avenue of classic design and proportions. It is the record of a glory that was short lived, but makes an illustrious event in Aarau's history.

The domination of Bern was thrown off without much trouble, a tree of liberty was planted in the Graben (Square) in the first flush of freedom, and in 1798, Aarau became not only the capital of the canton of Aargau, but the seat of the newly proclaimed Helvetian republic. The politicians, army officers, civil servants and government officials all descended and Aarau, of course, was too small to accommodate them in the style to which they were accustomed. So almost overnight, Aarau decided on a major expansion scheme, and work began on the Laurenzenvorstadt. All very enterprising, but within six months, with the builders not far advanced into the job, the Helvetian government decided to move to Lucerne. Undismayed, Aarau carried on with the building of the Laurenzenvorstadt to house its responsibilities as the capital of the canton. And that is how the town collected that surprising classical street which stands apart from all the rest.

Among the artisans who contributed to Aarau's fame in medieval times were the gunsmiths, swordsmiths, cutlers and bell-founders. And in recent years, the bell-founders, still active, have forged an important link of friendship with the people of the United States. A much-remembered day is 16 April 1976, when representatives of America and Switzerland met there to celebrate the handing over of the bell cast in Aarau for the United Methodist church of Washington, DC.

Aarau is sometimes called the garden town because there is so much green and such easy access to the open countryside through which the Aare curves. The canton of Aargau itself earned the title of 'the culture state' as early as the mid-nineteenth century, through its wise development of education (including one of the first teacher-training colleges) and the arts, a tradition which has obviously continued, judging by the numerous advertisements for concerts, and particularly the Fine Arts Museum in the Rathausplatz. A walk across the wooden bridge into the Schlössli in the heart of the town leads to another museum with a fascinating record of how Aarau life has developed.

Aarau is a kind town of warm-hearted, helpful people. You meet every consideration in the shops, and there is a most efficient tourist office where the staff give every assistance and, if asked, will produce an English speaking guide to show you round. But it deserves much more than 45 minutes. And before you leave, try the local chocolates. They're superb.

After Aarau, it really is a question of how far, how soon. Brugg, on a direct road to the north-east should be visited, and so should Baden, just off the motorway in roughly the same direction. So it may be best to stay off the motorway and see Brugg first, continuing on route 5 and following the Aare.

Brugg

The road from Aarau to Brugg passes through **Bad Schinznach**, a health resort with one of the richest sulphur springs in Europe. Brugg itself is an attractive town, situated at the meeting place of three rivers, the Aare, the Reuss and the Limmat. Its situation has made it an important centre for both trade and tourism. The town has some fascinating historical buildings, among which must be mentioned the old Town Hall with its Black Tower, the Latin school with its allegorical front, the salt house with its striking black and white shutters, the house where Pestalozzi, the Swiss educational reformer, died in 1827, a parish church dating from 1480, and a cluster of houses in a happy jumble of styles around the Heimatsmuseum. There are stylish fountains, too. The Romans had a settlement near here at *Vindonissa*, and Brugg's Vindonissa Museum has many relics of their occupation.

Brugg is a convenient place from which to explore an interesting and unspoiled area around. There are over a hundred miles of signposted walks, including those in the quaint Schenkenberger valley with its vineyard villages and farmers' inns. The Bozberg plateau has fine views of the Alps. Favourite excursions are to the Habsburg castle, the very cradle of the Habsburg dynasty, perched on a hillock among green woods; to several other castles in the area; and to the many attractions of the countryside on the doorstep of **Windisch**. This is a small town of 7,000 people through which the motorist passes on the way to Baden, itself only a short distance from Brugg on a direct road to the east. But don't pass too quickly. There is plenty to see around here.

Windisch gets its name from *Vindonissa*, where in the first century AD, the Romans built a military camp to protect the strategically vital crossing of the Rhine. They stayed for four hundred years, and left plenty to record their occupation. The most notable evidence is the amphitheatre. The grassed oval arena, with its high embankment against a background of slender trees, should be visited. There are remains of gates and watch towers, and a Roman water pipeline is still in use.

The monastery of Königsfelden today houses a psychiatric clinic. The Habsburgs laid the foundation on the site where King Albrecht was killed in 1308. The monastery church is one of the treasures of north Switzerland, and its eleven colourful fourteenth-century choir windows, with their deep reds and blues catching the morning light, have few equals for their richly contrasted beauty. Famed throughout the land, they merit a detour. Yet for most visitors from overseas, Windisch with its treasure is definitely off the beaten track.

Baden

Anyone approaching Baden with the built-in idea that all spa towns are alike is in for a surprise. Baden is different.

There are really two Badens. One is the elegant collection of hotels where, as the town's name suggests, you can bathe for your health just as the Romans did 2,000 years ago, but in much greater comfort and with considerably more expert supervision. But there is that other Baden, just a short walk away (or an even shorter bus ride) with a quaint medieval quarter where you can wander amid graceful patrician houses, delightfully styled and decorated, and admire the care with which they have been preserved.

Since those warm springs were the principal reason for the existence of Baden in the earliest days, perhaps they should be dealt with first. They are the most mineral-rich springs in Switzerland. The Romans put great value on the sulphur baths which they knew as *Aquae Helvetiae*. But they could never have imagined the extent to which their fame would spread, so much so that today, at certain times of the year, visitors to the spa almost double Baden's population.

Stroll around a spa (and the atmosphere of relaxation hardly invites you to go any faster) and you become lulled into a state in which you would hardly be surprised to see a monarch emerge from the portals of an hotel. Baden is not so different in that respect. There is still something of the well fed confidence of the years before World War I about it, and not a little of the self-deluding establishment

The medieval city of Baden

complacence of the years before World War II. Holidays in medicinal spas were then the privilege of the wealthy. But that is no longer the case. With characteristic business acumen, the Swiss spas saw the renaissance of the classical water therapy on the way, beckoning all sections of society, and they have turned it to good account. Baden has been in the vanguard. The crowned heads and aristocrats may be in short supply today, but Baden is busier than ever.

There are all sorts of package spa breaks on offer. They say it takes about three weeks for a cure to work, and most Baden packages are based on this, although some are streamlined to 14 days. All-in

arrangements include air fare, full board, initial medical consulta-
tion, thermal baths, mud-packs, massages, passes for various insti-
tutions and facilities in the town, and vouchers for the Baden bus
shuttle which links the spa with the old quarter and the shops. There
is also a beauty package based on a 7-days treatment.

It is a special feature of Baden that the hot springs belong to the
hotels. Originally, they were the property of the crown, but in time
they passed to the local aristocrats. They leased them to the spa
innkeepers, who eventually became rich enough to purchase them.
So every hotel has its own spring and therapeutic installations which
are, however, available to the general public at certain times of the
day. Full details of all the package offers and general spa facilities can
be obtained from the Baden Tourist Office.

But you can have a fascinating time in Baden without paying too
much attention to the spa. For Baden is one of the 'Ten Typical Swiss
Towns' and that in itself is a guarantee of something individual. In
1978, it was decided to select ten small towns which, because of their
beautifully preserved old quarters, ambience of arts and crafts, and
situation away from the routine tourist tracks, would be a family
unto themselves through their subtle relationship of styles, and give
a cross-section of Swiss life of today and yesterday. Baden is one, and
it is easy to see why it was chosen. The old quarter is indeed a
concentration of Swiss life as it once was. Baden has taken care of its
past, rescuing old houses from decay, restoring where necessary and
always taking care that new colours blend. As old houses are re-
paired, many new or forgotten treasures have come to light, such as
old frescoes which were once thoughtlessly painted over. Here the
visitor can wander around without hindrance, as most of the antique
area is now a pedestrian zone. The town had Switzerland's first
railway tunnel, driven deep under the ridge beneath the Stein ruins
(a considerable engineering feat in those days) and this has been
widened to take the road as well, so that Baden is virtually free of
through traffic.

An abiding memory of Baden is the harmony of the old town. The
lovely oriel windows, the shapely gables, the cobbled streets, the
carved doorways, the murals and frescoes, all add up to an artistic
totality. And as you would expect in a town of enterprise, some of
these buildings have been sensibly adapted to modern use. For
example, the Kornhaus, a former granary in Kronengasse, which is
now principally a young people's centre. On the top floor there is an
art gallery where the young artists can exhibit and sell their work, in
the cellar an experimental theatre where anything goes.

Bathing in the open air thermal pool, Baden

The Gothic room in the old town hall should be visited. It has an important place in European history for it was here that the peace treaty was signed that finally brought an end to the War of the Spanish Succession. The peace of Utrecht ended the war proper in 1713, but desultory skirmishes carried on until 1714. In that year, Prince Eugene of Savoy (representing the emperor) and Marshal de

Villars (representing Louis XIV) met in the Gothic room, and signed the final peace document. The room has some striking windows bearing the stained glass coats of arms of the Swiss cantons, and can be visited when the district court, which has been meeting there since 1876, is not in session.

There is a notable sculpture on the north front of the town church representing the Mount of Olives. It is by Bartholomäus Cades, a Wurttemberg sculptor who worked in Baden, and was given by a town councillor of the Dorer family in 1630. His coat of arms appears there and can also be seen decorating the Hotel Bären. The shutters protecting the sculpture are opened only during Holy Week.

The river Limmat flows through Baden and is crossed by an old wooden bridge. Next to it stands the former bailiff's castle which is now a historical museum housing several treasures, one of which has a link with America. This is the ornate Lion Bowl, designed in 1688 by the Rapperswil goldsmith Heinrich Dumeisen (1653-1723). This remarkable piece has historic as well as artistic interest, for the intricately worked base is the only contemporaneous illustration of the town's fortifications as they were after their re-building in 1675-88. Bernhart Silberysen was the mayor in charge of the restoration, and the town council presented him with this bowl in thanks. But the fortifications were demolished again in 1712, before any other record had been made. Later, the bowl was sold by the Silberysen family, and was next heard of when it was acquired by the American financier J. Pierpont Morgan. On his death it went to the Wadsworth Atheneum in Hartford. In 1978, it was returned to the Baden museum on loan.

Baden's railway station is the oldest in Switzerland, and owes its existence partly to the Swiss love of hot rolls for breakfast. The line from Zürich became known as the *Spanischbrötlibahn* ('Spanish roll line'). These rolls were a speciality of Baden, and the people of Zürich liked them so much that a special train used to leave Baden early every morning so that they were in Zürich fresh and in time for breakfast.

There are a number of industries around Baden, all sited with typical Swiss discretion so as not to bruise the town's charm. As it happens, Baden has more than commercial prosperity for which to thank its industries. One of the most important is Brown Bovary engineering, and Charles Brown, a descendant of one of the founders, has recently bequeathed his superb private art collection to the town. This is undoubtedly going to make Baden one of the most important arts centres in Switzerland (and there are many distinguished ones) for the collection is known to include works by Renoir, Monet, Cézanne, Corot, Degas, the Venetians, a priceless array of Asiatic porcelain, Greek ceramics, carpets and marble.

The next destination is Schaffhausen, famous for picturesque buildings, its excellent connections which make it so convenient a place from which to start an exploration of the Bodensee (Lake Constance) or trips into Germany, the warmth of its people, and of course, the Rhine Falls, among Switzerland's most spectacular sights. From Baden, those in a hurry might take the motorway east to the outskirts of Zürich, then pick up the northbound motorway, carrying on through Jestetten. Those who are not may choose the more attractive route, going north to Koblenz, turning right to follow the Rhine, turning left about 8km (5 miles) after Kaiserstuhl to pick up the same road through Jestetten. Either route will bring you close to the falls at Neuhausen.

Schaffhausen

There are not many more spectacular sights in Switzerland than the Rhine Falls of Schaffhausen. At a point where the Rhine is 180yd wide, it suddenly plunges 80ft in three steps, like a giant clumsily walking down uneven stairs. On each level there is an enormous splash, then the biggest of them all as the falls collapse into the basin below, there to boil and fume furiously, and send a cloud of white spray floating across the countryside. Quite apart from the deafening thunder of the falls, and the awe-inspiring sight of their dramatic descent, the effect can be sheer magic on a fine day, as the sunlight catches the spray in flight, and transforms it into an elusive pattern of shapes and colours that suggest in painting the Impressionism of Manet or the mists of Corot, or in music, the evocative nuances of Debussy. Statistics declare that 1,200 tons of water every second feed that tempestuous wrath beneath. But even that pales beside the truth that must be excited in every onlooker, the realisation of man's transitory insufficiency compared with the enduring might of nature.

There are several good vantage places from which to see the falls. One is from the gardens of Schloss Laufen, and there are others, including a convenient platform. But no matter how optimistic the weather forecast, keep a raincoat handy if you intend taking a close-up. The falls create their own showers if the wind is in the wrong direction.

The falls are at Neuhausen, an extension of Schaffhausen to the south, rather than a suburb of it. If you are not travelling by car, then

The Rhine Falls at Schaffhausen

regular buses from the town centre have you there in 15 minutes, stopping at the end of a lane which leads to a good viewpoint.

The Rhine rises in the Swiss Grisons, forces its way north-west, forming for part of its course the border between Switzerland, Liechtenstein and Austria, enters the Bodensee (Lake Constance) in the south-east, flows through part of the lake, then out into the Untersee, over the falls to Basle, then north up through Germany on its long journey to Holland and out into the North Sea. Of its 850 miles, 437 are in Germany, and it passes through many beautiful old towns. But surely none more picturesque than Schaffhausen. More than once it has been labelled the oriel town of the upper Rhine, and certainly the multiplicity of those beautifully shaped projecting windows, so delicately ornamented, are a significant factor in preserving the essentially medieval atmosphere of the place. So are the many coloured statues that rise either arrogantly, gracefully, or humorously above the fountains that are discovered in quiet corners and sleepy squares.

Schaffhausen received its charter in 1045. A free city for almost four centuries, it entered into alliance with eight Swiss cantons in the

The sixteenth-century Munot fortress dominates the Rhine at Schaffhausen

fifteenth century, sealing its permanent union with the Swiss Confederation in 1501. Thereafter, its story of growing commercial

importance and wisely harboured prosperity is much the same as other Swiss communities. Except that in the case of Schaffhausen, there was a rather different reason, at least at first. In the Middle Ages, the town was a point of transfer for river cargoes. Then, as now, the Rhine was an important trade artery. Coming from the lake, or down from the north, all the goods had to be unloaded because of the impassable barrier of the Rhine Falls, then taken to the waiting vessels on the other side. So, just as the falls are important to Schaffhausen's expanding tourist industry, so energetically fostered by a lively local tourist office, so they helped lay the first foundations of prosperity hundreds of years ago.

The magnificence of the houses the merchants built for themselves show that they had an eye for artistic effect as well as financial security. Zum Ritter is among Switzerland's most lovely buildings, set among several beautifully designed guildhouses in the Vordergasse. The frescoes by Tobias Stimmer date from the sixteenth century, and it all adds up to a quite wonderful example of late German Renaissance.

A walk down the Münstergasse to the Romanesque cathedral consecrated in 1103 takes you past a treasury of old houses, their oriels jealously preserved, and brings you to the shapely cloister archways of the former zu Allerheigen (All Saints) monastery, now transformed into a museum which is one of the most important in north Switzerland. Take a deep breath before you go in. The monks of old began a tradition of growing aromatic herbs which still survives. Schaffhausen is dominated by the sixteenth-century Munot fortress, perched on top of a hillock and towering over half-timbered houses sleeping by the water. Like so many Swiss towns which are left with a legacy of the past, so that many of its buildings are protected by law, Schaffhausen has quietly converted them to modern use while preserving the exterior. For example, if you take advantage of one of the tourist office's all-in weekends, you might find yourself staying at the Alte Rheinmühle. Built in 1674, this timbered building, renovated in good taste, has become a country inn of considerable charm. On the ground floor, where the large wheel of the former mill was driven by the waters of the Rhine, there is a restaurant famous for its cuisine, with a wooden ceiling and arched windows giving a scenic view of the Rhine. Nearby is a wildfowl sanctuary.

These all-in weekends are typical of the imagination with which the tourist industry has been developed here. For details, write direct to the tourist office or, alternatively, contact the nearest branch of the

Swiss National Tourist Office in the country of your departure. Once arrived, they have made it easy to explore the best of Schaffhausen. On Mondays to Fridays from early April until the end of October (Good Friday, Easter Monday and Whit Monday excepted) there are guided walks with expert English-speaking commentators, starting from outside the tourist office at 3pm. The tour takes 90 minutes. Groups of ten or more should make advance reservations. You can also hire personal guides if you wish.

From Schaffhausen, it is natural to turn east and make for Konstanz and the broad waters of the Bodensee. This can be done by direct road, passing through a number of attractive little towns on the way. But while in Schaffhausen, the visitor should really take a trip on the Untersee, the inner lake connecting Schaffhausen with the Bodensee. In either case, a prolonged stop should be made at Stein-am-Rhein, for this is something special.

Stein-am-Rhein

Stein-am-Rhein is in some ways a reproduction of all that is wonderful about Schaffhausen, but with enough added subtleties to give it an identity of its own. On no account should it be regarded as something through which the traveller passes quickly while hurrying on to the next destination. The Rhine passes through Stein-am-Rhein, crossed by an elegant arched bridge, and you could almost imagine it slowing down to take a good look at this delectable little town. Stein-am-Rhein is an architectural gem.

Cars are banned from its cobbled streets, which are flanked by a positively intoxicating profusion of old buildings. It is cosily concentrated, with the guildhouses seeming to nudge each other affectionately, and in every narrow street and old square there is something to invite the wanderer to stand and stare. Colourful houses are on every side, with frescoes celebrating heroes of long ago and episodes that are remembered from centuries back in Swiss history.

Before settling down to a tour of the old quarter (and Stein is almost entirely an old quarter), it is a good idea to face the climb to the Burg Hohenklingen, from the battlements of which there is a breathtaking view of the Rhine winding its way through flat green pastures and dense woodland, and of the closely clustered pointed roofs of Stein itself.

There is no point in suggesting an itinerary in a small town like Stein. You simply roam around, safe in the knowledge that round each corner there will be something to please. The oriel windows, particularly in the Rathausplatz have a delicate beauty and a rich

Stein-am-Rhein

variety of expression that somehow blends into a happy harmony. The timbered Untertor, crowned by its clock within a triangular roof, stands at the end of a narrow street. The Rheingasse gives a foretaste of the glories of the Rathaus (town hall). Turn down it, pass into the Rathausplatz itself, and the promise is confirmed. The hall was built in 1539, and its façade is a marvel of elaborate murals topped by a richly carved half-timbered gallery. This, more than any other single building, proclaims the character of the town.

Coats of arms of the merchants who built the houses four hundred years ago catch the eye, as do those of the guilds and craftsmen who flourished in old Stein. Everything conspires to whisk you back into the past, including the statue of a fierce bearded mercenary leaning on his shield and grasping his pike firmly as though challenging you to try to take it from him. He reminds the visitor that so famed were Swiss soldiers for their heroism that monarchs vied with each other

The old quarter, Stein-am-Rhein

to hire them, and that the Swiss guards of Louis XVI died to a man in his defence when the mob stormed the Royal Palace in August 1792.

Without bruising the town's unique flavour, Stein has found its old buildings a creative role in a modern world. A half-timbered

house here has become a library. Cross the threshhold of a building
elaborately decorated with murals and you are inside a bank. The
sixteenth-century merchant who was so proud of his oriel windows
would be astonished if he came back today to find that behind them
management was managing and typists typing. But outside he
would have known where he was. Nothing much has changed for
hundreds of years. The former Benedictine monastery of St George
has found a new life as a museum and is well worth visiting.

The most startling illustration of how things can stay the same
while they change is found in one of Stein-am-Rhein's many excellent restaurants. The sign on the door tells the visitor he can have a
tooth extracted for a trifling sum. Another says that if the diner
happens to put an elbow out, it can be put back at once. Neither seems
to say much for the tenderness of the steaks. Then there is a notice
advising that blood-letting sessions can be arranged. And another
recommends the visitor to take a bath. Three hundred years ago the
place was a *badstube*, where you tethered your horse outside (the
posts are still there) and took advantage of all these services which
were available. Today it is a restaurant specialising in several different ways of cooking fish fresh from the lake. In Stein-am-Rhein, the
past is always looking over the shoulder of the present.

The Rhine and the Untersee

Schaffhausen makes a good base for an exploration of this part of
Switzerland. Quite apart from the time demanded by the town itself,
a visit to the Rhine Falls and another to Stein-am-Rhein, you should
reserve a day for a trip by steamer down the Rhine, and on to the
Untersee and Konstanz and back. There are usually three boats a day,
sometimes more in high season. It takes 4 hours in each direction, and
there is plenty to see as you drift through a landscape where woodlands slope down to the water's edge, medieval towns seem to be
snoozing, vineyards look sweet with promise, and heights are
crowned mysteriously with fine old castles and monasteries.

There is history as well as scenic beauty all the way. Armies chose
these banks as suitable places for crossing the Rhine, and a particularly eventful time was around the end of the eighteenth century and
the start of the next. Going about their daily tasks, the people of these
villages must have grown tired of the tramp of marching feet. Before
Diessenhofen (on the right as you travel) is the spot where the
Archduke Charles, full of misplaced confidence, crossed with the
Austrian army in 1799. A little further on is where the distinguished
General Moreau led the French troops across the Rhine a year later,

on their way to the battle of Hohenlinden, the most important of his many successes against the Austrians.

Diessenhofen (the Romans called it *Gunodorum*) has a fine old clock tower, under which the road from Schaffhausen to Konstanz passes, then Stein-am-Rhein comes into view on the left bank. In midstream is the island of Werd. But look to the right, where the walls of Schloss Freudenfels (1359) are white against the green of the descending woods.

Mammern, hugging the right-hand shore and set amid fruit orchards, is a stopping place for the boats. It was first mentioned in 909 as *Manburon*, but the remains of defensive works and lake pile-dwellings indicate that it was inhabited in prehistoric times. The Seerücken hills rise at the back, and on them the forts of Neuberg (1270, now a ruin) and Liebenfels (1254) bear witness to wars and feuds now forgotten. Klingenzell priory, between the castles Lieben-fels and Freudenfels, was founded in 1333 and became a place of pil-grimage.

Now the Rhine widens into the Untersee, an offshoot of the Bodensee. **Steckborn**, on the right, is the next stop, and if you have time, deserves a brief visit for its superb Turmhof Castle (1320), with its copper bulb-shaped roof, and for its Rathaus (1669), with its half-timbered façade, and stepped tower. The emperor Henry VII granted Steckborn its charter in 1313, and you can still see the remains of the old town walls. In **Berlingen**, flanked by vineyards a little further on, fishing and farming still survive as major occupa-tions. The evangelical church is said to be Switzerland's first New Gothic building. The painter Adolf Dietrich (1877-1957) worked in Berlingen, and his former studio is open to the public. The island of Reichenau is German. Opposite is the village of Ermatingen, and above it, Schloss Arenenberg, where Hortense de Beauharnais, for-mer wife of Louis Bonaparte, king of Holland, lived from 1818 with her son, the future Napoleon III of France. It contains many replicas of France's second empire. **Gottlieben** is the last stop before Kon-stanz. Its Dominican monastery is where the Czech protestant re-former John Huss was imprisoned in 1415, despite having been given a safe conduct to appear before the Council of Konstanz. Refusing to recant his doctrines as heretical, he was condemned to be burnt at the stake at Konstanz.

The same journey can be done by car, as the road follows the river and lake all the way. But a leisurely trip by boat is recommended.

Further Information
— The North: From the Aare to the Rhine Falls —

Museums and Other Places of Interest

Opening times are those applicable at the time of compilation. But check locally as they are subject to variation.

Aarau
Aargauer Kunsthaus
Rathausplatz
☎ 064/21 12 44
Swiss paintings, prints and sculptures from 1750 to the present day.
Open: daily 10am-5pm; Thursday 10am-5pm and 8-10pm. Closed Monday.

Stadtmuseum Alt-Arrau
Schlossli, Schlossplatz 12
☎ 064/22 26 33
Panorama of Aarau life during seven centuries
Open: Saturday 2-5pm, Sunday 10am-2pm.

Aargauisches Museum für Natur und Heimatkude
Bahnhofplatz
☎ 064/22 29 48
Natural history and wildlife of the Aargau
Open: daily 10am-5pm, except Sunday 10am-12noon and 2-4pm. Closed Monday.

Baden
Historisches Museum
der Stadt Landvogteischloss
☎ 056/22 75 44
History of Baden, including exhibition of ceramics, porcelain, documents, folk arts, and crafts.

Open: daily 10am-12noon and 2-5pm. Closed Monday.

Brugg
Heimatsmuseum
Altes Zeughaus, Untere Hofstaff
☎ 056/41 57 13
Local arts and crafts
Open: April to October. Inquire locally for times.

Stäblistübli
Altes Zeughaus, Untere Hofstaff (in Heimatsmuseum)
Exhibition of the painter Adolf Stübli
Open: April to October. Inquire locally for times.

Vindonissa Museum
Museumstrasse 1
☎ 056/41 21 84
Roman discoveries
Open: January to March, October to December daily 10am-12noon and 2-4pm. April to September 10am-12noon and 2-5.30pm.

Hallwil
Schloss
Old castle with rooms decorated in eighteenth-century style
Open: April to October daily 9am-11.30am and 1.30-5.30pm. Closed Monday.

Olten
Kunstmuseum
Kirchgasse 8
☎ 062/32 86 76
Paintings and sculptures by Swiss artists of the nineteenth and twentieth centuries

*Schaffhausen,
north Switzerland*

*Remote Appenzell,
north Switzerland*

St Gallen, the largest city in north-east Switzerland

Open: daily 2-5pm. Saturday and Sunday also 10am-12noon. Closed Monday.

Historisches Museum
Konradstrasse 7
☎ 062/21 79 07
History and art of the region. Porcelain of the eighteenth and nineteenth centuries. Weapons, medals, costumes, goldsmith craft of the seventeenth and eighteenth centuries
Open: daily 10am-12noon and 2-5pm. Closed Monday.

Naturhistorisches Museum
Kirchgasse 10
☎ 062/21 39 39
Geological and mineral exhibits, fossils, botany, zoology
Open: daily 10am-12noon and 2-5pm. Closed Monday.

Rheinfelden
Oldtimermuseum
Beim Kurzentrum
☎ 061/87 20 35
Over a hundred cars and motorbikes from 1896 to 1975. Includes various famous racing cars
Open: Wednesday 2-5pm, Saturday and Sunday 10am-12noon and 2-5pm. Or by appointment.

Schaffhausen
Museum zu Aller Heiligen
Klosterplatz 1
☎ 053/5 43 77
Paintings by artists of the area and modern Swiss painting. Collection of prints from copper engravings of the sixteenth to twentieth centuries
Open: daily 10am-12noon and 2-5pm. Closed Monday.

Hallen für neue Kunst

Baumgartnerstrasse 23
☎ 053//5 25 15
Contemporary art
Open: May to October, Wednesday-Saturday 3-5pm. Sunday 10am-1pm.

Stein-am-Rhein
Puppenmuseum
Schwarzhorngasse 136
☎ 054/41 39 66
Collection of dolls and dolls' houses. Also automatic toys
Open: March to October daily 1-5pm. Closed Monday.

Klostermuseum St George
☎ 054/8 61 42
Former Benedictine monastery, now a museum.

Heimatsmuseum
☎ 054/8 61 27
Arts and crafts of the area
Open: March to November daily 10am-12noon and 1.30-5pm. Closed Monday.

Tourist Information Offices

Most tourist offices open at 8am and close around 5.30pm, but many, particularly smaller ones in remote areas, will be closed at lunch time, mostly between 12noon and 2pm.

Regional
North-Western Switzerland
Nordwestschweizerische Verkehrsvereinigung
Blumenrain 2
Basel
☎ 061/25 50 50

Local
Baden
Kur-und Verkekrsverein

Bahnhofstrasse 50
☎ 056/22 53 18

Olten
Verkehrsverein
Bahnhofpassage
☎ 062/26 16 16

Rheinfelden
Kur-und Verkehrsverein
Habich-Dietschy-strasse 10
☎ 061/87 55 20

Schaffhausen
Verkehrsbuero
Vorstadt 12
☎ 053/5 51 41

Useful Information

Banks
Most open Monday-Wednesday
8.15am-4.30pm, Thursday 8.15am-
6pm, Friday 8.15am-4.30pm. Some
open Saturday 9am-4pm. But
hours can vary from town to town.

Bicycles
Can be hired from, and returned
to, railway stations.

Camping
The Swiss National Tourist Office
publishes a complete guide to the
camp sites throughout the country.

Car Hire
It is assumed that travellers in
north Switzerland will hire a car
on arrival in Switzerland, probably
in Zürich. For details, see under
Car Hire in the Zürich chapter.

Changing money
At banks and tourist offices during
normal business hours.

Credit Cards
Most hotels and restaurants accept
the principal credit cards, as do the
leading stores, filling stations etc.

Facilities for the Disabled
The Swiss National Tourist Office
have a pamphlet dealing with
facilities for the disabled.

Shopping
North Switzerland has many
characteristic products which
make excellent souvenirs or presents. Wood carving, embroidery,
costume dolls, and, of course,
Swiss watches and chocolates are
famous. Swiss army knives are
remarkably versatile instruments,
able to open anything. Several
towns produce their own confectionery (Aarau, for example, has
some particularly mouth-watering
chocolates). Keep an eye open for
local markets. It is often cheaper to
shop there, and in any event, they
are generally colourful.

Sport
Facilities naturally vary with the
size of the town, but the people of
north Switzerland love the open-
air life, and every sport is usually
within reach, including water
sports in lake areas. There are
many sophisticated indoor sports
complexes. Inquire at your tourist
office.

Tipping
Don't. Gratuities are included in
the bill at most hotels and restaurants.

Winter Sports
The mountainous areas of north

Switzerland make this an ideal region for winter sports. It is a useful district for beginners, for there are ski schools in most resorts, and easy runs for learners. New downhill and cross-country runs (becoming more and more popular) are opening all the time making a definitive list impossible to compile. Curling, skating, ski-bob and tobogganing are all plentiful. Inquire at the local tourist office for up-to-date information.

Youth Hostels

Switzerland has always been in the vanguard of youth hostel development. The Swiss National Tourist Office publishes a special booklet giving full information.

2 • The North: Around the Bodensee

Along the Lakeshore

Strictly speaking, **Konstanz**, is not Swiss at all. It is an important piece of Germany on the Swiss shore of the Bodensee, overlooking the point where the Untersee joins it, but since it will inevitably be in the path of the traveller following those lakes, it had better be mentioned. But remember to have your passport with you. The odds are that you will not need it, but you never know.

So why is Konstanz German? Originally a Celtic settlement and later a Roman one, it has had a stormy history. It became a free city in 1192. The Council of Konstanz met here in 1414-18, sometimes in the cathedral, sometimes in the Kaufhaus, and here the Czech reformers John Huss and Jerome of Prague were burnt at the stake. Huss is remembered by a street named after him (the Hussenstrasse) and by his effigy on the house where he lived in the same street. The town was occupied by the Austrians in 1548, and besieged by the Swedes in 1633 during the Thirty Years War. In 1805 it was ceded to Baden in Germany under the Treaty of Pressburg (now Bratislava) and German it has remained. Its bishopric was suppressed in 1821.

The Romanesque cathedral was begun in 1052, considerably rebuilt four hundred years later, and the Gothic tower was added as recently as 1850. Inside, you can see the actual spot on which Huss stood so bravely to hear his sentence. Another building to note is the Renaissance Rathaus (town hall) with its frescoes commemorating historical events, and the old house where Frederick Barbarossa (or Redbeard) signed a peace treaty with the Lombards in 1183. More recent history is commemorated by the town's most prominent statue. It is of Count Ferdinand von Zeppelin (1838-1917), pioneer of the airship, who was born here. His dirigible balloons were built at Friedrichshafen, on the German shore of the lake, reached by direct boat from Romanshorn, which will be visited later.

Kreuzlingen is the smaller and adjoining Swiss cousin of Konstanz. There are many fine old houses and other links with the past. From here, you can make boat trips to many spots on the Bodensee, including the German flower island of Mainau. Once the home of the Grand Duke of Baden, Mainau's gardens, with their sub-tropical vegetation and lush colours in high summer, are reminiscent of the Isola Madre on Italy's Lake Maggiore, a little piece of Germany which is almost Italian.

Kreuzlingen's Augustinian priory, founded in the tenth century, was a victim of that siege during the Thirty Years War, and the present building, erected soon after, now houses a college.

Before leaving Konstanz and Kreuzlingen, a drive through the Thurgau is recommended. This is a happily unspoiled expanse of green countryside to the south of the Untersee, through which the Thur meanders on its way to join hands with the Rhine. Romantic villages nestle in the woods, fierce castles rise on the crags, and the further you penetrate, more tempting are the vistas of distant mountains.

You can explore part of the Thurgau in a round trip starting and finishing at Kreuzlingen. A direct road will bring you to **Weinfelden**, a town of about 9,000 inhabitants lying at the foot of the Ottenburg. There are many imposing old buildings and elegant fountains, and the castle has been renovated. The people of Weinfelden seem to have a flair for putting window boxes of scarlet and pink flowers in places where they blend with the half-timbered fronts. Winding paths lead into the surrounding woods, which in autumn are a riot of russet and gold. This is a colourful town at any time of the year, and one which has moved purposefully into the twentieth century. Small it may be, but as the centre of an area of prosperous little villages, it has become a thriving business centre, and is equipped with a wide range of sports facilities, while the admirably designed, flag-bedecked Thurgauerhof is a thriving centre for concerts, exhibitions and other events.

Frauenfeld is the capital of the canton of Thurgau, and you reach it by a road to the west, passing through Märstetten and Mülheim. The town was founded by the counts of Kyburg, whose name thrusts itself into so much history in north Switzerland, and their shadow lives on. The great white-fronted, red-roofed castle they built to defend their lands is mostly preserved. The tower was erected in 1227, and the town itself evolved around it in a triangular pattern from 1244 onwards. Up to as late as 1798, the district governors lived in the castle. From the top of the tower, there is a fine view of the Thurgau countryside.

There are, however, not so many medieval houses as you might expect to find. Frauenfeld was unlucky in the eighteenth century when two disastrous fires wiped out most of the town. Nevertheless, neighbouring cantons came to the rescue, mounted a re-building act, and the result is a mixture of Bernese, Lucernese and Zürich baroque frontages. The imposing white-faced Rathaus was built in 1790, and has recently been extensively restored, forming a harmonious group with the restored houses Sonne and Gambrinus. Outside the town, the St Laurentius church at Oberkirch is renowned for its medieval glass paintings, while the half-timbered house Guggenhürli, perched above its vineyard, is an attractive landmark. Back in the town, a visit should be paid to the popular Natural History Museum.

Frauenfeld is an excellent centre for a leisurely break. There are well signposted walks, some of them offering views of the snow-topped Alps. The Ittingen monastery, less than 4 miles distant, has a number of art exhibits. Return to Kreuzlingen either by the same route, or extend your run to Wil, then turn north for Weinfelden and Kreuzlingen. For scenery, these are the recommended routes. But if time presses, you can take a direct road from Frauenfeld.

All the way from Kreuzlingen to Rorschach the road follows the lake almost as though they were happy partners in some holiday excursion. This is a different Switzerland, an area where places to play and places to relax somehow live side by side with that never-to-be-suppressed Swiss past, which looks down on it all, smiling benevolently but quietly insisting that the twentieth century must keep its place and show respect. So elegant chateaux, some of them pressed into contemporary usefulness without loss of character, exist beside new swimming pools. Camp sites there are in plenty, but they are discreetly sited. Flower-fringed lakeside boulevards, places to stroll in the lake air, or sit quietly on a sunlit Bodensee afternoon, plentiful water sports, all proclaim modern resorts; half-timbered houses proclaim the past.

Alleys lead from sophisticated yachting harbours or strands where near-naked bodies soak up the sun, to carefully preserved old quarters where the houses have medieval frescoes, a sudden adventure in baroque here, a touch of Renaissance there, an unexpected quiet square with a decorated fountain somewhere else. All the small towns and villages on the edge of the lake seem to have solved the problem of living in two ages at once. There are excellent restaurants and hotels, many of them specialising in their own way of serving

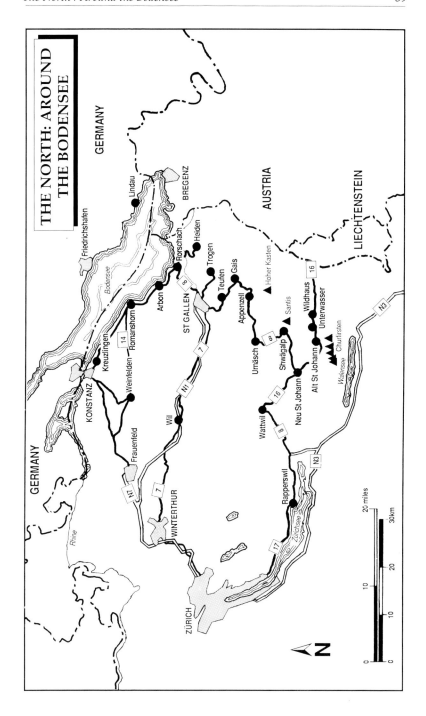

THE NORTH: AROUND THE BODENSEE

GERMANY

GERMANY

AUSTRIA

LIECHTENSTEIN

Rhine

Bodensee

Friedrichshafen

Lindau

BREGENZ

KONSTANZ

Kreuzlingen

Weinfelden

Romanshorn

Arbon

Rorschach

Heiden

Trogen

Teufen

Gais

Hoher Kasten

ST GALLEN

Appenzell

Santis

Wildhaus

Unterwasser

Urnäsch

Shwägalp

Churfirsten

Walensee

Alt St Johann

Neu St Johann

Wattwil

Wil

Frauenfeld

WINTERTHUR

Rapperswil

Zürichsee

ZÜRICH

14

8

7

N1

16

8

9

16

N3

N3

17

N1

7

Z N

20 miles

30km

0 · 10 · 20

0 · 10 · 20

fresh fish from the lake.

The first place of any size en route is **Bottighofen**. It is making the most of its favoured situation and gaining an increasing reputation as a bathing place and holiday centre. It has recently acquired a fine new harbour, and for those who prefer the delights of the country-side to those of the waterfront, several footpaths lead into the adjacent meadows and woodlands. **Scherzingen**, which also attracts its share of holidaymakers, has retained its village atmosphere, and has a baroque church as well as a former Benedictine monastery.

A peninsula reaching into the lake gives the first sight of **Romanshorn**, which today has spilled into the landscape behind, and along the gentle curve of a bay. From here, you can take the car ferry across the water to Friedrichshafen (take the passports). Romanshorn has some industry, but it is unobtrusive. It is noted for its healthy lake air and well organised holiday facilities. The climate is generous, and swimming, water-skiing, sailing and tennis are all available. The people of Romanshorn are proud of their park, and so they should be. Skilfully planned, for most of the year it is full of colour.

Like Romanshorn, **Arbon**, on another headland, seems to be sitting beside the lake with its big toe dipped cautiously into the water. It is perhaps the best example on the Bodensee of the success-ful marriage between the demands of a growing holiday trade and a carefully guarded past. Indeed, it is the historic old houses you are likely to recall long after the memory of the well kept gardens, water sports, smart promenades and bathing pools have faded. Spare time for a walk round Arbon's streets.

The castle is said to symbolise Arbon. If so, the town must have known turbulent times in the past. It stands gaunt and grey, but today has found a peaceful role in the new Arbon, housing a museum which illustrates life in the area right back to the time of the Romans and beyond. In fact, the Romans were not the first here. The Celts had been established for centuries before the Romans came in 60BC and built a military camp. There are Celtic remains in the museum as well.

The castle may cast its shadow, but the character of Arbon is formed equally by the half-timbered houses. One of the most striking of these is the Rathaus in the Promenadenstrasse, built in 1791 and renovated this century. Another is the Untertor, which is also deco-rated with several picturesque murals illustrating old country crafts and customs. And there are many others at which to point the camera. St Martin's church, with its Gothic tower rising behind the pink-walled vicarage, has its own collection of local relics. The St

Ittigen monastery

Gallus church, wedged between tall trees, has something vaguely Scandinavian about its outline, and has notable stained glass windows. Arbon's surrounding countryside is attractive at all times, and at its best in spring when the orchards on the town's doorstep are heavy with blossom.

Five minutes driving brings the traveller to **Horn**, an ancient fishing village lying in a slight recession in the coast, and then the road continues to **Rorschach**.

This well established town is a fitting climax to the lakeside journey. Its proximity to Austria, just a few miles away, and to Lindau, the old German city on the opposite shore reached in a short journey by direct lake steamer, has cast its influence and given it a faintly cosmopolitan atmosphere. It is Switzerland's largest port on the Bodensee, and lies in a bay beneath the pine forests of the 3,000ft-high Rorschacherberg. The reason for its traditional importance as a

Rorschach

trading centre is obvious from a glance at the map. Its position stands astride an international route, and traders were meeting here 1,000 years ago. They came by road, they came by water, and the arrival of the railway much later added to Rorschach's significance. Today, evidence of its past prosperity mingles with that of today, a prosperity to which the expansion of tourism has added its quota.

In 936, King Otto I (Otto the Great) was crowned King of the Germans at Aachen. He established a considerable empire through central Europe, in the course of which he conferred on the Abbot of St Gall the right of market holding, coinage and excise. From this the importance of Rorschach grew in the Middle Ages, a story told by the town's many handsome old houses, with their enchantingly carved oriels. Later, in 1746, the Kornhaus was built, now a well stocked museum of local history. The former Mariaberg cloister has also been faithfully restored.

A car ferry on Bodensee

With its numerous holiday facilities, coupled with history and glamorous country, Rorschach invites a stay. There are footpaths wandering away into the countryside, where wonderful views of the mountains of three countries (Austria, Germany and Switzerland) can be enjoyed. And it is a convenient starting point for several excursions. You should certainly cross the border (remember the passports) for a taste of the Vorarlberg, and particularly of **Bregenz**, squeezed into that tiny corner of Austria which intrudes on to the Bodensee between Switzerland and Germany. It is a beautiful and lively little Austrian town with a fine waterfront, and the Vorarlberg at its back is an area of delightfully unspoiled woods, picturesque villages, clearly marked footpaths and gushing rivers and waterfalls. It is easily reached by car, train or boat. Bregenz has another claim to fame: during July and August it is the home of the celebrated Bregenz Festival, where opera becomes aquatic. The performances are given on a floating stage in the lake, and the audience is accommodated in an open-air auditorium on the shore. International singers take part, and the orchestra is usually the Vienna Symphony. There are also concerts and recitals in the town's municipal theatre and halls. *The Flying Dutchman* is an obvious choice for water-borne opera, and at Bregenz it can become very realistic indeed. But many other operas seem to take naturally to water. Unique spectacle means a lot at this festival, but is hardly ever at the expense of artistic quality.

If you stay in Rorschach, a visit across the lake to **Lindau** is also recommended. This fascinating German town has an abbey founded in the ninth century, several other medieval churches, well preserved guildhouses, and a fifteenth-century town hall. In the Middle Ages, Lindau was an essential link in the commerce between the German states and Italy. Goods would be unloaded at Lindau, taken across the Bodensee to Rorschach, and from there go on through the passes to the south, to Milan or on to Venice for further shipment. Swiss money is acceptable in Bregenz and Lindau, and prices in Swiss francs are usually quoted in restaurants and shops.

No visitor can claim to have had a totally Swiss experience until he or she has travelled on one of the many cogwheel railways that whisk the traveller from ground level to the heights. As they rumble up the steep slopes, they unfold a gradually widening panorama of countryside, mountain and forest. So though it is perfectly practicable to take a trip to Heiden by car (a direct road leads from Rorschach) you would do much better to leave the car behind, go along to the station of the Rorschach-Heiden mountain railway near the harbour, take a cogwheel train, sit back in one of the red coaches and enjoy the gradually changing view. As the train ascends, the port gradually recedes, the wide expanse of the Bodensee comes into view, dotted with white sails and the frothy wakes of the steamers, and the length of the German shore is revealed. You pass through orchards, over farms where the people wave greetings, catch glimpses of castles that were there centuries before the railway was built and of huddled villages, then go higher through woodlands where the trees brush the carriages, and on to views of snow clad peaks shimmering on the horizon.

Heiden is one of those places which, though famous and well developed, can still claim to be off the beaten track. It is blessed with a sunny position high above the Bodensee, and some of its fame is owed to its standing as a health resort, offering electrotherapy and treatments designed for those recovering from heart attacks, nervous disorders, stress and circulation problems. With its splendid climate and stimulating air, it is also ideal for holidaymakers who like a generous ration of open-air activity combined with relaxation. It also has prestige as the place where Henri Dunant (1828-1910), the Swiss philanthrophist and founder of the Red Cross, did important work. He was so moved by the sufferings of the wounded at the battle of Solferino (the Lombard village where the French and Sardinians defeated the Austrians in June 1859) that he published a book urging the formation of permanent voluntary aid societies to succour the wounded in time of war, and this so caught international imagination that in 1863, sixteen European nations met at a conference in Geneva to launch the plan. The Red Cross was born, its flag a red cross on a white background, reversing Switzerland's national flag. There is a museum devoted to Dunant's work at Heiden. It seems happily appropriate that the contemporary role of this charming village should still involve healing.

Return to Rorschach, and from there the tour continues to St Gallen.

St Gallen

From Rorschach a direct road to the south-west brings the traveller quickly to St Gallen, the largest city in north-east Switzerland, the capital of the canton which bears its name, and a place whose prestige rests securely on a joint foundation of industry, its role in Switzerland's cultural life, scholarship, expanding tourism, its success in preserving an inherited past, and its development as a congress centre. It is dealt with in detail here because visitors in search of out of the way spots are almost certain to pass through it on their way to Appenzell, or even to break their journey here.

The city's origins have distant links with the British Isles. In the seventh century, the Irish monk Gallus left his cell, and travelling by way of Scotland, arrived in what was described as 'the green wilderness between the Lake of Constance and Säntis'. There, in 612, he established his hermitage, which was soon a place of pilgrimage. By the following century, it had become the nucleus of a Benedictine abbey which grew to become one of the leading centres of learning in central Europe. Around it grew the Villa Sancti Galli, a settlement of craftsmen and small farmers which developed steadily into the St Gallen of trade and commercial importance. In 1212 it received the charter of a free imperial city. Allegiance to the abbot was ended when St Gallen joined the Swiss Confederation in 1454. In the next century Vadin brought religious freedom (his memorial stands in a corner of the Marktgasse).

St Gallen's standing as a centre of commerce gradually became more dominant, particularly in the growth of a healthy textile industry. The end of the eighteenth century and the first years of the nineteenth brought a time of confusion and revised Swiss administration in the wake of the Napoleonic wars, and in 1803, St Gallen's monastery was secularised along with others in Switzerland, the new canton of St Gallen was formed, and the city became its capital.

St Gallen

The traditional association with textiles is preserved. Even today, a third of the population of the city is employed in industry, many of them in the one in which their families have worked for generations. The Textile Museum in the Vadianstrasse has on show a remarkable range of products made in St Gallen from the sixteenth century to the nineteenth. It should certainly be visited. And in the summer, there are processions involving thousands of children in costumes made in the city down the ages.

The old town is the very heart of St Gallen, concentrated in an oval formed roughly by the Moosbruggstrasse, Oberergraben, Marktplatz and an extension of the Torstrasse from the Brühl Tor to the Spiser Tor. Within this area, there are many gems. Approach the old quarter from any direction, and the twin towers of the baroque cathedral dominate. The best route is through the Marktgasse, from which the full effect of the cathedral's symmetry can be felt. As cathedrals go, it is hardly one of Switzerland's oldest, but it is very beautiful. Cheerful, too, as a place of worship ought to be. On a sunny day, the interior, tastefully restored and maintained, glitters with light. Another church to visit is near at hand. St Laurence is on the

The cathedral, St Gallen

corner of the Zeughausgasse immediately facing the cathedral pre-
cincts. St Mangen, at the end of the Goliathgasse (which leads off the
Marktplatz, near the Unterergraben), is another.

The streets around are for wandering slowly. Many of the older
houses have been affectionately restored in the Riegel style peculiar
to north Switzerland and south Germany. Conical turrets, oriel
windows and frescoes make a picturesque decoration to the winding
alleys, many of them now reserved exclusively for pedestrians. But
the most remarkable antiquity in St Gallen is surely the Stiftsbibliothek, the library of the former abbey, situated at the rear of the
cathedral. Here there are 100,000 old books and illuminated manuscripts, some dating back to the tenth century. Another essential for
visitors to St Gallen.

In fact, for a city of its size, St Gallen is particularly rich in
museums and you need never fear a wet day. There is much to see
and admire indoors. It is a lively place in the evening too. Opera and
ballet, operetta and musicals, plays and cabaret, discos and night
clubs all play a part in a varied programme of entertainment. St
Gallen's opera has always been recognised as one of Switzerland's
best, and performs in the imposing Stadttheater in the Museumstrasse. The municipal orchestra gives regular concerts in the

The Stiftsbibliothek, St Gallen

Tonhalle opposite. There are puppet shows, too, in the Puppen-theater in the Lämmlisbrunnenstrasse.

St Gallen has several parks and gardens, notably the Stadtpark situated off the Museumstrasse. Take the children to the Peter and Paul Wildlife Park off the Dufourstrasse where there are wild boar, deer and chamois. The city is lucky in its proximity to unspoiled woodlands, some of them not much more than ten minutes walking from the centre.

A variety of cuisine is offered in the city's numerous restaurants. Some are situated in the old quarter, which is just as colourful by night as it is by day, and have a characteristic local atmosphere. Dishes special to the canton are a feature, but many have an international menu, in which French and Italian cuisine are both prominent. It is also noted as a shopping centre, and here again the old town is

Säntis, 8,000ft high and reached by cablecar from Swägalp

The lake boat at Flüelen, at the head of the Urner See

Lake Uri, south of Brunnen

a rewarding area, with its many boutiques and busy market stalls, and pavement cafés where you can break your journey.

St Gallen has become expert at the organisation of congresses and trade fairs, for which the Schützengarten Congress Centre in the St Jakobstrasse has been specially designed. Olma, the Swiss Agriculture and Dairy Fair brings around half a million visitors to St Gallen each year. Quite an influx for a city whose own population is around 75,000.

From many vantage points near the city, exciting views of the Austrian Vorarlberg and the Säntis can be had. The city is well placed for many excursions to well known Swiss beauty spots and cities because of its excellent road and rail communications. Nearer at hand, a pleasant short run from St Gallen is to **Trogen** by road to the east. The journey is scenically attractive, and Trogen is a neat village where white-fronted, red-roofed villas spread up the green slopes of the Gäbris. It has some elegant buildings, and is the centre of the Pestalozzi Children's Village, named after Johann Heinrich Pestalozzi (1746-1827), the Swiss educational pioneer and reformer, which was founded in 1946 for war refugee children of several nationalities. In 1956, refugees from the tragic Hungarian revolution were accepted there. The groups are educated by teachers from their own countries.

Another attractive trip is to **Herisau**, a picturesque village easily reached by road from St Gallen, yet off the beaten track. It has many red-roofed old houses, is the centre of colourful processions, has facilities for children in the Kinderparadies, a nature reserve, peaceful walks by the Gübensee and fine views of the Säntis range.

Return to St Gallen, and from there leave for Appenzell.

Appenzell

It may come as a surprise to learn that in the last years of the twentieth century there is still a part of one of Europe's most enlightened democracies where women cannot vote in their local elections. But then, the region of Appenzell is different in many respects from other parts of Switzerland.

Down on the lakeside at Rorschach, or wandering in the fields around St Gallen, the highlands to the south-east look sometimes invitingly mysterious, sometimes defiantly forbidding according to the weather. Peaks that on one day will glitter like jewels against the sky, on others appear like a strange mirage, then vanish at the whim of scudding clouds. This is the remote area of Appenzell, known to many for the unique flavour of its celebrated cheese, but for many

Appenzell

tourists, not much more than that. Appenzell really is off the beaten track.

You can reach it from St Gallen by road, climbing steadily to Teufen, then ascending through a valley on up to Gais. Turn right here, and the road gradually descends to the little town of Appenzell. But you are brought closer to the real nature of Appenzell and its people if you catch a train on the narrow gauge railway from St Gallen. It winds its slow way ever higher through first one valley then another, rumbling past waterfalls, passing over bubbling streams, stopping at mountain villages to pick up farmers with weather-beaten faces. Suddenly, you feel part of a special commu-

An Appenzell folk band

nity. This sense of belonging is even stronger in Appenzell itself. One never feels like a stranger or some visiting curiosity. It is a welcoming little town, but it also has a sturdy independence. This is an area where old customs die hard. It keeps rather apart from the conventional order of things.

Swiss women got the vote on the federal level in 1971, rather late, you might think, considering the record of humanitarianism and tolerance in Swiss affairs. It was left to the cantons to decide whether to follow suit on the local level. Most did. But not the region of Appenzell, which is divided into two cantons. Women were still excluded, and there's no sign of a revolution yet.

There's nothing very secret about the elections. They are conducted in public, by a show of hands. Nobody bothers to count the votes. The conducting officer just looks around and assesses the result. The high attendance at the annual *Landesgemiende*, as it is called, certainly makes it look as though there's a healthy interest in public affairs generally and these annual meetings in particular. Probably there is. But actually, every enfranchised citizen under 60 is expected to turn up, and there is a fine waiting for anyone who fails to attend without good reason.

Appenzell is different in many other ways. The region where

A bell saddler exhibits his craft at Appenzell. It takes 25 hours of meticulous work to finish one of the bell straps with leather laces, woollen frills and brass engravings

women can't vote in the local elections, and seats on the council depend on how a show of hands looks to the official in charge, is also the region where men were wearing a ring in the right ear long before it became a youth fashion elsewhere. Usually, it is of silver and gilt with a rural motif. It is also the area where you will often see the men

The annual Landesgemiende

smoking the handsome *lendauerli*, the pipe whose wooden stem is engraved with white metal figures, with the bowl similarly decorated, and an ornate lid. The pipe is filled in the usual way. Then the top is sealed, and it is smoked upside down.

This is a district where old crafts are handed down from father to son. You may meet a saddler who is the sixth generation of his family to carry on making bell harnesses. It is a region where handweavers still exist, where the women preserve their own style of embroidery, and where milk churns are still decorated by craftsmen. Here they have their own special cakes, *chlausebickli*, honey cakes baked in October with scenes painted on the surface illustrating peasant life. They are on sale from All Saints Day until Christmas. They also have their own folk music. An Appenzell band consists of two violins, cello, double bass, and a *Hackbrett*, a kind of dulcimer special to the

The Säntis range near Appenzell. In 10 minutes the cablecar climbs 3,300ft to a point near the summit

area. Most of their music is unattributed, passed down for centuries. The bands come into their own on the Sunday nearest to the feast of St Jakob (25 July) when the holiday of the alpine herdsmen is celebrated, and again during the *Alpstobete*, a noisy celebration to close the summer grazing season.

The most colourful of Appenzell's many processions is the ascent

The Churfirsten range looking from the Toggenburg valley

to the mountains, when the cattle are moved up to their summer quarters. A goatherd leads the way, followed by his unique white Appenzell goats. Next comes a cowherd in a bright yellow uniform, carrying a richly carved wooden milking pail, cows with their bells jangling, a group of lusty yodellers, then the farmer, leading his bull by the nose.

Strange figures haunt the streets on New Year's Eve and on 13 January, New Year's Eve in the old calendar, still respected in the Appenzell cantons. These are the 'handsome-ugly ones', whose origins probably descend from ancient fertility rites. The demonic figures wearing ugly masks and straw and brushwood clothes are intended to scare away evil spirits. The beautiful ones wear ornate regional head-dresses, chime bells and yodel to welcome the New Year, while nature mummers appear in costumes of pine-cones, moss and snail shells.

The Appenzell countryside is a fairyland where the sun plays tricks with the tall firs and casts elusive shadows in a forest noon, where picturesque cottages straight out of story books have murals telling of local legends, where there are numerous footpaths through green meadows and around the fruit orchards, and the sound of

tinkling cowbells drifts across the air. It is flanked by a dramatic ridge
of mountains to the south, white-clad needle points that are silhouetted against the blue sky. The nearest to the town itself is Hoher
Kasten (6,000ft) easily reached from the tiny holiday village of Brüli-
sau. At the summit there is a wonderful view of the mountains of four
countries. Säntis is the dominating peak of the range.

While in Appenzell, a visit should be paid to Retonio's Mechanical Music and Magic Museum. Retonio, a well known ventriloquist,
has collected an assortment of music boxes, parlour organs, fair-
ground organs, automatic violins and other mechanical instruments, the result of touring the fairgrounds of the world.

And, of course, there is Appenzell cheese, with a taste all its own.
To find out more about it, pay a visit to nearby **Stein**, situated on a
sunny hill top with attractive views of pastures dotted with neat
farms, and the far-spreading, softly undulating hills. Here they have
established the Appenzell Showcase Cheese Dairy. From a specta-
tor's gallery, visitors can watch the production of the famous cheese
step by step, from the delivery of the milk right through to the
ripening of whole cheeses in the cellar. There are also sound-slide
shows, and a restaurant decorated with old farm implements. The
cheesemakers are quite happy to share their secrets, so make sure
you come away with a few useful recipes, such as those for making
Appenzell cheese tarts, Appenzell *Rösti*, Appenzell cheese pillows,
cheese soufflé and *Appenzellerei*, a luscious blend of ham pork, on-
ions, parsley and cheese.

Appenzell has a sixteenth-century town hall and a number of
picturesque houses. Several of the hotels and guest houses in the area
have been owned and managed by the same families for generations,
and a tradition of personal service has grown up. And despite its
comparative remoteness, the town is well connected to adjacent
resorts and holiday spots by the faithful Swiss yellow postal coaches.

Add to old traditions a welcoming people, glorious mountains
and soft fields, attractive houses and well run hotels and guest
houses, a predominantly mild sub-alpine climate, a surprising
wealth of holiday facilities, and mile upon mile of easy walking in
stimulating mountain air, the bonus of an efficient local tourist office,
and Appenzell is an ideal centre for a break that is as relaxing as it can
be exciting.

From Appenzell to Zürich

The route now heads west in the direction of Zürich. But this does not
mean an end to sightseeing. There are many delights on the way.

Climbers on the Churfirsten range

And it will not be a straight run, as Switzerland has a habit of putting mountains in the way. The reward is many a spectacular view, nature at its most proud and colourful.

From the town of Appenzell, follow the road to **Urnäsch** and make a stop here. There is an excellent museum which summarises all the characteristics of Appenzell's past and present. After Urnäsch, take the road to the south for Schwägalp. Ahead, the mountains rise more superb with every mile. This is Swiss alpine scenery at its most glorious. Stop again at **Schwägalp** and take the cablecar, which brings you close to the summit of Säntis, the 8,000ft high monarch of the range. From there the visitor has a thrilling view over the entire alpine range, taking in Germany's Zugspitze, Austria's Weisse Kugel, Italy's Monte Disgrazia and Switzerland's celebrated Jungfrau. On particularly clear days (the locals will tell you that mid-winter provides the best of them) the view reaches as far as the Vosges in France and Switzerland's Jura. From near the peak, there are several safe and well maintained paths. In winter, this is a popular skiing area with snow guaranteed until late spring.

Continuing the journey, the road follows the mountainside to **Rietbad**, a holiday village, thence to **Neu St Johann**, to enter the Toggenburg valley. This is a popular skiing area in winter, and wonderful walking country in spring, summer and autumn. Those to whom time is of no object (and given this countryside, it ought not to be) might take the road to the right on reaching Neu St Johann. This goes to **Alt St Johann, Unterwasser** and **Wildhaus**, the birthplace of Ulrich Zwingli, the fierce preacher of the Reformation, whose house can be visited. Each of these three places is a pleasantly sited holiday village, sharing between them nearly two hundred miles of sign-posted footpaths. Some lead to sunny picnic spots, others to exciting vantage points, others to restful spots by the Thur, and another to the waterfall near Unterwasser.

There is more glamorous mountain scenery ahead, but this unfortunately is not the way to Zürich. It would make a wonderful return journey if you could now turn south and pick up a return road by the dark green waters of the Walensee, an attractive unspoiled shore unaffected by its growing holiday business. But nature has decreed otherwise. The Churfirsten range, nearly 7,000ft at its highest point, bars the way. Nothing for it but to go back the way you came, to Neu St Johann, thence down the Toggenburg valley through the resorts of Nesslau and Ebnat-Kappel to Wattwil. From there a good road leads to Rapperswil and the northern shore of the Zürichsee. A stop at **Rapperswil** is recommended if only to sample the restaurants serving fresh caught lake fish cooked in a variety of local recipes. But there is much more to Rapperswil than fish. The castle, silhouetted against the sky, was first built in the thirteenth century, but was destroyed in 1350 in one of the local quarrels of the period. Earlier, the Habsburgs had sacked Zürich, and the people of Rapperswil had given them plenty of help in doing it. So in revenge, Zürich sent their own army to Rapperswil and destroyed the castle. Nothing daunted,

Rapperswil

the people of Rapperswil built the castle again within 4 years. The town has much evidence of its Middle Ages importance, brought about by its strategic position at the end of the lake. There are several well preserved medieval houses and a handsome town hall with carved Gothic portals. The spire of a monastery rises high above the town. From Rapperswil follow the lake to Zürich.

Further Information
— The North: Around the Bodensee —

Museums and Other Places of Interest

Appenzell
Appenzeller Schaukäserei
(Appenzell Cheese Dairy), Stein
☎ 071/59 17 33
Open: daily 8am-8pm.

Heimatsmuseum
Rathaus Hauptgasse
☎ 071/87 15 95
Appenzell history and folklore.
Open: May, June and mid-September to early November, Sundays
1.30-5pm; July to mid-September
daily 1.30-5pm.

Retonio's Mechanisches
Musikmuseum
Bankgasse 6
☎ 071/87 41 22
Mechanical musical instruments,
automatic dolls and toys. Magic.
Open: July to October daily
10.30am-3.30pm; November to
June daily 2.30-4pm. Closed
Mondays.

Arbon
Historisches Museum
Schloss
☎ 071/46 13 28
Comprehensive exhibition of the
life of the area from prehistoric
times to the present day.
Open: daily 10am-12noon for most
of the year, also 2-5pm in summer.

Berlingen
Adolf Dietrich Haus
Seestrasse 26
☎ 054/8 23 23

The Swiss painter Adolf Dietrich
was a Berlingen man, and his
former studio is open to the public,
with some of his work on view
Open: Wednesday and Friday
2-6pm, also most Saturdays and
Sundays 2-6pm.

Frauenfeld
Natural History Museum
Freistrasse 24
☎ 054/7 91 11
Natural history and geology of
Thurgau canton
Open: Wednesday, Saturday and
Sunday 2-5pm.

Heiden
Henry Dunant Museum
Alterspflegeheim, Werdstrasse
☎ 071/91 12 55
Open: daily 10am-4pm.

Herisau
Museum, Altes Rathaus
Dorfplatz
☎ 071/512373
Appenzell folk art and history.
Open: April to November,
Sundays 10am-12noon.

Rapperswil
Heimatsmuseum
Brenyshaus am Herrenberg
☎ 055/27 71 64
Folk arts and crafts of the region.
Open: Easter Monday to October
daily 2-5pm. Closed Friday.

Polenmuseum
Schloss
☎ 055/27 44 95

Polish art and culture.
Check opening times locally.

Rorschach
Heimatsmuseum
Kornhaus
☎ 071/41 40 62
Local life, history and crafts.
Open: daily 9.30-11.30am and
2-5pm, Sunday 10am-12noon and
2-5pm. Closed Monday.

Salenstein
Napoleonic Museum
Schloss Arenenberg
☎ 073/64 18 66
The house where Napoleon III
spent his childhood is full of
souvenirs of his life.
Open: May-September daily 10am-
12noon and 2-4pm. Closing time
extended to 5pm in April and
October. Closed Monday.

St Gallen
Kunstmuseum
Kirchoferhaus, Museumstrasse 27
☎ 071/24 75 21
Swiss paintings of the nineteenth
and twentieth centuries, French
and German paintings of the
nineteenth century.
Open: January to May, October to
December 2-4pm, also 10am-
12noon on Sundays; June to September daily 10am-12noon and
2-5pm.

Museum in Kirchoferhaus
Museumstrasse 27
☎ 071/24 75 21
Collection of silver vessels from
the High Renaissance and baroque
periods.
Open: January to May, October to
December, Thursday-Sunday

2-4pm. Sunday also 10am-12noon;
June to September, Thursday-
Sunday 10am-12noon and 2-5pm.

Textilmuseum
Vadianstrasse 2
☎ 071/22 17 45
Embroidery and lace from the
sixteenth to nineteenth centuries.
Open: Monday-Friday 10am-
12noon and 2-5pm. April to September daily 10am-12noon and
2-5pm. Closed Sunday.

Spieldosen Kabinett Lebhart
Marktgasse 23
☎ 071/22 70 95
Collection of musical boxes.
Open: Tuesday-Saturday, guided
tour at 11am.

Historisches Museum
(History Museum)
Museumstrasse 50
☎ 071/24 78 32
Cultural and historical inheritance
of the region.
Open: October to May, Tuesday-
Saturday 2-4pm, Sunday 10am-
12noon, and 2-4pm. Closed Mon-
day; June to September daily
10am-12noon and 2-5pm. Closed
Monday.

Stiftsbibliothek
(Monastery Library)
Klosterhof
☎ 071/22 57 19
Medieval books and manuscripts.
Inquire locally for times.

Urnäsch
Museum für Appenzeller
Brauchturm
Dorfplatz
☎ 071/58 23 22
The rural arts, crafts and way of

life of the people of Appenzell.
Open: April to June, Wednesday,
Saturday and Sunday 2-5pm; April
to October daily 2-5pm.

Wil
Stadtmuseum
Hofgebaube
☎ 073/22 38 55
Life of Wil and surrounding countryside. Includes several baroque
prints, relics of religious art and
old documents.
Open: Monday, Wednesday and
Friday 2-5pm, Saturday 9-11am
and 2-5pm, Sunday 10am-12noon
and 2-5pm.

Wildhaus
Zwinglihaus
☎ 074/5 21 78
Commemorates the life of Ulrich
Zwingli, Swiss protestant reformer.
Open: daily 2-4pm. Closed Mon-
days.

Tourist Information Offices

Most tourist offices open at 8am
and close at 5.30pm, but many, especially smaller ones in remote
areas, will close for lunch, usually
between 12noon and 2pm.

Regional
Eastern Switzerland
Verkehrsverband Ostschweiz
Bahnhofplatz 1a
St Gallen
☎ 071/22 62 62

Sub-Regional
Appenzell Ausser-Rhoden
Verband Verkehrsvereine
Dorf 33
Stein
☎ 071/59 11 59

Appenzell Innerrhoden
Kur-und-Verkehrsverein
Appenzell Innerrhoden
Hauptgasse 19
Appenzell
☎ 071/87 41 11

Obertoggenburg
Werbegemeinschaft
Obertoggenburg
c/o Verkehrsbuero Wildhaus
☎ 074/5 27 27

Canton Thurgau
Thurgauische
Verkehrsvereinigung
Gemeindehaus
Amriswil
☎ 071/67 68 51

Local
Appenzell
Verkehrsbuero
Hauptgasse 19
☎ 071/87 41 41

Arbon
Offizielles
Verkehrsbuero
Bahnhofstrasse 26
☎ 171/46 65 77

Bad Ragaz
Kur-und
Verkehrsverein
☎ 085/9 10 61

Glarus
Verkehrsbuero
Kirchweg 18
☎ 058/61 13 47

Heiden
Verkehrsbuero
Seeallee 813
☎ 071//91 10 96

Herisau
Verkehrsbuero
Oberdorfstrasse 1
☎ 071/51 44 60

Rapperswil
Verkehrsverein
Seequai
☎ 055/27 70 00

Romanshorn
Verkehrsverein
Bahnhofplatz
☎ 071/63 32 32

St Gallen
Verkehrsverein
Bahnhofplatz 1a
☎ 071/22 62 62

Wildhaus
Kur-und Verkehrsverein
☎ 074/5 27 27

Useful Information

Banks
Most open Monday-Wednesday
8.15am-4.30pm, Thursday 8.15am-
6pm, Friday 8.15am-4.30pm. Some
open Saturday 9am-4pm. But
hours can vary from town to town.

Bicycles
Can be hired from, and returned
to, railway stations.

Camping
The Swiss National Tourist Office
publishes a complete guide to the
camp sites throughout the country.

Car Hire
It is assumed that travellers in
north Switzerland will hire a car
on arrival in Switzerland, probably

in Zürich. For details, see under
Car Hire in the Zürich chapter.

Changing Money
At banks and tourist offices during
normal business hours.

Credit Cards
Most hotels and restaurants accept
the principal credit cards, as do the
leading stores, filling stations etc.

Facilities for the Disabled
The Swiss National Tourist Office
have a pamphlet dealing with
facilities for the disabled.

Shopping
North Switzerland has many
characteristic products which
make excellent souvenirs or presents. Wood carving, embroidery,
costume dolls, and, of course,
Swiss watches and chocolates are
famous. Swiss army knives are
remarkably versatile instruments,
able to open anything. Several
towns produce their own confectionery (Aarau, for example, has
some particularly mouth-watering
chocolates). Keep an eye open for
local markets. It is often cheaper to
shop there, and in any event, they
are generally colourful.

Sport
Facilities naturally vary with the
size of the town, but the people of
north Switzerland love the open-
air life, and every sport is usually
within reach, including water
sports in lake areas. There are
many sophisticated indoor sports
complexes. Inquire at your tourist
office.

Tipping
Don't. Gratuities are included in the bill at most hotels and restaurants.

Winter Sports
The mountainous areas of north Switzerland make this an ideal region for winter sports. It is a useful district for beginners, for there are ski schools in most resorts, and easy runs for learners. New downhill and cross-country runs (becoming more and more popular) are opening all the time making a definitive list impossible to compile. Curling, skating, ski-bob and tobogganing are all plentiful. Inquire at the local tourist office for up-to-date-information.

Youth Hostels
Switzerland has always been in the vanguard of youth hostel development. The Swiss National Tourist Office publishes a special booklet giving full information.

3 • Zürich

Zürich could hardly be described as remote, either in terms of situation or events. There it is, standing astride an international crossroads, straddling routes through which the traffic of many nations must pass, and giving rapid access to all of the most famous places with which we associate the name of Switzerland. The Bernese Oberland, Lake Lucerne, Lake Geneva, cities like Bern and Basle, the Jura mountains, the shores of the Bodensee, are all within easy reach by road or rail.

Of its relationship with the rest of Europe and with contemporary history, something similar could be written. Zürich is always in the news, not merely on the map of world affairs, but usually right at the heart of it.

So what is it doing in a book devoted to places off the beaten track in Switzerland? It is here for a number of reasons. Zürich is an essential part of one of the regions inviting exploration, north Switzerland, which tourists are inclined to pass through with no more than an approving nod, rather than lingering to find out.

It is the most likely place of arrival and departure for most visitors from overseas. And having arrived in Zürich, or having returned there at the end of a tour round north Switzerland, visitors will probably want to spend a little time in a city about which they have heard so much. They are recommended to do so, for Zürich is hardly what one has been led to expect.

The first thing to get straight about Zürich is that it is not the capital of Switzerland, though there are times when one thinks it ought to be, and others when one gets the impression that it would not mind at all if it was. But that distinction belongs to Bern. The

Zürich rooftops

second is that you must not expect a large metropolis. By modern European standards, Zürich is not a big city, not yet 400,000 people at the time of writing, but it is still the largest in Switzerland.

A visitor arriving in Zürich for the first time will almost certainly do so with a preconceived idea of a feverishly busy city where austere-faced financiers wearing dark suits hurry past in search of the next billion dollars, where bankers huddle together in back rooms like a secret society, a place resembling a web from the centre of which threads reach out to manipulate the money markets of the world, and everything is subordinate to profit.

Judge, then, the surprise of the visitor who arrives on a fine spring day to find the scent of the linden trees on the Bahnhofstrasse filling the air. The cafés have their pavement tables out, nobody seems to be in a hurry, and the atmosphere is that of a relaxed Mediterranean

Ninety-nine steps lead to the Old Town of Zürich

city. Somebody must be locked away somewhere totting up figures, or how would they make all that money? But somehow, it's difficult to imagine.

There are other surprises too: swans in the city centre, for example, and leisurely, old-fashioned steamers. For soon after descending from their international express at Zürich's main station, new arrivals may be standing on the bridge where Zürich's river, the Limmat, joins its lake, the Zürichsee, looking up at green fields and trees, at ancient towers, or perhaps down-lake to a wide expanse of blue water criss-crossed by the wakes of pleasure steamers, decorated by the white sails of holidaying yachtsmen.

The point is that years of hard work and steady application, the rocks on which Zürich's prosperity and influence have been built, have not spoiled the city or its people. The Zürichers know how to work, but they also know how to play. With growing success has also come a more informed understanding of the quality of life. The city wears a smile, and the arts that endure are valued. So is having a good time. It is a very human place.

And though Zürich could never be described as off the beaten track of tourism, there are plenty of quiet corners close to the city centre which are off the beaten track of Zürich itself.

You come across them unexpectedly. Zürich is a city of squares, in many of which time seems to have edged forward by only a few hours since the Middle Ages. There are winding alleyways, old guildhouses clustered together, sleepy sidewalks, and steps. Plenty of steps, most of them with a rich reward for the climber, such as those that lead to the Lindenhof. Walk down the Bahnhofstrasse towards the lake, turn left when you come to the Rennweg, left again into the Fortunagasse, up the inevitable steps to the **Lindenhof**. There are fine views of the old town from here, and the remains of the original Roman customs house are near at hand.

A fountain catches the eye. Erected in 1912, it commemorates a strange event in Zürich history. In 1292, the Habsburgs were making one of their periodic assaults on the turbulent Swiss. Their forces encircled the city, and the Swiss were out-numbered. But the women of Zürich donned armour, marched to the Lindenhof and manned the battlements. The invaders thought it must be a reinforcing army, and decided to go home. Zürich was saved by the inventiveness of its women.

This is the beginning of the classic route to follow on a walking tour of Zürich, starting from the main railway station through the sophisticated poise of the Bahnhofstrasse and branching off for the

Parade Square, Zürich

Lindenhof. But before going on, perhaps some time should be spent considering its history.

The Lindenhof, in fact, is not at all a bad place to do it, since this is where Zürich's recorded history begins. In 15BC the Romans established a settlement on this very spot, no doubt with its commanding strategic position in mind, and called it *Turicum*. In the third century AD Zürich collected its patron saints. Roman power was declining generally, but it was still strong in Zürich, and the beheading of Felix and his sister Regula, two Christians, was ordered by the governor. They were executed on a small island in the river. That much is established fact. The rest of the legend states that Felix and Regula picked up their heads, waded through the water, and walked up to the hill where the Grossmünster now stands, before expiring.

After the Romans were driven out by the Alemanni in the fifth century, the history of the area is misty until the ninth, when Zürich is mentioned as a town for the first time with the building of a palace there by Charlemagne. But this was out of character with Zürich's later history. It was never to become a place of palaces and princes. Its strength was a nose for commerce which soon manifested itself, so that by the twelfth century, the authority of an effete aristocracy began to dwindle as the power of the merchants correspondingly grew. Zürich became famous for its accumulating wealth and as a place where merchants flourished and silk, wool and leather industries were all securely established. Zürich, in the Middle Ages, was Switzerland's most important city, and it was to stay that way.

The merchants had the cash, but the weakening aristocracy held on to the reins of government. It was a situation which could not be tolerated, and in a revolution led by Rudolf Brun the nobles were overthrown, and Brun, as Zürich's first burgomaster, divided the power between the patricians and the craft guilds. The town eventually joined the new Swiss Confederation and played its distinguished part in the final expulsion of the Habsburgs. Hans Waldman, another great Zürich burgomaster, led the Swiss forces to victory at Morat during the Burgundian war in 1476, defeating the formerly all-conquering Charles the Bold.

Enter Ulrich Zwingli (1484-1531), one of the most zealously dedicated of all the religious reformers, a man whose opposition to traditional beliefs and practices was so extreme as to make Luther (with whom he quarrelled) look mild. In 1519, Zwingli became preacher at the Grossmünster, and he used its pulpit to launch savage attacks on Catholic doctrines. His teachings appealed to the Zürichers. His quarrel with Luther meant that he had little influence in Germany, but there was something about his insistence on thrift, application, and hard work for its own sake that struck sympathetic chords in the Zürich temperament. No doubt, too, the Zürichers, always a theatrically-minded people, were won by the threatening sense of drama with which his philosophy was delivered. Long after his death, Zwingli's influence persisted, so that spirituality and commerce met conveniently on common ground.

Zürich's importance as a business centre grew, as did its reputation as a place of refuge, so that it rivalled even that of Geneva. Huguenots brought their skills to augment those of Zürich's own craftsmen, and other refugees enriched its artistic life. Wagner, in retreat from pursuing creditors and political enemies, was one. By the end of the nineteenth century, Zürich had grasped the nettle of industrial development to become a leader among the world's banking centres, thanks mainly to the foresight of Alfred Escher, and, at the centre of a skilfully developed network of communications and engineering feats, was ready to take full advantage of the transport explosion.

Although Switzerland had no part in them, the two World Wars left their mark, but when the conflicts were over, Zürich quickly resumed its place in the forefront of the world's business and cultural affairs. Hand in hand went successful economic policies, wise co-operation between management and workers resulting in productive years of economic peace, and an enlightened appreciation of the arts, all making Zürich a rich city, not just in terms of finance, but in the variety of its life.

Time to re-commence the walk. Near the Lindenhof there is **St Peter's church**, which is said to have the largest clock face in Europe (nearly 29ft in diameter). There was a church on this spot in the ninth century, and part of the existing building dates back to the thirteenth century (including the tower which houses the record-breaking clock). Of more interest is the **Fraumünster**, which shares with St Peter's a ninth-century origin, and a thirteenth-century construction of the present edifice. But the Fraumünster's appeal is more artistic than historic. The choir has some superb stained glass windows by Marc Chagall, there is a notable painting by the Swiss artist Augusto Giacometti, and fine modern frescoes by Paul Bodmer.

In this part of Zürich, one is often reminded that the power of the guilds lasted until the end of the eighteenth century. The **Zunfthaus zur Waag**, where the linen craftsmen used to meet, survives from the early seventeenth century, and the **Zunfthaus zur Meise**, built approximately a century later, was the meeting place of the wine merchants. From here, it is a short walk to the river. Go along the Stadhaus Quai to the right, to Quai bridge, and one of Zürich's most invigorating views awaits. Cross over to the east bank, and on the way, look right. There is a superb panorama of the lake and its traffic, with the peaks of distant mountains glistening in the background. Look left, and there are the spires and clustered roofs of the old town.

When you reach the far bank, the renovated **Opera House** is away to the right. For the Kunsthaus and its distinguished collection, cross Bellevue Platz, keep on up the Rämstrasse and the **Kunsthaus** is on your left. But the collection here is best left for another day, as it merits a special visit. Turn left and come to the **Wasserkirche**, the Water Church, as lovely a piece of late Gothic architecture as you could wish to see. This, too, boasts a Giacometti stained glass window, and near here, Zürich's patron saints were martyred.

Turn right, and the **Grossmünster** is before you. This is where Zwingli preached the message which swung the Züricher to his line of thinking, and its grave façade seems to reflect the severity of his teaching. So, for that matter, does the glum look on the face of Charlemagne, whose statue is on the south tower. The architecture of the Grossmünster ranges from the eleventh to eighteenth centuries, and once more there is some Giacometti stained glass.

Go back to the river, turn right and some of Zürich's finest buildings can be seen. There is the thirteenth-century **Gesellschafsthaus zum Rüden**, the Hall of the Noblemen, with its ancient wooden ceiling, and nearby stand the baroque **Zunfthaus zur Zimmerleuten** (Guildhouse of the Carpenters, 1708) and the **Zunfthaus zur Saffran** (Guildhouse of the Haberdashers, 1723). It is as though the historic opponents of medieval times, the aristocrats and the guildsmen, had been brought together in harmony. Both the guildhouses and the House of the Noblemen are now restaurants.

Near at hand is the seventeenth-century **Rathaus**, the Town Hall, imposing from the outside and positively beautiful inside, with its fine baroque Banqueting Hall. Then wander through the maze of streets leading into the old town on your right, to enter a world as far from the busy twentieth century as it is possible to be. There are drowsy old houses, sleepy alleys and squares, intimate cafés, and the air of medieval Switzerland envelopes you.

Next make for Rindermarkt, and stop at No 9. Here lived Gottfried Keller (1819-90), the Swiss poet and novelist whose carefully crafted short stories embrace both humour and a touching romanticism, and make him one of the most important figures of Swiss literature. The restaurant in which he used to take his lunch, Zur Opfelchammer, is still there.

The picturesque Neumarkt is worth a visit before heading back to the Limmatquai. Cross the Bahnhof bridge, and you will have come full circle back to the starting point. On route you will have found plenty of cosy little cafés for a mid-morning coffee, cheerful pubs, and in the Bahnhofstrasse, confectionery shops whose wares are displayed with such imagination that it seems a sin to pass them by.

To help visitors who are in Zürich for the first time, the tourist office has worked out four planned itineraries. 'The Sights of Zürich' gives a good general idea of the city, and takes about 2 hours. 'Zürich and Vicinity' includes an aerial cableway trip to Felsenegg. This runs daily from May to October, and the tour lasts $2\frac{1}{2}$ hours. 'Goldtimer' is a very special way of getting to know the city centre. This is an

The record-breaking clock of St Peter's

hour-long conducted tour in an old tram car, nostalgia every inch of the way. This also runs from May to October, departing from Uster-istrasse/Bahnhofstrasse. 'Zürich by Night' is a daily tour of the city's night spots from folklore to strip-tease, and lasts about $3^1/_2$ hours. A conducted 'Stroll around the Town' starts from the tourist office every day, and takes $2^1/_2$ hours. Or you can hire your own personal hostess, also from the tourist office.

Don't let the ultra-sophisticates put you off the guided city tour. Regularly one hears a traveller say 'I don't want to be herded around with a lot of tourists'. Fair enough. It's more fun finding out on your own, and the best experiences are usually those you seek out for yourself. But it's not at all a bad idea to have a quick guided tour on your first day to get an idea of the layout, saving a lot of time asking the way and taking the wrong turning. Then go it alone on another day, taking as long as you like over whatever you like.

Every kind of entertainment thrives in Zürich after dark. Its opera has an international reputation, both for its musical standards and its progressive attitude to production. It is open for most of the year, but you need to book well in advance for any specific performance.

The Zürich Tonhalle is the city's principal symphony orchestra, and one of Europe's oldest. It numbers Brahms and Wagner among its past conductors, and is the centre of the city's musical life, with a long annual season of subscription concerts from September to the following summer. Other Swiss and leading foreign symphony orchestras also appear regularly, while the world's best known chamber ensembles and solo recitalists stop at Zürich on their travels as a matter of course.

The Zürich Festival in June has taken its place among the most highly regarded events of its kind in Europe. Opera, ballet, symphony concerts, chamber recitals, art exhibitions and plays all have their part in this 4-week programme. Here again, it is advisable to book well ahead. The nearest branch of the Swiss National Tourist Office in your home country can help.

Traditional drama, contemporary theatre, experimental theatre, farce, musical comedy, operetta, revue and poetry reading all have their places in the regular round. So do rock concerts, folk, jazz (with a special 5-day jazz festival every October), discos, strip-tease shows and late night cabaret. Most Zürich cinemas show films in the original language, and these are very diverse, so there are always some showing English language films. The Schauspielhaus is Zürich's most important theatre, and it has a legendary reputation. During World War II it was the only German-speaking theatre where free speech was possible. Traditional classics and modern plays are performed here, as well as experimental theatre, but performances are in German.

You could hardly leave Zürich without seeing one of the Swiss floor shows. One of the best of these is at Baggli's Swiss Chalet at Marktgasse 14 (☎ 01/252 15 30) where you can eat Swiss cheese fondue and see an authentic Swiss folklore display, with dancing, singing, alpine horn-blowing, zither music and yodelling. For a complete up-to-date list of what's on in Zürich, pick up a copy of *Zürich News* which is published each week. Most hotels will give you one on arrival, or it can be collected from the tourist office.

Bürkliplatz

The view from the Quai bridge will have whetted your appetite for a trip on the lake, and a visit to Zürich is not complete without at least one water-borne day out. The Zürichsee is the third largest lake which is entirely in Switzerland, covering an area of nearly 35sq miles, and measuring 25 miles from the Bürkliplatz at the end of Zürich's Bahnhofstrasse to Schmerikon, where the lake tapers to its end. Like most of the lakes of Switzerland it has its own character. Look not for the romantic glamour of Lake Geneva, the dramatic backcloth of Lake Lucerne, or the fascinating cosmopolitanism of Lake Constance (the Bodensee). Instead, the shores of Zürich's lake have a more intimate charm, comparing to those of Lucerne and Geneva as a well kept garden might to an alpine panorama or a royal park. Not that Zürich's lake is without romance. It intrudes when the distant views of the snow-clad Mürtschenstock first become visible.

It does so when the eye catches the castle of Rapperswil towards the end of the lake on the eastern shore. But Rapperswil is treated in more detail in the section on north Switzerland.

So take a boat trip. There's no more relaxing way of travelling, and passenger ships leave the Bürkliplatz daily from April to October. The 'Long Tour' goes all the way from Zürich to Rapperswil and back, which takes 5 hours. The afternoon 'Short Trip' last 1 $^1/_2$ hours, while the 'Lunchtime Trip', departing just after mid-day, is a 75 minute run. Every day during the season there is also an 'Evening Tour' with dancing on board (around 2$^1/_2$ hours) and a 'Lake Fondue Party' (about 2$^1/_2$ hours in the evening).

For those interested in shopping, the best area is concentrated in a small part of the city centre. Start at the Bahnhofstrasse, leading from the main railway station towards the Paradeplatz and the lake. Zürich people will tell you that this is one of Europe's most elegant shopping streets, and they are probably right. Here there are famous department stores, fashion shops, retail shops with high quality goods, confectioners and pavement cafés. In the old town, streets such as Rennweg, Strehlgasse, Augustinergasse and St Peterhofstatt have enticing smaller boutiques and antique shops. The Limmatquai, on the right-hand bank of the river, has old guildhouses overlooking the shops. The Langstrasse is renowned for variety and competitive prices. The Löwenstrasse area with the neighbouring Bahnhofpassage has become so popular with shoppers that now they call it 'Shopville'. Explore the medieval side streets where prices are often lower. For all the elegance and elaborate façades, Zürich is a city where you can find value for money, so it pays to be patient and spend time comparing prices.

Articles for which Zürich is famous are antiques and *objets d'art* (Neumarkt area) and of course Swiss watches. Its pastries and confectioneries are unsurpassable (Bahnhofstrasse, Rennweg, Bellevue). Embroidery and lace products are of high quality, and Swiss chocolates need no recommendation. Folk products, particularly wood carving, are delightful souvenirs to take home. A particularly good buy is the Swiss army knife, able to open anything, and equipped with gadgets to deal with every domestic crisis.

Zürich is a book lover's paradise. In the centre alone, there are thirty bookshops with an international reputation, including many second hand ones. A shop specialising in children's books is on the Grossmünsterplatz.

It is natural that Zürich, as an international centre of finance, business and tourism, should be well equipped with numerous

A quiet oasis only a few steps away from Zürich's business centre

hotels in all categories. By the same token, it follows that these hotels are heavily booked. So if Zürich is to be the centre of your Swiss exploration, be sure to book a hotel well in advance. You get what you pay for. Don't expect five-star facilities in a one-star hotel. What is certain is that in each category the hotel will be excellent of its kind: the five-star hotel a very good five-star hotel, the one-star hotel a very good one-star hotel. The welcome will be warm, the service professional. The people of Zürich have been playing host to the world for a long time, and you reap the benefit of matured experience. In the smallest Swiss guest house, you may have a delightful and characteristic Swiss experience.

The city's restaurants and cuisine also cover a wide variety. The visitor who seeks something elegant and sophisticated, or a discreet corner, or a lively atmosphere, will find it. Cooking in the classical French style, something spiced with the flavour of the Orient, an evocation of the Arabian nights or India, national dishes from the Balkans, Greece or the Mediterranean, the Italian pizza, the Spanish paella, the Hungarian goulash or a genuine American hamburger, are always within easy reach.

Enjoy the traditional Swiss dishes: the Zürich way with chopped veal or fresh fish from the lake, and many others. Zürich cooking is well flavoured but not over-spiced. Swiss wines are consistent. The best are excellent, and the most modest are never less than attractive. And remember that the most characteristic meals are not necessarily found behind the most imposing façades, nor do they necessarily carry the highest price tags. Remember, too, that there are literally scores of cafés in Zürich where you can have a quick and cheap snack. Don't tip unless for some unusual or special service. Gratuities are included in the bill.

Zürich has several exciting vantage points from which superb views of the city, the lake and the far-off mountains can be obtained. All can be reached by public transport and offer quiet and relaxing woodland walks. These include Dolder, Zürichberg, Rigiblick, Waidberg, and Käferberg. The tourist office can provide informative brochures. For the more adventurous, an excursion to Uetliberg, the mountain on Zürich's doorstep, is recommended. Foot travellers can take a tram from the main railway station to Albisgüetli, then walk to Uetliberg-Kulm (2,756ft, 871m). The walk takes a little over an hour. Or take the Uetliberg railway from Selnau station to Uto-Kulm. If you're lucky enough to have a clear day, the view of the distant Alps, the city and the lake beneath is quite unforgettable.

Excursion to Winterthur

Winterthur is easily reached from Zürich, and it is a good idea to make it the destination of an excursion from there. But you will probably need to spend more than a single day in Winterthur. It would, for example, take more than that to see in detail its museums and art galleries, for Winterthur is world famous as an arts centre, a

Winterthur

town which has been lucky in its collectors and benefactors. Then there is its well preserved old quarter, and on the doorstep a romantic, well wooded and castle-adorned countryside.

Winterthur is one of the ten towns chosen as typically Swiss. In the way in which, down the years, it has kept its responsibilities as a cultural centre sensibly in step with its growing commercial importance and prosperity, it is something of a model. It is astonishing that it should have preserved its character so well when it is close to Zürich. One might have expected it to be either suffocated or swallowed up. But nothing of the kind has happened.

To get there, take one of the trains that run every hour from Zürich to St Gallen. The journey takes only 20 minutes. Allow just a little longer if you go by the motorway leading to the north from Zürich.

Winterthur is first mentioned during the history of the third century, though the present town was founded in 1180. For two centuries it was under the Habsburgs, but in the fifteenth it passed to Zürich. Despite this, it became a mecca for craftsmen and merchants, and by the early nineteenth century, the domination of Zürich had been thrown off.

From then onwards, Winterthur's development into the city of today was rapid. An early regard for the quality of life was shown when the walls of the medieval town were pulled down in the early nineteenth century. Many of Winterthur's wealthier citizens had already built their villas outside in the country, and it was assumed that the space cleared by destroying the walls would go the same way. But the authorities had more far-seeing ideas. Where the walls had stood, they ringed the town with schools and dignified public buildings, of which the neo-classical Town Hall is an imposing example. Something similar happened in Vienna later, when the Emperor Franz Josef ordered the removal of the city's walls, and replaced them with the famous Ring, with its parks, university, public buildings and what is now the Vienna State Opera.

Winterthur's prosperity was built on business acumen and new industries. Textiles was one, but more famous was engineering. Locomotives for the railways of the world and huge engines for transatlantic liners carried the town's name everywhere.

Today, industry and commerce are still prominent. Sulzer and Rieter are names known all over Europe, and so are Volkart and Winterthur Insurance. And from the affluence they have brought has come Winterthur's other fame as a cultural centre.

When one considers the proximity of Zürich (so easy to go there for a show or a concert, have a meal, and arrive back home at a reasonable hour), the thriving variety of Winterthur's night life is surprising. Opera and symphony concerts, cabaret and musicals, discos and night clubs, plays and experimental theatre all appear on the weekly list.

There is a new theatre of almost alarming contemporary design which shows that the town is prepared to take an adventurous chance with new ideas as well as preserving its inheritance. And in the summer, the tree-fringed open-air theatre is a major attraction.

Winterthur's symphony orchestra has achieved a reputation outside Switzerland through its recordings. It has one activity which

Winterthur market

must make Winterthur the envy of other musical centres. There is a distinguished series of subscription concerts from autumn to the succeeding summer (they still talk with pride of the day in 1934 when Richard Strauss came to conduct his *Don Quixote* and *Alpine Symphony*) but there are also free symphony concerts most weeks in the year, very popular particularly with Winterthur's younger generation.

But it is Winterthur's art collections that almost dwarf the rest of its cultural life. The most proud possession among these is the collection of Oskar Reinhart (1885-1965) at the gallery Am Römerholz, a country house in what was once a vineyard on the edge of the town. On a fine day, it is a pleasant walk from the centre of the town taking from 15 to 20 minutes. Or take a taxi from outside the railway

The castle of the counts of Kyburg near Winterthur

station.

Oskar Reinhart's father Theodor was head of the international company Volkart Brothers. This trading concern, based in Winterthur and Bombay was started in 1851 by Salomon Volkart (1816-1893) and was so successful that it was soon founding banks and insurance companies, and was one of the stalwarts of Switzerland's growing influence in world business affairs.

Theodor Reinhart was himself an art collector, and was undoubtedly a strong motivating influence on his son. While still at grammar school, Oskar Reinhart suspected that art was where his future lay, rather than the commercial life for which he was intended. Soon he was able to devote himself to it full time. From 1924 on, his collection

Inside the castle of the counts of Kyburg

became his life. He had the shrewd selective instinct and the artistic taste. And he had the money to exploit both. Art treasures flowed steadily to Am Römerholz.

In the gallery today, the visitor is confronted with one of the most comprehensive collections of impressionist painting anywhere in the world. Manet, Monet, Corot, Renoir, Delacroix, Van Gogh, Cézanne, Daumier, are just a few of the names. But this is only half the story. A second collection in the gallery includes work by Goya, Greco, Rubens, Rembrandt, Holbein, Bruegel and others. When he died shortly after his eightieth birthday, Oskar Reinhart bequeathed the entire Am Römerholz treasury of painting to the people of Winterthur.

And even that does not complete the story of Winterthur's artistic debt to him. In the city itself there is the Oskar Reinhart Foundation, which he set up for Winterthur in his lifetime, and which houses over six hundred works by Swiss, German and Austrian artists of the sixteenth, seventeenth and eighteenth centuries.

There is also a fine collection of Swiss and German masterpieces in the municipal art gallery, much of which is owed to enlightened patronage by other leading local entrepreneurs down the years. Winterthur is Switzerland's sixth largest town, but none surpasses it in artistic richness.

When you have had your fill of art galleries, there still remains the Konrad Kellenberger collection of clocks in the renovated Town Hall, and the Swiss Technorama, where contemporary technology is skilfully related to everyday life in a way the visitor can understand. There is a chance to carry out your own experiments, a steam railway, and a special laboratory for young people. The Swiss Technorama is some distance from the town centre, but regular buses take you there.

Winterthur is a green town, with plenty of parks and quick access to the unspoiled country around. The old quarter is a delightful mixture, with charming Renaissance houses and quiet corners set amid the bustle of the narrow shopping streets, many of them reserved for pedestrians. Sometimes, turning a corner from some leisurely alley, you feel you have been thrust into the coruscating life of a country fair. On Tuesdays and Fridays, for example, the old quarter is busy with the fruit, flower and vegetable markets, and on the last Saturday of every month, it is enlivened by the traditional flea market. On these occasions, it is hard to realise that not so very far away, industry and commerce are hard at work. Hard to realise too that another contrasting world, that of a tranquil countryside is close at hand.

Here there are many fine castles. Probably the most historic and also the most photogenic is that of the counts of Kyburg, perched high above woodlands and looking down fiercely on the river Töss. The counts were considerable powers in north Switzerland, with widespread properties. They held on to this fortress until 1264, when it passed to the Habsburgs, who in turn lost it to the canton of Zürich in 1452. It is still theirs today, which is surprising when one considers how regularly the winds of change have blown across the cantons. It has a Romanesque chapel and some medieval frescoes. The most picturesque approach to Kyburg castle is through the Eschenberg forest, past the Bruderhaus deer park. The castle looms on the other side of the river.

Wüflingen castle is older. Its history begins in the last years of the ninth century. The Gerichtsstube, today a restaurant, was painted by Kühn in 1767, and the most famous of its rooms is the upstairs Herrenstube, with its walnut panelling and rococo decorations. The stoves, decorated with stories from history and the Bible, are master-pieces of tile craft work.

Hegi castle is a typical example of the moated castles of north Switzerland. The tower dates from around 1200, and the manor house was probably added at the end of the fifteenth century. The owner, Professor Friedrich Hegi of Zürich, carried out considerable renovations, and the town of Winterthur took possession of the castle in 1947.

The counts of Kyburg and the royal family of Habsburg figure prominently again in relation to Mörsburg castle. They owned it consecutively until, in 1598, Winterthur took it over. It was reno-vated in 1931 and today has many relics of Winterthur's past.

Inquire locally at the tourist office of Winterthur for opening times of these castles, as they are likely to be subject to variation from time to time.

Further Information
— Zürich —

Museums and Other Places of Interest

Haus zum Rech
Neumarkt 4
☎ 01 69 20 81
Zürich architecture.
Open: Monday-Friday 8am-6pm,
Saturday 8am-12noon. Closed
Sunday.

Indianer Museum der Stadt
Schulhaus Feldstrasse
Feldstrasse 89
☎ 01/241 00 50
Cultural heritage of the North
American Indian.
Open: Saturdays 2-5pm, Sundays
10am-12noon. Closed during
school holidays except summer
vacation.

Jacobs Suchard Museum
Seefeldquai 17
☎ 01/38512 83
History of coffee.
Open: Friday 3-6pm, Saturday
10am-4pm. Closed on public holi-
days, Saturdays before Easter and
Whitsun, and between Christmas
Day and New Year's Day. Groups
by appointment only.

Keramiksammlung
Zunfthaus zur Meisen
Münsterhof 20
☎ 01/221 10 10
Swiss eighteenth-century ceramics
and porcelain.
Open: daily 10am-12noon, except
Monday 2-5pm.

Kulturama
Espenhofweg 60
☎ 01/493 25 25
Prehistory and anatomy of ani-
mals.
Open: Monday-Friday and first
Sunday in each month 10am-5pm
or by arrangement.

Kunstgewerbemuseum der Stadt
Austellungsstrasse 60
Museum of applied arts.
Open: most days 10am-5pm, but
check locally.

Kunsthaus
Heimplatz 1
☎ 01/251 67 65
Dutch and Italian paintings;
French and Zürich artists; Dada
movement.
Open: Monday 2-5pm, Tuesday-
Friday 10am-9pm, Saturday,
Sunday 10am-5pm.

Medizinhistorische Sammlung der Universität
Universität
Ramistrasse 7
☎ 01/257 27 04
Medicine from the witch doctor to
the present day.
Open: Wednesday, Thursday 2-
5pm, Saturday 10am-12noon, or by
arrangement.

Mühlerama
Seefeldstrasse 231
Fully operational mill complex.
Open: daily 2-5pm, except Sunday
11am-5pm. Closed Monday.

Museum Bellerive

Höschgasse 3
☎ 01/251 43 77
Crafts, glass, jewellery, textiles.
Open: daily 10am-12noon and 2-5pm. Closed Monday.

Museum der Zeitmessung Beyer

Banhofstrasse 31
☎ 01/221 10 80
Timepieces from 1400BC to the present day.
Open: Monday-Friday 10am-12noon and 2-4pm, Saturday 10am-12noon. Closed Sunday.

Museum Rietberg

Gablerstrasse 15
☎ 01/202 45 28
Attractive villa setting for display of non-European art.
Open: daily 10am-5pm, Wednesday 8am-8pm. Closed Monday.

Pestalozzi-Gedenkzimmer

Pestalozzianum
Beckenhofstrasse 33
☎ 01/362 04 28
Memorial museum to the work of Johann Heinrich Pestalozzi, famed Swiss educational reformer.
Open: daily 2-5pm, except Sundays.

Puppenhaus und Spiel-zeugmuseum Martha Volleweider

Birmensdorferstrasse 38
Old dolls' houses and toys, interesting for children.
Open: Monday, Wednesday, Friday 2-4.30pm, or by arrangement.

Puppenmuseum Sasha Morgenthaler

Bärengasse 22

☎ 01/211 17 16
Collection of the well known Swiss puppet artist. 160 dolls and other toys. Film show. Interesting for children.
Open: mid-September-early June, daily 10am-12noon and 2-5pm. Mid-June-mid-September, daily 10am-12noon, except Monday 2-5pm.
At same address is the Wohnmuseum (see below).

Sammlung E.G. Bührle

Zollikerstrasse 172
☎ 01/55 00 86

One of Zürich's finest exhibitions. Private collection of the family Bührle, now open to the public. Splendid display of French nineteenth-century paintings, including work by Renoir, Cézanne, Gauguin, Toulouse-Lautrec, Van Gogh, Manet and others. Out of town, but conveniently placed on tram routes 2 and 4.

Open: Tuesday and Friday 2-5pm, first Friday of the month 2-8pm.

Schweizerisches Landesmuseum

Museumstrasse 2
☎ 01/221 10 10

Swiss history. Rooms furnished in period styles. Ceramics, paintings, weapons.

Open: June-September, Tuesday-Friday and Sunday 10am-12noon and 2-5pm, Saturday 10am-4pm. Closed Monday; October-June daily 10am-12noon and 2-5pm, except Saturday 10am-12noon and 2-4pm.
Closed Monday. Guided tour by arrangement.

Stadtische Galerie zum Strauhof
Augustinergasse 9
☎ 01/216 33 39
Swiss art in atmospheric old house.
Open: Tuesday-Friday 10am-6pm.
Closed weekends and Monday.

Volkerkundmuseum
Pelikanstrasse 40
☎ 01/221 31 91
African, East Asian and Indonesian art.
Open: Tuesday-Friday 10am-12noon, Saturday and Sunday 10am-4pm. Closed Monday.

Wohnmuseum
Bärengasse 22
☎ 01/211 17 60
Museum of domestic art.
Open: daily 10am-12noon and 2-5pm, Saturday 10am-12noon and 2-4pm. Closed Monday.
At same address is the Puppenmuseum Sasha Morgenthaler (see above).

Zinnfiguren Museum
Obere Zäune 19
☎ 01/69 57 20
Tinware, including toys, military objects, animals.
Open: Monday-Saturday 2-5pm, except Thursday 2-7pm. Sunday 10am-12noon and 2-5pm or by arrangement.

Zürcher Spielzeugmuseum
Fortunagasse 15
☎ 01/211 93 05
Toys from the past, dolls, dolls houses, mechanical toys, railways, steam engines, books. Ideal for children.
Open: daily 2-5pm except Saturdays, Sundays and public holidays.

Winterthur

Sammlung Oskar Reinhart (Oskar Reinhart Collection)
Römerholz, Haldenstrasse 95
☎ 052/ 23 41 21
One of the outstanding collections of paintings in Europe, 5 minutes drive by car or taxi (from outside the Bahnhof)
Open: daily 10am-4pm. Closed Monday.

Stiftung Oskar Reinhart (Oskar Reinhart Foundation)
Stadthausstrasse 6
☎ 052/84 51 72
Another magnificent collection of art treasures bequeathed to the public by the great Swiss collector.
Open: daily 10am-12noon, and 2-5pm, except Monday morning.

Kunstmuseum
Museumstrasse 52
☎ 052/84 51 62
Swiss and German paintings of the nineteenth and twentieth centuries. French art since Impressionism.
Open: daily 10am-5pm, except Monday morning.

Technorama
Technoramastrasse 1
☎ 052/27 27 21
Striking exhibition of modern technology, including laboratory for young people. Also miniature steam railway. Out of the city, but regular bus service from the Bahnhof.
Open: daily 10am-5pm.

Uhrensammlung
Rathaus, Marktgasse 20
☎ 052/841 51 26
Clocks and watches down the centuries.

Open: daily 2-5pm, also Sunday
10am-12noon. Closed Monday and
public holidays.

Tourist Offices

Winterthur
Verkehrsverein
Bahnhofplatz 12
☎ 052/22 00 88

Zurich
Bahnhofplatz 15
☎ 01/24 40 40

Useful Information

Accident Department
Cantonal University Hospital
Schmelbergstrasse 8
☎ 01/255 44 11

Banks
Most are open Monday-Wednesday 8.15am-4.30pm, Thursday
8.15am-6pm, Friday 8.15am-
4.30pm.

Swiss Bank Corporation (SBC)
Banhofstrasse 70
Open: Monday-Friday 9am-
6.30pm, Saturday 9am-4pm.

Credit Suisse
Banhofstrasse 89
Open: Monday-Wednesday 7am-
6.30pm, Thursday 7am-9pm,
Friday 7am-6.30pm, Saturday 9am-
4pm.

Bicycles
Can be hired at the main railway
station.

Car Hire
Avis
Gartenhofstrasse

☎ 01/242 20 40

Zürich airport (☎ 01/814 38 04)

Budget Rent-a-Car
Tödistrasse 9
☎ 01/209 26 70

Zürich airport ☎ 01/814 38

Europcar
Badenstrasse 812
☎ 01/65 28 20

Zürich airport ☎ 01/813 20 44

Hertz
Lagesstrasse 33
☎ 01/241 80 77

Zürich airport ☎ 01/814 05 11

Also see the Zürich city telephone
directory (14) under *Autovermei-
tungen.*

Camping
The Swiss National Tourist Office
publish a comprehensive guide to
camp sites throughout Switzerland. If you intend to use them,
this booklet should be obtained
before departure.

Changing Money
At most banks and principal travel
agencies. Also daily at the main
railway station 6.30am-11.30pm.

Chemist (all-night)
Bellevue-Apotheke
Theatrestrasse 14
☎ 01/252 44 11

Cinemas
Zürich has many. Most show films
in the original language, so there
are usually several on show suitable for English-speaking visitors.

See 'What's On' below.

Consulates
American
Zollikerstrasse 141
☎ 01/55 25 66

British
Dufourstrasse 56
☎ 01/47 15 20

Credit Cards
Most hotels and restaurants accept
the principal credit cards, as do the
railway station, most leading
stores, filling stations, etc.

Dental Emergency
See medical.

Keep Fit
Zürich has seven woodland jog-
ging routes. The nearest to the
centre is on the Allmend Fluntern.
Ask about this and other keep fit
facilities at the tourist office.

Lake Trips
Bürkliplatz Ticket Office
☎ 01/482 10 33

Lost Property
Werdmühlerstrasse 10
☎ 01/216 51 11
See also 'Railway Information'
below.

Markets
At Burkliplatz, Helvetiaplatz,
Milchbuckstrasse, and Markplatz
Oerlikon on Tuesday and Friday
6-11am. During the summer there
is a market on Saturday morning
on the Limmatquai. The flea market is at Bürklianlage from May to
November.

Medical Emergency, including
dentist
☎ 01/47 47 00

City ambulance
☎ 01/361 61 61

Music
Tonhalle
Gotthardstrasse 5
☎ 01/201 15 80

Zürich International Festival
International Juni-Festwochen
Präsidialabteilung der Stadt Zürich
CH 8002 Zürich
☎ 01/216 31 11
Book as far in advance as possible.

Night Life
Consult the current weekly programme when you arrive (see
'What's On' below). The tourist
office will have up to the minute
information and help you to
choose.

Opera and Ballet
Opera House
Schillerstrasse 1
☎ 01/251 69 22

Parks and Gardens
Arboretum: lakeside gardens;
botanical gardens: exotic plants in
hot houses and 150,000 others on
show.
Open: daily March-September.

Belvoir Park: in the Enge district,
and the city's biggest.

Muraltengut: lovely rose garden in
summer.

Platzpromenade: conveniently
located popular public garden
behind the National Museum,

between the rivers Limmat and
Sihl, in city centre.

Rieterpark: magnificent trees, and
the Villa Wesendonck.

Zürichhorn: rhododendrons.

Post Offices
Conform to usual business hours,
but close Saturdays at 11am.
Urgent counter stays open most
days at the Sihlpost in Kasern-
strasse until 11pm.

Railway Information
Main railway station
☎ 01/211 50 10
For railway lost property,
☎ 01/211 88 11

Shopping
The main shopping centre is
concentrated in a small area of the
centre of the city.

Sport
Billiards: information from Bil-
liard-Club Zürich.
☎ 01/241 07 11

Boccia: numerous pitches
☎ 01/491 30 50

Bowling: seventy restaurants and
hotels have alleys.

Bridge: information from Bridge-
Club Zürich.
☎ 01/252 70 53.

Golf: Dolder Golf Club
(nine holes)
☎ 01/47 50 45;

Golf and Country Club, Zürich
(eighteen holes)
☎ 01/918 00 51

Ice-skating: Heuried and Dolder
artificial rinks open October-
March.

Riding: Fifteen riding schools in
and around Zürich. Inquire at
tourist office.

Rowing, sailing and motor boats:
can be hired along the Seequai
grounds, on the Upper Limmat
quay, and the Stadthaus quay. No
licence necessary.

Skiing: nearest region Hoch-Ybrig.
One hour train journey to Einsiedeln, bus to Weglosen, aerial
cableway to Hoch-Ybrig. There is a
$7^1/_2$ mile cross-country skiing trail
on the Albiskamm.
☎ 01/201 24 24 for information.

Squash: fifteen locations. Inquire
tourist office.

Swimming: in addition to the lake
(average summer temperature 68°F
(20°C) Zürich has six indoor swimming pools.

Tennis: courts can be hired by the
hour at ten municipal courts.

Theatres
Schauspielhaus
Rämistrasse 34
☎ 01/251 11 11

Bernhard-Theater
Comedies, cabaret, musicals.

Kammertheater Stok
Contemporary plays.

Komödienhaus
musicals, operettas.

Puppentheater Sonnenhof
Puppet shows for adults and
children.

Theater 11
Drama.

Theater am Hechtplatz
Musicals.

Theater am Neumarkt
Plays both repertory and contemporary.

Theater Heddy Maria Wettstein
Poetry readings.

Theater an der Winkelwiese
Cellar theatre, experimental productions.

See 'What's On' below.

Taxis
Taxi-Zentrale Zürich
☎ 01/44 44 41

Taxiphone
☎ 01/44 99 44

Taxi Union
☎ 01/47 30 37

AG Züritaxi
☎ 01/44 11 22

Also wheelchair taxi service Monday-Friday, prior booking required, but at no extra fee.
☎ 01/44 11 22

Tours
Inquire main railway station or at tourist office.

Traditional Festivals
Sechseläuten
Third Monday in April. Procession of guildsmen in historic costumes. Burning of the 'Böögg', the straw dummy symbolising winter. Torchlight procession.

St Nicholas Day (6 December)
Traditional Santa Claus

processions.

Fasnacht
The characteristic carnival after Ash Wednesday. Exuberant bands, parades, public masked balls, wild goings-on.

Lake Night Festival
In July on the banks of the lake.

Trams and Buses
Before any journey starts, tickets must be obtained from the automatic vending machine located at every stop. One day tickets giving unlimited travelling for 24 hours are recommended for visitors. Enquire at the tourist office about new facilities available to holders of the Swiss Holiday Card, which must be obtained before arrival in Switzerland.

Veterinary
Cantonal Veterinary Clinic
Winterthurstrasse 260
☎ 01/365 11 11

What's On
Every week *Zürich News* is published giving all you need to know about Zürich's life for the next 7 days. Most hotels can give you a copy, or ask at the tourist office. It's absolutely invaluable.

Youth Hostels
The Swiss National Tourist Office publishes a complete guide to all the youth hostels in the country. Switzerland has always been in the vanguard of the youth hostel movement and those intending to use youth hostels should obtain this very easy to follow guide before arrival in Switzerland.

4 • Central Switzerland

Lakeside

C entral Switzerland is a name used regularly by the Swiss themselves for one of their country's major regions — and it fairly well explains itself. What sometimes causes a little confusion to strangers is the fact that virtually the same region often goes under other names. The Swiss often define it with both geographical and historical precision as the region round the shores of the lake they call the Vierwaldstättersee — Lake of the Four Forest Cantons. The reference is to the three cantons (Uri, Schwyz and Unterwalden) which originally got together to form the Swiss Confederation, along with the fourth that soon joined them, Luzern. To add further complication, English speakers rarely give that lake the name used by Swiss, French, Germans and Italians, calling it instead the Lake of Luzern, a name which the Swiss only apply to one arm (and almost the smallest at that) of this many-armed lake.

The lake's many arms, and its very irregular shape with constrictions here and twists of direction there, contribute greatly to its fascinating charm as they combine to provide a series of dramatic changes of vista and of interest. The well known city of Luzern, possibly one of the country's greatest tourist attractions, lies at the head of the north-west arm, and the small town of Flüelen, gateway to the Gotthard Pass route, lies 38km (24 miles) away at the end of the long south-east arm which is called the Urner Lake after the name of the Uri canton in which it lies. Although there are notable mountain peaks within sight of every arm of the lake, the western end — the Luzern end — has more gentle, more settled and more 'tamed' scenery than the more awe-inspiring scenic grandeur that surrounds the Urner branch in the south-east.

Whatever the specialised interests of visitors to this region, they can gain a reasonable general orientation of it before starting their particular excursions, by taking the 3 hour boat trip from Luzern to

Flüelen or vice versa. (This full-length trip is available from early April to mid-October.)

Luzern to Flüelen, by Boat

Shortly after leaving the Luzern steamer-quays, the lakeside lido can be seen on the northern shore, and just behind it the city's camp site. Once clear of the Luzern lake-arm the ship enters an open stretch of water which is known locally as the 'Cross Funnel'. It lies in the centre of the cross formed by four branches of the lake meeting: the Luzerner See (the word *See* means lake) to the north-west, the Küssnachter See to the north-east, the main body of the lake due east, and the southern basin that leads to the Stansstad narrows and the Alpnacher See beyond. (It is called a funnel because it is open to so many wind directions.) From here two mountains, famous as viewpoints, are in sight. The elephantine mass of the Rigi (1,800m, 5,904ft) fills the angle between the Küssnachter See and the main lake body; in the opposite direction, to the south-west, is the jagged outline of Pilatus (2,120m, 6,954ft), Luzern's 'local' mountain, accessible by cogwheel railway from Alpnachstad. Due south is the Bürgenstock cliff, topped by Europe's highest outdoor elevator lift up to the Hammetschwand (1,128m, 3,700ft), a magnificent viewpoint over the lake.

The boat sails east past the Hertenstein peninsula to call at **Weggis**, the first of three resort villages that enjoy a mild climate under the shelter of the Rigi's bulwark on the north. The second is the boat's next calling place, **Vitznau**, where, immediately behind the pier, is the bottom station of Europe's first-established cog-wheel railway which climbs via Rigi Kaltbad and Rigi Staffel stations to the summit, Rigi Kulm. From here, instead of returning by the same route, it is possible to descend the mountain's opposite side by taking the other cog-wheel railway from the Rigi Kulm to Arth, the bottom station near the Arth-Goldau junction station on the Swiss Federal Railway main line from Luzern, Basel, Zürich and the Gotthard line.

From Vitznau the boat passes through a narrow channel formed between two promontories from the north and south shores, called the Upper and Lower Nose respectively. Beyond this channel the great main expanse of the lake towards the east opens out. The boat's course normally heads south into the Bay of Beckenried to make calls at Buochs and Beckenried. The mountains immediately ahead are the Klewenalp (1,600m, 5,248ft) on the left and the Buochserhorn on the right. At Beckenried is an aerial railway to the Klewenalp, a winter sports and summer resort on the high plateau.

The boat now heads back to the north shore to call at **Gersau**, the third of the lakeside resorts sheltered by the Rigi massif. By a curious historical freak, this village was an independent republic for four centuries; it was only after the French Revolutionary Wars that it was incorporated into canton Schwyz. After Gersau the boat crosses diagonally to call at **Treib**, a pier beside a picturesque timber boatman's cottage, adjacent to the bottom station of the funicular line that runs to the mountain terrace of **Seelisberg**. This lies on top of a buttress cliff which forms the turning corner of the lake's south shore, which here swings into a long south-pointing branch, the Urner See. On the north shore's corresponding corner lies **Brunnen**, situated on the alluvial valley-mouth of the Muota stream which here enters the lake. Brunnen is a long-established resort and former fishing village. It is well placed for excursions to the most spectacular part of the lake, and a region through its position at the corner, where the main lake turns south to face the high massif of the Gotthard and

A view of Brunnen looking towards the Great Mythen

the route which has always beckoned northern traders, adventurers, mercenary soldiers — and nowadays tourists — towards the southern lands.

Here on the shores of the Urner See is the very heart of Switzerland. For it was the people of the three original founding cantons, Uri, Schwyz and Unterwalden, who took the first steps to free themselves from external domination and start what was to become an independent confederation of communities, unified in a unique fashion, which in their early years were mostly called simply the Confederates but later became known as Schweizer after the name of one of the original component areas, Schwyz. The Urner See is William Tell country. Modern historians are quite uncertain whether an individual of that name existed here and carried out the exploits attributed to him; or whether he is a representative figure around

The lakeside village of Bauen, in Central Switzerland

Lungern, on the way to Brünig, Bernese Mittelland

Rampart walk at Murten, now in the canton of Fribourg but previously part of Bernese Mittelland

Brunnen, on the 'Lake of the Four Forest Cantons'

whom have accreted the age-old memories of a people's struggles to maintain inherited liberties in the face of alien subjection. Possibly the question is unimportant. The outcome of the struggles was definite enough.

The first two landing stages touched by the excursion ship after leaving Brunnen and heading south into the Urner See are part of the story. After rounding the imposing sheer cliff face of Seelisberg, it is rather surprising when the boat draws inshore to moor at a little pier with no sign of village or community in sight. The landing place is for a meadow lying on a shelf or terrace beneath the cliffs: the Rütli meadow where representatives of the three founding cantons met in 1307 to take a solemn oath confirming their Everlasting League to defend the liberties their valleys had inherited against tyrants.

The next landing stage, this one at a tree-covered spur projecting from the opposite shore of the lake, bears the sign 'Tellsplatte'; nearby is a memorial chapel to the folk hero who is reputed to have leapt ashore at this spot escaping from an Austrian-manned boat that was carrying him to prison.

The Tellsplatte lies at the base of the Axenberg mount, part of the precipitous east face of the Urner See. More than a century ago tunnels and galleries were cut into the cliffs here by the engineers who constructed the Axenstrasse road which enabled vehicular traffic to pass along the lakeside towards the Gotthard and obviate the need for lake transhipments.

Here the view down the Urner See, with its many cliff faces and behind them serried mountain peaks, some with perpetual snows and ice, is most dramatic. At the head of the lake is Flüelen, on the delta of the river Reuss, which there enters the lake after flowing down from the Gotthard. (The same river makes its exit from the lake some 30 miles away to flow through Luzern on its way north).

The Gotthard as North-South Corridor

From northern Europe the routes into Central Switzerland, both road and rail, come via either Basel or Zürich and their first lakeside destinations are either in the neighbourhood of Luzern or in that of Brunnen. Until comparatively recently the Axenstrasse traffic still passed through the streets of Brunnen. Later a bypass was provided for the Gotthard traffic, and since the Swiss through-road from Basel to Chiasso (on the Italian frontier) was finally completed in 1986, fast through traffic using the road from Basel has no longer passed by way of canton Schwyz and Axenstrasse. The N2 is routed to bypass west of Luzern, run along through canton Unterwalden on the south side of the lake, passing under the Seelisberg in a 9km (5$\frac{1}{2}$ mile) tunnel, and beyond Flüelen running parallel with the old Gotthard road (and rail) up the valley of the river Reuss. Among other effects this has freed the old Gotthard road between Flüelen and the Gotthard Pass from most through traffic (as, indeed, it also freed the southern section of that road beyond the pass into the Ticino).

Today a majority of those travelling south over the Gotthard are heading either for the popular lakeside resorts of the Ticino, or beyond that into Italy. So although no route can more truly be called a 'beaten track' than the one which heads for the Gotthard Pass, now that the old Gotthard road has been supplanted so far as through traffic is concerned by the Basel-Chiasso motor expressway (E9, N2), many towns and villages on the old road can be rated as 'off the beaten track'. In 1988 this was recognised by Swiss Federal Railways' promotion of a stretch of former 'Gotthard Road' between Flüelen and Göschenen as one suitably traffic-free for use by those who seek to combine touring and sightseeing with cycling, which in Switzerland has become popular as part of a current 'fitness' movement.

The scheme is based on Göschenen and Flüelen railway stations. At any time up to midday of the day before travel, phone Göschenen station and reserve a cycle for hire. On the day agreed, travel from any station to Göschenen by rail on a special round-journey ticket, take over the reserved hire-cycle there, and set off on the journey of

Lake Uri with Rütli Meadow in right foreground

exploration downhill on the old cantonal road, taking as much time, and with as many halts, as suits you. At journey's end in Flüelen the cycle is returned to the SBB (Swiss Federal Rail) station and the round-ticket covers the return journey to the station you started from. (A subsequent section will describe some of the places on the Uri section of the Gotthard road.)

The 'Heart' of Switzerland

In 1991 the 700th anniversary of the Swiss Confederation was celebrated. To mark the occasion a 'Swiss Trail' for walkers was opened in the 'Heartland' around the Uri Lake south of Brunnen. All of the cantons were involved in the creation of this path, parts of which are quite new. It starts on the Rütli in Uri canton, runs via Seelisberg, Bauen, Isleten, Seedorf, Flüelen, Tellsplate, Sisikon, then through Morschach in Schwyz canton to end in Brunnen. Two units of this Path are incorporated in excursions to Rütli and Bauen (see pages 102-4). To keep route descriptions in this area reasonably compact and unambiguous, Brunnen, on the north-east corner of the lake, will be assumed as the starting-point, but visitors based on other centres between Luzern and Brunnen should be able to make necessary adjustments.

As the earlier reference to the Rütli Meadow implied, the lake steamer service provides the simplest and most direct access to this property of the Swiss nation, which has its own jetty. However it can also be the goal of a not very demanding walk, embodied in a short but rewarding circular excursion full of interest and variety. Take the steamer, not to Rütli direct but to the calling place round the corner of the Seelisberg cliff face, **Treib** (pronounced like the English word 'tripe'). At Treib there is just a small harbour and a very picturesque house, to the right of which through the trees can be glimpsed the car of a funicular railway. The little harbour has existed since at least the fourteenth century, and the house was a place of shelter for sailors caught by the sudden tempest so typical of the *Föhn* south wind in these parts. In the period 1637-1767 it furnished accommodation for smaller diets of representatives of the Confederate Forest Cantons; its assembly room still boasts a handsome tiled heating stove of the period. In recent time it has been thoroughly renovated, and serves still as a place of shelter and of refreshment for travellers.

The *Föhn* is the name given to the south wind from the Mediterranean which, when it meets the Alps, precipitates much moisture on the southern aspects and brings dry warmth to areas immediately to the north of the Alps. In the spring it has a near miraculous effect

The house at Treib, a fishers' refuge, ferry house and occasional meeting place

on snow accumulations. It is usually accompanied by a clarity of distant visibility which is almost eerie at times. When the *Föhn* is channelled through such a 'funnel' as the south-north troughs of the Ticino and Reuss river valleys which form the 'Gotthard Route', it develops at times a violence that is awe-inspiring, and with such suddenness that alpine lakes such as this one have shore-based warning 'flashers' at strategic points to let navigators know when a storm is imminent. Because the Urner Lake's fjord-like outline continues the south-north 'funnel', this corner is notably vulnerable. (The William Tell story's emphasis on the escape opportunity given to Tell and the disorder caused to the Austrian boat crew by the 'sudden squall' has a ring of conviction hereabouts!)

Immediately behind the Treib-haus a good footpath leads up to
the left, soon passing into an asphalted track which enters the Treib-
Seelisberg vehicle road. This road is followed for a short distance to
a hairpin bend, where there is a signpost which clearly points the
direction of Rütli. A gently ascending forest track leads up through
woods and comes out into the open at the summit of the trail, to give
a fine view of the whole length of the Urner See, framed by the
Fronalpstock (1,922m, 6,304ft) and Rophaien (2,078m, 6,816ft) peaks
towering over the bluffs of the opposite (east) shore. The Rütli
meadow is soon seen ahead. The descent is easy and well shaded.
Rütli can be reached at leisurely pace in $1\frac{1}{2}$ hours from the start of
the walk. Towards the back of the meadow stands the Rütli House,
a traditional timber building characteristic of the region, where there
is catering for visitors.

Switzerland's National Day, 1 August, is a great occasion at the
Rütli. The place seems to enshrine for the Swiss their national ideals
from the earliest days of the Confederation onward, and there is an
element of pilgrimage attendant on the crowds of citizens from all
parts of the country, wearing many varieties of national costume,
who come here, ferried across from Brunnen by relays of lake steamers, to join in the observations of the day, commemorating the solemn oath of 1307 which confirmed the earlier League Covenant of
1291 to defend inherited liberties.

An alternative way of reaching Rütli from Treib is to take the
funicular car (a ride of 8 minutes) to Seelisberg on its high terrace at
801m (2,627ft) above sea level, and to walk through the straggling
village past church and holiday hotels to the outlook point provided
with benches where there is a panorama of the lake as well as a
glimpse of Rütli far below. This can be reached by a well maintained
serpentine path down the steep slope.

In both cases return to Brunnen direct by boat from the Rütli
landing stage (a special ticket can be taken out to allow an outward
journey to Treib and return from Rütli). On the journey to Brunnen
as the boat passes near the sheer face of the Seelisberg cliff, look out
for the Schillerstein: a 24m (80ft) high outrider crag, rising from the
lake in obelisk shape, inscribed in letters of gold to the memory of
Friedrich Schiller, author of the _William Tell_ poetic drama.

Those who are travelling by private car might wish to drive to
Seelisberg. Assuming a starting point on the north shore, drive to
Gersau (one of the resorts sheltered by the Rigi) from where a
vehicular ferry operates across the lake to **Beckenried** approximately hourly from April to mid-October. (At Beckenried is the

Bauen, remote in its sheltered site

bottom station of the Klewenalp aerial railway.) The modern Basel-Chiasso motorway N2 bypasses Beckenried: drive east from the ferry and shortly passing under the motorway, follow the winding road up and onto the terrace where Emmetten stands; the road continues to climb then dips to cross the Klön valley, and rising again passes a tunnel and descends to the neighbourhood of the mountain tarn of Seeli, south of Seelisberg, before ascending past the pilgrim-age church of Maria Sonnenberg (dated 1666, with a baroque high altar) and on to the village of Seelisberg. Rütli is reached on foot by the marked path from Seelisberg in half an hour; if for the return walk an easier ascent is preferred, take the gentle ascent-descent to Treib previously described in reverse direction; then back to Seelisberg by funicular.

Treib-Seelisberg to Bauen
From Seelisberg there is a longer walk which is particularly reward-ing in the sustained panoramic views it offers. Its destination is the lakeside village of Bauen (which has a lake steamer service from April to mid-October). The excursion can start by arriving at Treib by boat (car drivers would reach Seelisberg via Beckenried). Arriving at Treib those who wish to reach Seelisberg on foot rather than travel up by funicular will find the footpath to the village clearly marked and

well maintained. It starts behind the Treib-haus and takes just under an hour for a climb of 370m (1,214ft) altitude difference. There is a stroll up the long main street as far as the last houses of the village. At the post office there is a clear indication for the turn off to the left, which very soon becomes a forest track that comes out on to a metalled road after 10 minutes walk. The road is only used briefly before the footpath branches off and upwards to the right, breasting a slope which is the highest point of the walk. The Urner See now comes into view, 400m (1,312ft) below, and it remains in view for the rest of the ramble. The footpath passes (on the right) the Beroldingen castle which probably occupies the site of the earlier castle of 1530; attached is a chapel added to it in 1546 by Josua von Beroldingen when he was accepted into the Order of Knights of the Holy Sepulchre in Jerusalem. The footpath is now pointing due south and the panorama is magnificent, with rock faces rising almost vertically from the lake. There is a view beyond the lake's end to the distant alluvial plain in which the course of the river Reuss glints like a silver bar. As backdrop to the scene is the distant pyramid of the 3,072m (10,076ft) Bristen. The descent of the footpath to Bauen starts in easy fashion but becomes quite steep. However, solid timber steps help to cope with it (walking-time $1^3/_4$ hours).

Bauen enjoys an unexpectedly mild climate thanks to a sunny situation and also to its openness to the *Föhn* wind which brings Mediterranean warmth down from the Gotthard in spring. Magnolias and palm trees flourish here! The village has some fine timber houses, among them an outstanding seventeenth-century one, the Obere Baumgarten (Upper Orchard). Bauen was the birthplace of the composer of the Swiss national anthem to whose memory there stands a small monument in the village.

Until 1953 Bauen's only transport access was by the lake, and although today's motorway N2 Basel-Chiasso passes within 2km (just over a mile) of the village, it does so in a tunnel through the mountain rock. Bauen's modern connection with the outer world is the 1953 lakeside road covering the 15km (9 miles) from Altdorf via Isleten, which is used by the postbus service (Table No 600. 33 ☎ Altdorf 044 2 21 85). For visitors interested in making the journey to Bauen by private transport the route could be combined with a trip from Brunnen along the Axenstrasse to Flüelen and Altdorf. The excursion can also be carried out by public transport by taking an SBB train (a 'regional' ie, stopping at all stations) from Brunnen to Altdorf (Official Timetable No 600) and a postbus to Bauen (Timetable No 600. 33) from which a return by boat would add variety.

(Lake Navigation Timetable is No 2600. It cannot be over-empha-
sised that the official timetable volumes take in railways, mountain
railways, lake and riverboat services as well as bus services.)

Brunnen to Altdorf

From Brunnen landing quay go past the Casino on the road which
soon joins the bypassing main road from Luzern. This stretch on the
Urner See to Flüelen is called the Axenstrasse, as it was blasted and
tunnelled through the rock faces of the Axenberg. It runs roughly
parallel to the Gotthard railway line. Between tunnels there is a view
across the lake of Rütli and Seelisberg. At the village of Sisikon
(which has a camp and caravan site) the road crosses the cantonal
boundary from Schwyz into Uri. After further tunnels comes Tellsplatte, where parking is possible, and a path leads down to the Tell
chapel, with its frescoes depicting the Tell story, near the lake
steamer quay.

The small resort village of **Flüelen** at the end of the lake was for
centuries an important lake port and customs station where goods
were trans-shipped from the lake to mule transport for carriage over
the Gotthard. As a terminus nowadays of the lake excursion service
during the season it is today a main stop for many international train
services. About 1km (half a mile) further on, the road has a right-
hand turn off for entry to the motorway N2 which has emerged from
the Seelisberg 9km ($5^1/_2$ mile) tunnel to run up the Reuss valley
between railway and river for a considerable stretch. Disregarding
this turn, the road for Altdorf continues straight on for 2km (just over
a mile).

Altdorf is capital of Uri, canton of mountains and glaciers. Town
and canton rose in importance after the early thirteenth century
when the bridging of the Schöllenen gorge opened up the Gotthard.
Of the old forest cantons, Uri was always the leader in policies of
expansion over the Gotthard into the Ticino. Nowadays it is the
centre of the William Tell cult, the place where, according to tradition, the national hero shot the apple from his son's head. A huge
bronze statue commemorating him stands in the Town House
Square in front of a thirteenth-century residential tower, renovated
and given a dome roof in the early nineteenth century. There is a Tell
theatre too, where the Schiller play is performed during the season
by local players. The town has many picturesque corners and interesting buildings although it sustained much damage by fire in 1799
when the town was fought over by French, Austrian and Russian
armies. One of the sixteenth-century houses which survived the fire

is known as the Suworow House, as it served as the Russian general's quarters after he succeeded in getting his troops north through the notorious Schöllenen gorge in the face of fierce French resistance. The town's Capuchin friary was the first founded in Switzerland (1581) to strengthen the Counter Reformation movement which Uri strongly espoused; the church was rebuilt after the great fire. A regional historical museum is housed in the Gotthardstrasse 18.

Altdorf to Bauen
To reach Bauen take the road that crosses the Reuss valley to the far side of railway, motorway and river heading for Seedorf. Near Seedorf on the valley plain stands a picturesque gabled eighteenth-century castle called A Pro after the Ticinese knight who had it built; it is now used for occasions of state by the canton. From Seedorf the road runs round the south-west corner of Lake Uri to Isleten, continuing from there along the shore to Bauen. At Isleten a narrow mountain road (used by the postbus) also swings off to the left, running for 19km (12 miles) to the rocky and romantic Isenthal from which the ascent to the ice-capped Uri Rotstock is approached.

Beyond the Lakeside

An Excursion into Canton Schwyz
From Brunnen it is only 5km (3 miles) distance to **Schwyz** — the cantonal capital which gave its name to the whole country with only a slight change of vowel. Its delightful situation in a wide fertile valley framed by the twin craggy peaks of the Mythen standing behind is particularly picturesque when the cherry orchards that surround it are smothered in spring blossom. The old town well merits a day's visit, with its many handsome seventeenth-century patrician mansions and Town House façade, painted with frescoes of significant moments in Swiss history. It is appropriate, too, that an attractive modern building here houses the country's Federal Archives — containing among other items the solemn pact of 1291, the signing of which by representatives of Schwyz, Uri and Unterwalden was the decisive step in the evolution of Switzerland as we know it. Also here is the earlier deed from the Holy Roman Emperor (1240) granting privileges and liberties to the people of Schwyz — the document which was the constitutional basis of the stance taken by the people of Schwyz in refusing to accept subjection to the powerful Austrian Hapsburgs. Recent scientific investigations have established that an old timber dwelling-house in Schwyz called Haus Bethlehem, previously thought to be sixteenth century, in fact was

constructed in the thirteenth century and is the oldest timber 'chalet' in Switzerland. It lies on an estate run by the Ital-Reding Foundation, and its main building is the Ital-Reding mansion, built in 1609, which combines features that are typical of local farmhouse architecture with baroque trends befitting the town houses of families of that era which had 'done well' in mercenary service abroad. The baroque St Martin's church is generally accounted the most beautiful parish church in Switzerland.

A change of scene both from lakeside and historic town is to be had by leaving Schwyz on the road which ascends southward into the valley of the Muota (the river which enters the lake just west of Brunnen). Shortly after entering the mouth of the valley, at Schlattli, is the bottom station of a funicular which rises to Stoos, a settlement on an alpine terrace at upward of 1,300m (4,265ft).

Stoos provides a tempting side-trip. The terrace lies on the east side of the Fronalpstock — the bluff, stumpy mountain which forms the corner buttress where the main lake turns into the Urner See, its long south arm. Stoos is an automobile-free summer and winter resort. Modern skilifts run up from the alpine terrace to the Fronalpstock. In summer the skilifts convert to chairlifts and, combining the use of two stages of chairlift with some walking it is possible to ascend to the 1,922m (6,304ft) summit with its commanding oversight of this corner of the cantons of Schwyz and Uri. Stoos has a heated open-air swimming pool in summer, in alpine surroundings.

Before leaving the Schlattli neighbourhood, not far from the funicular station is an old wooden, roofed bridge across the Muota gorge. It is known as the Suworow bridge. The name of the Russian General Suworow keeps coming up in this region because of the marches made by the army he brought up from Italy into Switzerland in 1799 during the Napoleonic Wars, forcing the Gotthard Pass against bitter French resistance, but later driven to retreat back up the Muota valley when the French blocked his path at the passage of the Schlattli bridge.

The river exhibits some fine rapids and waterfalls as the road continues up the steep-sided valley to the hamlet of Ried and to the village which bears the valley's name, **Muotathal**, which boasts a late eighteenth-century parish church with a particularly striking rococo interior. There is also the seventeenth-century Franciscan convent of St Joseph. Further on by 2km (just over a mile) at the hamlet of **Hinterthal**, the road crosses the river and forks where the stream is joined by a tributary. The main road, bearing right, continues into the

Spectacular alpine scenery between Urnerboden and the Klausen Pass summit

spectacular Bisis valley and comes to its end at the picturesquely situated hamlet of **Bisisthal**. (This hamlet is the terminus of a bus route from Schwyz (Table 600. 16).

After 2km (just over a mile) the left-hand branch of the road from Hinterthal reaches the entrance to the remarkable Hölloch Caverns (the labyrinthine passages of which are calculated to extend some 93km (58 miles); 1km (half a mile) of the caves are open to visitors). Shortly after this point the road becomes little more than a bridle path or cart track which, however, provides an intriguing pass-walk of about 4 hours duration over the Pragel Pass to Richisau's alpine pasture leading down to the beautiful Klöntal valley in the canton of Glarus. This was the route marched by Suworow's army, incidentally, when their Muota valley passage was blocked. Nowadays the walk is a favourite with high-level hill walkers. It can be organised by using the Muota valley bus from Schwyz to Hinterthal on the one side, and on the other the postbus mountain-postroad service Glarus-Klontal (Table 902. 20, ☎ 058/63 52 30). From Glarus — a canton shut in by mountains on three sides — a circular return to Schwyz by train is possible, or by postbus to Altdorf or Flüelen via the Klausen Pass, the reverse of the route next to be described.

Altdorf into Canton Glarus

Altdorf is sited on alluvial soil where the Schächen side valley enters the Reuss valley from the east. An interesting excursion consists in the trip up this side valley and over the Klausen Pass road from Uri into the canton of Glarus.

Leaving Altdorf by the Gotthard road to the south there is a turn off left almost immediately for road No 17, which, within 3km (2 miles) reaches the sizeable village of **Bürglen**. This is a very old settlement, as its two sentinel towers of medieval period suggest. In AD857 King Ludwig the German placed the village under the protection of the Zürich Fraumünster abbey, and one of the towers, the Meierturm is thought to have been the seat of the abbey's bailiff in Bürglen. Nowadays the other medieval tower houses the William Tell Museum. Tradition attributes to Bürglen Tell's place of birth; and the Tell chapel, erected in 1582, is reputed to be on the site of Tell's house. The fine early baroque church has substructures remaining of Romanesque date and style.

Beyond Bürglen at **Brugg** is the bottom station of a cablecar which, in two stages, runs up to the Biel mountain inn below the Kinzig Pass which provides a track through to the Muota valley at Hinterthal. This was the route taken by Suworow's army in 1799 when he discovered there was no road along the east shore of the Urner Lake (along the line of the present day Axenstrasse) from Altdorf.

The road ascends to **Unterschächen** (994m, 3,260ft), a climbing centre at the mouth of the Brunni valley gorge, giving a spectacular view of the towering Windgallen cliffs. Now comes a swinging zigzag of a rise to Urigen (1,280m, 4,198ft). The road passes through rock galleries, then there is a view of the 90m (295ft) Stäubi waterfall. Soon the Klausenpass hotel is reached and within another kilometre the pass summit of 1,948m (6,389ft), dominated by mountains on both sides. It then descends in nearly a dozen zigzags, traverses a gorge and continues along the Urnerboden high valley of near-level alpine meadow, crossing the stream which is the cantonal boundary. In further steep zigzags of descent, passing the Fätschbach falls, the road reaches Linthal, Glarus canton, 23km (14 miles) beyond the pass summit, and 65km (40 miles) from Altdorf.

Linthal takes its name from the river Linth which drains the beautiful transverse valley that largely makes up the canton of Glarus. The Linth's tributary streams are fed from the slopes of the wall of mountains that form the Glarus Alps, Clariden (3,268m, 10,719ft), Tödi (3,614m, 11,854ft) and Bifertenstock (3,425m, 11,234ft)

The Klausen Pass

which form the south-west boundary between this small canton and its neighbours Uri and Grisons. There are splendid views of this great alpine barrier to the south from the twisting road between Urnerboden and Linthal.

The canton of Glarus lies between this mountain barrier in the

A postbus on the Klausen Pass

south and, in the north, the Walensee (lake) and the Linth Canal which in the short northern plain links Walensee with the eastern extension of Lake Zürich which is known as the Obersee, (ie, Upper Lake). The canal also drains former marshland between these two lakes. Glarus, though one of the smallest cantons, is often described as an epitomy of Switzerland as a whole in that it has three geographical sectors: a vast area of mountain country, a moderate stretch of rolling upland plateau capable of settlement — what the Swiss call *Mittel-land* (literally, middle-land) and a small area of real lowland. In Glarus the south is spectacularly alpine, and the canton is bounded by mountain ranges on three sides; only from the north is access easy — as the line of the railway illustrates. For centuries agriculture was the main economy of the Glarus. Today it is, paradoxically, industry; for textile industries were early in being located here because of the ample availability of water power, and the Linth plain in the north has also attracted modern industries.

The Klausen Pass trip from Uri to Glarus can be made by a postbus service which operates July to September from Flüelen via Altdorf, the sector Bürglen to Linthal being classed as a mountain postroad. For details consult Official Timetable No 600. 30. At all times seat reservation in advance is necessary.

From Linthal train services are available down the valley via Glarus, cantonal capital, to Ziegelbrücke (junction with the Chur-Zürich main line); most trains also continue beyond that junction to Rapperswil at the east end of Lake Zürich, from where in turn a train may be taken (via Pfäffikon on the south-east corner of Lake Zürich) to Arth-Goldau (for Schwyz, Brunnen, Luzern). Motorists with private transport who have come over the Klausen Pass road may wish to return by the same route to see the opposite angles of view. Others may be tempted to explore the Glarus canton (perhaps using this excursion as their exit route from the region of the Vierwald-stättersee for further explorations in north or north-east Switzerland, in cantons Zürich, St Gallen or Grisons).

Linthal to Walensee

Within 2 minutes of the SBB main station at Linthal is a funicular bottom station. Its cars climb in 10 minutes to **Braunwald** (1,256m, 4,120ft), a traffic-free climatic resort, well equipped for both winter and summer sports, which lies on an extensive terrace-plateau beneath the slopes of the Eckstock and the Ortstock, facing south across the Linth valley to the Hausstock massif on the Grisons frontier. This noise-free holiday and sports region is a great favourite with the Swiss themselves.

About 10km (6 miles) down the main valley road from Linthal is **Schwanden**, a small industrial town where the Sernf valley joins the Linth. This is the starting point for excursions in the Kärpf district, lying in the angle between these two valleys. The Kärpf is the oldest wildlife reserve in Switzerland, dating back to the sixteenth century, where chamois, ibex and marmots can be seen in the wild. The Sernf valley, which curves round in the shape of a crook, is served by a postbus service (Timetable No 902. 45) to a number of village resorts, the terminal one being **Elm** (at 977m, 3,205ft) where springs the source of one of Switzerland's widely distributed natural mineral waters. It is in a peaceful and idyllic countryside offering a great variety of walking paths.

Six kilometres (4 miles) on from Schwanden the main valley road reaches the cantonal capital, also named **Glarus**, set at the foot of 2,331m (7,646ft) high Glärnisch. In 1861 the town was largely destroyed by fire (fanned by the *Föhn* wind) and was thereafter rebuilt. It is a small town, with a textile industry, and on the first Sunday of May each year it is the scene of the meeting of the Landsgemeinde — the formal assembly of all vote holding citizens of the canton and its

The Reichenbach Falls, near Meiringen in the Bernese Oberland

Mountain-top, Les Diablerets, Bernese Oberland

Adelboden, at the head of the Engstligental, Bernese Oberland

Upper Valais

law-giving governing body. Voting is by show of hands and the agenda is circulated to householders one month ahead of the meeting.

Eight kilometres (5 miles) on from Glarus, near the mouth of the valley, is another little industrial town, **Näfels**. Its name is associated with the site of the battle in 1388 when the men of Glarus defeated a greatly superior Austrian army and so regained their independent liberties. There is a memorial chapel to this event. The town also boasts, in its main street, a remarkable seventeenth-century mansion, the Freuler Mansion or Palace as it is locally known, built for a local man who acquired riches in the service of the French crown as a colonel of mercenaries (a not uncommon employment for the Swiss in those days). The building, with magnificent Renaissance-style exterior and baroque interior furnishing and decoration, is now the cantonal museum and has, in particular, a unique collection of the printed textiles for which Glarus has long been famed.

To the east of Näfels is an entry/exit to the motorway N3 which, running west-east, links Zürich with the southern shores of the Walensee (flanking for part of the way the Linth canal referred to above) and on to Chur in the Grisons. For motorists who intend to travel west by road on N3 to Zürich or beyond, a short side-trip is to be recommended. The famous Benedictine abbey of Einsiedeln — Switzerland's greatest place of pilgrimage, set in the pre-Alp country of canton Schwyz — cannot be described as 'off the beaten track' but it would be unthinkable to omit the possibility of visiting it when in this neighbourhood. Carry on along the N3 motorway west beyond the exit for Rapperswil and Pfäffikon to the exit indicated for Einsiedeln and Schwyz. Turning south in some 6km (4 miles) the Biberbrugg crossroads are reached. For Einsiedeln turn off left onto road No 8 for Schwyz, offering the possibility of completing a round trip from canton Schwyz via Altdorf, Klausen Pass and Glarus with return by the N3 and national road No 8 to Schwyz. Schwanden, Glarus and Näfels all have stations on the Linthal-Ziegelbrücke railway. The line from Rapperswil and Pfäffikon to Arth-Goldau also has a branch to Einsiedeln from the station at Biberbrugg.

There has been a monastic community at Einsiedeln for more than a thousand years, for most of that time a Benedictine monastery. In its present form it was rebuilt in mid-eighteenth century and is one of Europe's greatest baroque buildings, with the monastery church embodied as centrepiece of the great façade. Its Gnadenkapelle, Chapel of Grace, enshrines the Black Madonna venerated by pilgrims.

Altdorf to Andermatt on the 'Old Gotthard Road'

The Reuss valley floor is comparatively wide and level for a considerable stretch south of Altdorf (447m, 1,466ft above sea level) and only begins to narrow at Erstfeld (472m, 1,548ft), by which point the new motorway N2 has parted company with the old Gotthard road No 2 as well as the railway, having crossed to the west bank of the river. For this stretch the pyramid of the Bristen (3,072m, 10,076ft) occupies the valley horizon.

Amsteg (7km, 4 miles on) lies at the entrance to the Maderaner valley, another beautiful transverse valley to the east, which the railway crosses on a 53m (175ft) high viaduct. Amsteg's position makes it a well placed base for climbers and hill walkers. There is a steep mountain road — served by mountain postbus (route 600. 38) from June to September — leading to the village of Bristen (6km, 4 miles) and beyond it to the Golzern cablecar station (Timetable 1595) which gives an altitude start to climbers. For high-pass walkers there is also from that road end a track up the spectacularly wild little valley of the Etzli which climbs up to the south. This leads to the Krüzli Pass (2,347m, 7,698ft) which descends on the other side to Sedrun on the Vorderrhein (anterior Rhine) valley of canton Grisons about 10km (6 miles) from Disentis.

At Amsteg motorists who are in haste to reach a further destination have an opportunity to leave the old Gotthard road in favour of entry to the fast N2 motorway before the old road enters the steepest and most tortuous part of the route. It is at this point that the old Gotthard road and the railway line both cross to the west side of the valley while the modern motorway in galleries and tunnels cuts through the steep rock-flank of the massive Bristen, which was seen on the horizon earlier in the route. Remaining, however, with the old road makes possible a visit to **Wiler**, in the valley near Gurtnellen, where there is a seventeenth-century church of St Anna with a massive canopied porch (a snow shelter) through which the earlier historic Gotthard pack-trail actually passed.

As Wassen, the next village after Gurtnellen, is approached, it is possible to see from the road the manner in which the railway line (now running on the opposite side of the valley from both roads) climbs the steep 'steps' in the valley floor which occasion waterfalls. The line penetrates into the mountainside and tunnels a wide upward spiral in the heart of the mountain, to emerge again on the same mountain face at a level 35m (115ft) higher. Opposite the village the Gotthard line executes two further tunnel-loops in succession — almost carrying out a figure-of-eight — while all the time gaining a

The famous abbey of Einsiedeln

further height of 122m (400ft) inside the rock. It is the unique experience of rail travellers on the Gotthard to glimpse the same, unmis-
takable baroque-domed village church three times in a few minutes
as the train passes it at different levels above and below. For the
motorist on the 'old road' now relieved of traffic frenzy, the village
of **Wassen** repays a short visit. The church mentioned above, which

is sited on top of a steep hill, was built in 1735 and has beautiful inlaid wooden altars of that era.

Wassen lies at the mouth of the Meien valley and for the motorist with a day in hand to spare it can be an ideal starting point for the famed Three Alpine Passes round trip. That trip is by no means 'off the beaten track' and will not be detailed here. As it may be a tempting detour, however, for any who have not previously toured the passes of the glacial Alps, an outline of the circuit is briefly summarised:

The Meien valley road climbs up west from Wassen through varied alpine landscape including tunnels, through one of which it traverses the Susten pass summit (2,224m, 7,295ft). It descends into Bernese Oberland territory in sweeping bends that present a close view of the Stein glacier, then along the Gadmen valley to the gentler scenery of the valley of the Aare at Innertkirchen (near Meiringen). Next turning south, it ascends the wooded approaches to the attractive Hasli valley which becomes barer and wilder in the ascent. On thereafter toward the Grimsel Lake and then the summit of the Grimsel Pass (at 1,652m, 5,419ft). Descending from the pass, sharp, steep bends afford good views of the Rhône glacier before reaching Gletsch to join the great upper Rhône valley road which links western Switzerland with Grisons and the east. The road, now heading east once more, climbs onward to within a short walk's distance from that same awesome Rhône glacier before tackling the highest pass of the trio, the Furka (2,431m, 7,974ft), which forms the boundary between cantons Valais and Uri. Splendid views here to east and west. From the Furka summit the road is by way of Hospental and Andermatt and so back to the Gotthard road and to Wassen.

The Three Pass circuit is usually feasible from mid-June to mid-October. Having so many bends and so much climbing in the thin air however, it is quite demanding on vehicle and driver. Depending on the driver's experience of mountain roads, anything from 7 to 9 hours' driving is involved.

From Wassen the 'old Gotthard road' crosses and re-crosses the valley before reaching (in 5km, 3 miles) **Göschenen** in its impressive situation where the Reuss river is joined by a main tributary just as it has emerged from the Schöllenen gorge. If the Göschenen rail station appears disproportionately large for the size of the village, this is accountable to the control functions exercised here for the traffic through the 15km (9 mile) long Gotthard railway tunnel which begins here. For very many years the loading of vehicles onto railway trucks here was the only means of overcoming the Gotthard barrier

Wassen

when the pass road was closed by winter snows. Nowadays the motorway tunnel, which also runs from Göschenen through the Gotthard massif into canton Ticino, is the route taken by the overwhelming majority of motorists in summer as well as in winter.

Göschenen then is the place of decisions: whether to take the tunnel through to Italian-speaking Ticino and southern climes, or to proceed to Andermatt on the old Gotthard road which now climbs sharply up to cross the Reuss tributary and after some hairpin bends enters the forbidding rock walls of the Schöllenen gorge which took centuries for road builders to master, first by bridle paths on suspended plank bridges and in more modern days by tunnels and galleries as well as daring bridges. Emerging from the gorge the road crosses the Reuss waterfall on the 'Devil's bridge' and enters the wide Urseren valley in which Andermatt lies, occupying the strategic position at the 'crossroads of Switzerland' — or even of Europe — where the main west-east route carved out of the high alpine massif by the Rhine and Rhône rivers crosses the north-south route gouged out by rivers Reuss and Ticino. Andermatt itself is an attractive town. Many months of snow availability and a good sunshine record make it a favourite winter sports centre; and a multitude of varied excursion opportunities and walking trails attract summer visitors. Andermatt too is a place for travellers' decisions: whether to return north back to Uri, or to choose one of the other three cardinal points of the compass for further travel.

Further Information
— Central Switzerland —

Entertainment

Altdorf
William Tell historical plays in dedicated theatre, July to September.
Information: Tellspielbüro
CH-6460 Altdorf
☎ 044/2 22 80

Beckenried
Afternoon concerts in square during season.

Brunnen
Kursaal Casino
Daily dancing from 9pm.

Eden Hotel
Live music, entertainment and dancing in 250 year old wine cellar. From 8pm except Sunday.

Museums and Other Places of Interest

Note: many of the places of interest 'off the beaten track' are villages of small population; consequently they do not always find it possible to man, for instance, local folk museums for the number of hours and with the regularity that would be taken for granted in a larger town. On the other hand they usually take it as a compliment if visitors interested in their community's art treasures, village church or other place of interest take the trouble to inquire where keys, caretaker or a guide may be found. Even when opening hours are stated, you do well to check the hours by tele-

phone if your visit to a museum, for instance, involves travel.

Altdorf
Town Hall
Collection of historic banners

St Martin's church
Priceless museum collection of sixteenth-century gold and silver ecclesiastical treasures.
To be seen by prior appointment through pastor.
☎ 044/2 11 43

Historical Museum
Gotthardstrasse
Art and folklore collections.
Open: beginning April to end September 10am-12noon, 2-5pm, closed Mondays.

Guided tours of town from Tell Memorial, Wednesdays June-September 9.30-11am.

Bürglen
Tell Museum
Wattigwiler Tower, near the parish church.
Exhibits illustrate the Tell story and history of Uri.
Open: June to mid-October, 9am-12noon and 2-6pm daily.

Näfels
Battle Chapel (Schlachtkapelle)
Memorial to the dead in the Battle of Näfels against the Hapsburgs, 1388.

Cantonal Museum
Freuler Palace

Includes collection of Glarnish printed fabrics.
Open: daily except Monday, April to November 9-11.30am and 1.30-5.30pm.

Schwyz
Swiss Federal Archives (Bundesbriefarchiv)
Holds originals of federal documents 1291-1513, also historic flags and banners.
Open: daily 9.30-11.30am, and 2-5pm.
☎ 043/24 11 24

Ital-Reding Haus, 1609
Mansion and estate maintained by a Trust.
Open: May to October

Turm Museum
Medieval tower-house which formerly housed federal archives, now holds a local museum collection.

Public Transport

The lake shipping timetable is to be found in the comprehensive Swiss Official Timetable, Tables 2600 to 2605; the boats are operated by:
Schiffahrtsgesellschaft des Vierwaldstättersees (the initials SGV usually suffice!)
CH-6002 Luzern
☎ 041/44 34 34
Note: The phrase 'Off Timetable' followed by a number frequently occurs in connection with transport. The reference is to the publication (obtainable from SNTOs in Switzerland and abroad) 'Official Timetable' of all public transport. There are three volumes, one containing trains, cable railways and boat services, the second dealing entirely with bus services and the third with international connections. Every timetable has a number for identification, eg, 600 for the Gotthard rail route. Explanatory notes are in five languages, including English.

Note for Hikers
Canton Schwyz was a pioneer area for a travel 'package-deal ticket' for walkers/hikers known as the Reka Wanderpass. It is an extension of the regional travel ticket. Operating between May and October, adults' and children's passes are issued for durations of 2, 4 or 7 days, allowing unrestricted second class use of all regional public transport services, coupled with coupons covering bed-and-breakfast provision for the corresponding nights in participant hotels and inns in the region — lists of such are issued, and advance bookings are advisable. The transport network included in the Schwyz region extends beyond cantonal boundaries as far as rail is concerned, extending west to Luzern and north to Zug and to Rapperswil, for instance. Details — with maps and with suggestions for routes — may be obtained from main Verkehrsbüros, such as those in Schwyz and Brunnen, and from Schweizer Reisekasse, Neuengasse 15, CH-3001 Bern.

Sports

Altdorf
Indoor swimming pool
☎ 044/2 58 25

Andermatt
Mountaineering school, guided
mountaineering and horse riding.
☎ 044/67130 for information.

Brunnen
Indoor swimming pool adjacent to
Lido beach
☎ 043/31 18 87

Gersau
Sailing
☎ 041/84 17 40 for information.

Linthal
Walking and hiking trails, also
mountaineering.
Funicular rail to resort of Braunwald
☎ 058/84 13 26
☎ 058/86 19 19 weather report

Sisikon
Windsurfing
☎ 043/31 30 23 for information

Vitznau
Waterskiing
☎ 041/83 13 22 (Park Hotel) for
information

Tourist Information Offices

Swiss National Tourist Offices
(which in German speaking regions are usually designated by the
term Verkehrsbüro or
Verkehrsverein followed by the
resort name) are available for
national, cantonal and local information. Verkehrsvereine are often
voluntary associations.

Regional Office
Verkehrsverband Zentralschweiz
Alpenstrasse 1
CH-6002 Luzern
☎ 041/51 18 91

Canton Uri has an information
office in a motorway rest area
which also deals with postal and
telephone enquiries:

Information Uri
Gotthard Raststaette
CH-6467 Schattdorf-Uri
☎ 044/2 53 53

Alpnachstad
Verkehrsverein
CH- 6055 Alpnach Dorf
☎ 041/96 12 44

Altdorf
Verkehrsverein
CH-6460 Altdorf
☎ 044/2 28 88

Andermatt
Verkehrsbüro
CH-6490 Andermatt
☎ 044/6 74 54

Bauen
Verkehrsverein
CH-64 66 Bauen

Beckenried
Verkehrsbüro
CH-6375 Beckenried
☎ 041/54 31 70

Brunnen
Verkehrsbüro
CH-6440 Brunnen
☎ 043/31 17 77
Open: Sundays 10am-12noon
during July and August.

Bürglen
Sporthaus Imholz
Dorfplatz
CH-6463 Bürglen
☎ 044/2 26 43

Elm
Verkehrsbüro
CH-8767 Elm/Glarus
☎ 058/86 17 27

Flüelen
Verkehrsbüro
CH-6454 Flüelen/Uri
☎ 044/2 42 23

Gersau
Verkehrsbüro
CH-6442 Gersau
☎ 041/84 12 20

Glarus
Cantonal Office:
Verkehrsverein Glarnerland and
Walensee
Kirchweg 4
CH-8750 Glarus
☎ 058/61 13 47

Goldau
Verkehrsbüro
CH-6410 Goldau
☎ 041/82 11 29

Göschenen
Verkehrsbüro
CH-6487 Göschenen
☎ 044/6 51 96

Linthal
Verkehrsbüro
Gantenbein Bazar
CH-8783 Linthal
☎ 058/84 38 26

Muotathal
Verkehrsbüro Schwyz
Postplatz 9
CH-6430 Schwyz
☎ 043/21 34 46

Näfels
Verkehrsbüro
Kantonalbank Glarus
Agentur Näfels
☎ 058/ 34 21 88

Schwyz
Verkehrsbüro
Postplatz 9
CH-6430 Schwyz
☎ 043/21 34 46

Seelisberg
Verkehrsbüro
CH-6446 Seelisberg/Uri
Open: May-September 8.30-
11.30am and 2-6pm.
☎ 043/31 15 63

Sisikon
Verkehrsbüro
CH-6452 Sisikon
☎ 043/31 30 23

Stoos
Verkehrsbüro
CH-6433 Stoos/Schwyz
☎ 043/21 15 50

Vitznau
Verkehrsbüro
CH-6354 Vitznau
☎ 041/83 13 55

5 • Bernese Mittelland

The Bernese Oberland is perhaps the Swiss region best known to English speaking tourists because of the dramatic massif of mountains, high valleys and ridges that lies south-east of Lakes Brienz and Thun, and between these the popular centre of tourist traffic, Interlaken.

Yet the very large canton Bern consists of much more than its Oberland. Only a fraction of those who know the Oberland are acquainted with the Bernese Mitelland — except perhaps for the capital city, Bern itself, which lies near the centre of it. The concept of Mittelland is very important to the Swiss. In Switzerland there are very few real plains, and the term Mittelland (in which Mittel means something like 'betwixt and between') is applied to the great areas of pre-alpine hills and of rolling plateau country which over millenia have been settled and cultivated by the ancestors and predecessors of the Swiss, and on which have grown the great historic centres of agricultural civilisation as well as the civilisation of cities.

At the opposite end of the Lake of Thun (or Thunersee) from Interlaken lies Thun. In terms of political and administrative boundaries, Thun is counted as part of the Oberland. Indeed, long before the clusters of nineteenth-century hotels arose in Interlaken, Thun was the gateway to the Oberland for the earliest alpine travellers. Yet in geographical and historical terms Thun could almost serve as the model of a Mittelland town. It has a long history of urban culture as a market centre for a pastoral and agricultural hinterland, as a garrison town and a centre of services and administration, and it is equally well placed as the gateway to the Mittelland. Within minutes by car or bus, are characteristic Mittelland areas of great charm and interest that are not only off the beaten track but do not even receive passing mention in standard English-language guide books. A striking example is the road into the heights of wooded, pastoral and agricultural countryside to the north of the town.

A roofed sluice bridge at Thun

Thun to Goldiwil and Heiligenschwendi

Note for walkers: The first section of the road is a fairly consistently steep uphill gradient for 6km (3½ miles). However, a bus service offers an alternative if the going proves too taxing. The walk from Thun to Heiligenschwendi should require about 1 hour 40 minutes.

Leave Thun by the Berngate, turning right into the Steffisburgstrasse and right again shortly on to the Goldiwilstrasse. The steeply climbing road very soon affords views over Thun, dominated by the impressive, massive square keep with corner turrets of the castle built by the Zähringen Dukes from 1191, with the Stockhorn mountain (2,190m, 7,183ft) forming a backdrop across the wide valley. Within 2.5km (1½ miles) the road forks and the right-hand branch dips across a hollow towards Schwendi; but continue forward, climbing on the left-hand (main) road which ascends towards Goldiwil at a higher level with even more rewarding views. At 6km (3½ miles) the straggling village of **Goldiwil** is reached at an altitude of 1,000m (3,280ft). A hotel-restaurant with its terrace overhanging the slope gives splendid views over the Lake of Thun and the Stockhorn group. This attractive hill village has in the past decade become favoured as a 'dormitory suburb' for people employed in Thun. As the road twists uphill, following a ridge with the ground falling away to the right, panoramic views are revealed through clearings of the

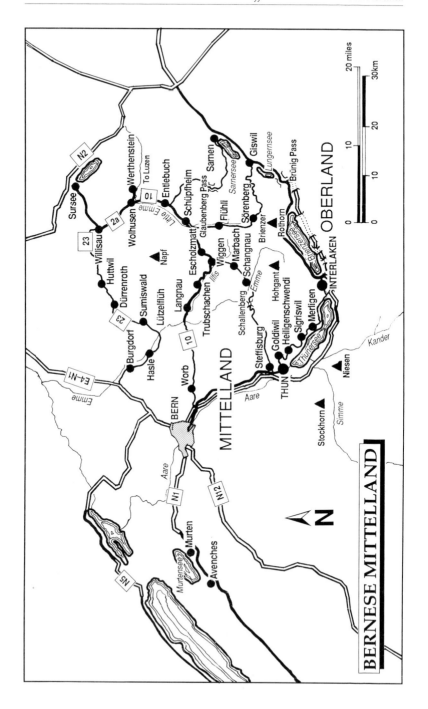

BERNESE MITTELLAND

Heiligenschwendi

lake down below and the backdrop of the Oberland mountains behind. The pre-alpine pastures in the immediate neighbourhood, dotted with mature cherry trees, make the foreground equally attractive, as does the sound of the cow-bells. Immediately beyond the church and school the road has a less steep section, and soon passes a small cheese dairy where, depending on circumstances of the season, there may be an opportunity to see something of the work that is typical of this type of country.

In about a kilometre (just over half a mile) the road reaches a terrace plateau, well wooded in places, and curves slowly to the right giving ever-changing angles of view until it reaches **Heiligenschwendi**, lying on a sun-terrace at 1,100m (3,608ft), sheltered from the north by wooded hillside. More of the Oberland mountains including the Niesen and Blümlisalp have now come into the panoramic view, and can be seen from a number of vantage points in striking perspective across the Lake of Thun. Continuing through the scattered little climatic resort the road leads to the Heiligenschwendi Klinik, a large hospital originally treating respiratory diseases but in more recent times catering for a wider variety of patients. The *Klinik* is the terminus of the bus service referred to

(Official Timetable 310. 55) which runs between here and the Station Square at Thun. A less demanding way of doing this excursion on foot is, of course, to take the bus from Thun to Heiligenschwendi and do the walk downhill.

Walkers can also extend the excursion by continuing from Heiligenschwendi downhill in a southerly direction on the edge of the woods to Oberhofen on the lakeside (approximately 40 minutes). On the way there are fine views of the pyramidal Niesen (2,360m, 7,741ft) which dominates the central section of the south shore of Lake Thun, separating the mouths of the Simme and Kander valleys which poke into the Oberland.

Although the bus route terminates at the *Klinik*, a road for motorists continues east from there, then swings south again, through wooded terrain with occasional clearings, via Ringoldswil to **Sigriswil**, a farming village and peaceful climatic resort on a sun terrace. From here there are magnificent panoramas over the lake of the great mountain groups of the Oberland. (Sigriswil has a charming church of St Gallus, rebuilt in the late seventeenth century with a baroque interior.) From Sigriswil the road leads down to **Gunten**, an attractive lakeside resort facing the Niesen across the lake, with very active sailing and windsurfing schools. (Sigriswil, it should be added, can also be reached by a bus service from Gunten, Official Timetable 310. 65, which in turn is served by a very frequent bus service (Official Timetable 310. 60) along the north shore of the lake between Thun Station Square and Interlaken.) The motorist, however, who has reached Gunten from Heiligenschwendi and Sigriswil will almost certainly be interested to continue along the lakeside to the next village to the east, **Merligen**, a former fishing village at a sheltered sun-trap situation on the lakeside where the Justis valley meets the lake at right angles. Merligen was traditionally a stage on the pilgrimage route to the Beatus Caves (see Bernese Oberland chapter).

From Merligen (or from the Beatus Caves) an expeditious but interesting return to Thun can be made by car or by the bus service noted above. The north shore road is an attractive one, passing through colourful lakeside villages with lush floral growth because of their favourably sheltered south-facing exposure. Many houses have picturesquely sited balconies overhanging the lake, or terraces supported on lakeside boat houses. One of the villages is **Oberhofen**, with its spectacular and colourful lakeside castle (see Bernese Oberland chapter). A particularly fine view of the castle — and indeed of most aspects of this shoreline — can be obtained from the deck of the

A steamer trip from Merligen passing Oberhofen Castle

lake steamers which in the season call frequently at all lakeside villages between Thun and Interlaken. Incidentally, the Oberhofen boat station is next to the castle.

The excursion as described from Thun via Heiligenschwendi to Merligen above is the most straightforward route for making acquaintance with a most attractive pre-alpine landscape with a very favoured southern exposure. There exists however a very great number of variant routes on the numerous well defined walking paths that make this area a great favourite with Swiss visitors who enjoy walking holidays off the beaten track

An Emmental Circuit

For tourists residing in the Oberland a favourite excursion is a visit to the capital of Central Switzerland, Luzern, by way of the dramatic Brünig Pass route. The route is substantially the same whether carried out by road or by the narrow-gauge Brünig railway; it follows the shore of Lake Brienz before turning north to climb over the Brünig Pass and then descend by steps via the Lungern and Sarnen Lakes to the shores of the Vierwaldstättersee. On the return journey to canton Bern some people may, for variety, choose to take by road or rail the faster route from Luzern to Bern (or Thun) by way of the Emmental. And for many visitors to Switzerland the fast through journey via Langnau may be the only experience they have of the Emmental (literally the valley of the river Emme), a district which illustrates the charm of the Berner Mittelland in high degree. With the Swiss themselves it is a great favourite as one of the most varied and beautiful walking areas in the country; in addition when it comes to food, the country towns and inns of the Emmental enjoy an exceptional reputation even for Switzerland, a reputation that one tends to link with the Emmental farming communities' repute as the foremost pioneers of Swiss agriculture. (It is said that distinguished foreign guests of the Swiss Confederation visiting Bern are invariably taken out to dine somewhere in the Emmental.) A fair example of the region can be had from a round trip, carried out from Thun or from Bern, extending to about 130km (80 miles).

From Bern take the N1 road to the north, heading for Olten/Basel. (Motorists starting from Thun by road can skirt Bern to join the N1). Leave the N1 after 19km (12 miles) turning right (east) for **Burgdorf**. This is a historic town, its nucleus occupying an imposing and consequently strategic position on an eminence commanding the river Emme. It is still generally known as the gateway to the Emmental. It has a long tradition of settlement, the hill having been a fortified place since the mid-tenth century. The Zähringer Dukes extended the castle from 1127 onward, and it is one of Switzerland's earliest

Burgdorf, the 'gateway to the Emmental'

brick buildings; the town alongside it on the ridge grew in proportion to its strategic importance and was in fact incorporated in the walled defences by the Kyburg dynasty which followed the Zähringers. When the Kyburgers sold Burgdorf to Bern in 1384 the townsfolk had already acquired burgher rights. From that date forward until the French Revolutionary wars (which had quite a momentous impact on Switzerland) the castle was occupied by a Bernese governor. The triple-towered castle which is today still a prominent landmark now serves as a historical museum. The late fifteenth-century parish church (Reformed) is a fine example of late Gothic and possesses a notable rood screen of 1512. The residential part of the castle has a Romanesque hall and a chapel with fourteenth-century frescoes. There is much of the old town that is well worth seeing, with its handsome merchant houses in the Höhengasse and Kronenplatz, of Gothic and baroque style.

From Burgdorf take the road south, along the west bank of the Emme. Within 5km (3 miles) on the right hand side is the village of **Hasle**, a small junction station on the local railway system. Just to the north of the village there is a bridge over the Emme that is a particularly interesting example of the characteristic rural Swiss timber-built covered bridge. (The timber roofing is not merely picturesque but intensely practical as it prevents heavy winter snowfalls from rendering passage over the bridge either impossible or very hazardous.) The Hasle bridge is the longest of its type in Europe, with a timber-vault span of 58m (190ft). It was designed in 1839. Hasle's parish church is an example of the baroque hall-style of Reformed church, specifically designed to lay emphasis on the primacy of the preaching aspects of divine service.

Leaving Hasle behind, in about 2km (just over a mile) turn left to cross the river into **Lützelflüh** near where the Langete tributary joins the Emme. This little town is best known to the Swiss and to others acquainted with Swiss literature as the 'Gotthelf-village'. It was here that Jeremias Gotthelf (1797-1854), whose novels portrayed early nineteenth-century life in the Emmental, served as village pastor. A *Gotthelf-stube* in the village exhibits memorabilia of the author during the season (April to October). The former grain mill of the village, one of the finest in the region built in 1821, serves nowadays as a community cultural centre and is known as the Kulturmühle.

From Lützelflüh the road heads north-east to reach **Sumiswald** (in 8km, 5 miles) on its broad sunny terrace. This market town and centre of its district has been a notable village of craft workers since the eighteenth century. Perhaps it owes that to influences from its earlier history. Its church of St Maria was built in the early sixteenth century as a church of the military and religious Teutonic Order of knights, priests and serving brothers. (The church has some superlative stained-glass windows from that period.) The town has also an institution called the Spittel, built from an endowment of 1225 which laid an obligation upon the Teutonic Order to maintain a hospice for tending the poor and providing hospitality to pilgrims. In its present form it is substantially an early eighteenth-century building, and now serves as a local nursing home. Sumiswald's hinterland of rolling hills and streams has around 75km (46 miles) of well defined walking trails.

Motorists travelling in this area at some leisure should feel encouraged to make detours and deviations from the minimal itinerary here outlined to visit the beautiful hamlets and the large unitary farmsteads that are so characteristic of this area, with its long history of settled agricultural civilisation. In the Emmental region the local customary laws of inheritance differed markedly from most of their neighbours. Farm estates, on the death of the owner, were not here divided up among several offspring, but were passed on undivided to a sole heir. This has had the effect that for centuries Emmental farmsteads and lands have had great historical continuity as units of accumulated agricultural wealth and skills; and they have given the landscape very impressive and characteristic features: the majestic farmsteads with enormous double-thatched roofs extending like half-folded wings nearly to ground level at the sides and encompassing under one giant roof not only living quarters but also stables, barns and other ancillary accommodation. A *stöckli* — ancestor of the modern 'grandmother's flat' — was invariably part of the complex, providing separate quarters for the older, retired generation of the family. Traditionally pioneers in agriculture, these were the families which at the beginning of the nineteenth century concluded that the making of good cheese need not be confined to the high alpine dairies as was then generally accepted, but could be practised in the rich pasturelands of the Mittelland. The outcome was that 'Emmentaler' became a common European word for Swiss cheese.

The visitor here soon realises that the unit of community is less commonly a village composed of the homes of farm workers, small-holders and other craftsmen, than a large unitary farm-estate with its branches of workers accommodated. It is well worth a deviation from the main road into part of the network of good minor roads that lead to these farm-estates. One important by-product of this style of organisation is that cheese is still largely made in the farm villages, instead of in some more or less distant town cheese factory to which milk is conveyed by road.

From Sumiswald road No 23 leads to Huttwil, 15km (9 miles) distant to the north-east. But on the way an opportunity arises after about 10km (6 miles) to make a detour to visit a community which exemplifies some splendid large-scale, almost manorial, farmstead-ings, as well as two magnificent late baroque inns (*Gasthöfe*) of the turn of eighteenth-nineteenth century, with the imposing hip-roofs of the best Emmental tradition. The community is signposted 'Dürrenroth' at a side road that goes off to the right (and later rejoins the main road further on).

Huttwil is nowadays a small market and industrial town. Originally a fortified town from the mid-thirteenth century, it was burned down in 1834 and, rebuilt in the neo-classicist town plan style of that era, presents a pleasing unified small town image. About 4km ($2\frac{1}{2}$ miles) further east of Huttwil on road 23 is the village of **Hüswil**, where there is an eighteenth-century granary, typical of the region, but particularly renowned for its handsomely carved door. Shortly beyond Hüswil, at Gettnau (10km, 6 miles from Huttwil) road 23 continues straight ahead east to Sursee (on the Sempacher Lake), but take instead a branch that goes off to the right for **Willisau**, a thirteenth-century foundation. Parts of its medieval walls survive, including the 1551 Upper Gate at the west end of the Hauptgasse (Main Street). A rebuilt Lower Gate matches it at the other end. Just outside the Upper Gate is the attractive Heiligblut (Holy Blood) pilgrimage chapel of 1674-5, with a series of biblical scenes on its wooden ceiling which are of the period. Inside the same city gate on a little hillock stands the neo-classical Catholic parish church, which was rebuilt in 1801 but retains its original thirteenth-century bell-tower (although now capped with a baroque dome!).

Shortly after leaving Huttwil, road 23 crossed the cantonal boundary from Bern to Luzern canton. In so doing it also crossed what the Swiss recognise as an ancient cultural frontier which in this part of the country runs not as a straight line but in a curve in clockwise direction, through the Brünig Pass, the centre of the highland massif known as the Napf, and the river Reuss which flows out from the Vierwaldstättersee at Luzern. (The Napf is in fact the mountain core of the region round which this excursion route executes a nearly circular path, and from which radiate the streams and glens which have intersected the route.) The cultural frontier that here lies between canton Bern and the original Four Forest Cantons has been described thus: 'though not a boundary between language groups, it does form a more significant division in everyday affairs, separating one set of customs and traditions from others.'

The road now continues to the industrial town of **Wolhusen** (10km, 6 miles) on the Little Emme river. (It is rather confusing that in this area there exist two rivers Emme. The Great Emme — mostly called simply the Emme — rises away to the south on the Hohgant (2,197m, 7,206ft) north of Lake Brienz and flows north-west to join the Aare. The Little Emme rises further east on the slopes of the Giswiler Stock (near the Lungern Lake) and flows roughly north and then east to join the Reuss.) From Wolhusen the circular itinerary now continues south on road 10 which has come in on the left (ie east) from Luzern. However, before resuming the circular journey it is worthwhile to take a short deviation along the Wolhusen-Luzern road for about 2km (just over a mile), following the river (as does also the Bern-Langnau-Luzern railway) to admire the strikingly beautiful site of the convent of Werthenstein, poised on a high bluff dominating a bend of the river. There is a lovely pilgrimage church of the early seventeenth century and a handsome cloister. But above all the setting is lovely, and is a temptation to find a picnic place.

The road, resumed south from Wolhusen, leads in 8km (5 miles) to the pretty village of **Entlebuch** through what is called the Entle-

The village of Trub in the Napf region

buch valley, although the river which actually traverses it is the Little
Emme river referred to above. The valley takes its name from the
Entlen torrent, a tributary of the Little Emme, which races down to
join it from the slopes of the Glaubenberg mount which separates this
valley from the parallel valley in which lie the Lungern and Sarnen
Lakes (and the road from Brünig Pass.) The Glaubenberg Pass, at
1,543m (5,061ft), is traversed by a mountain road which provides an
interesting hill walk backed up by public transport to starting and
finishing points. Transport to Entlebuch railway station is by the line
Bern-Langnau-Luzern (or Thun-Konolfingen-Luzern). Then a postbus from Entlebuch (Official Timetable No 460. 75) takes walkers
well up the Entlen valley beyond Entlenmatt, leaving them with a
6km (3$^1/_2$ miles) ascent to walk to the pass. On the far side a mountain
bus route (Timetable No 470. 30) operates to Sarnen, which has a
railway station on the Interlaken-Brünig-Luzern line.

From Entlebuch the main road (No 10) continues along the south
bank of the Little Emme to reach in 7km (4 miles) the main place of

Hohgant from the Schellenberg Pass

the Entlebuch valley, **Schüpfheim**. Here there is a local history museum, Entlebucher Heimatmuseum, dealing with the valley; its opening hours are irregular.

From Schüpfheim a spectacular minor road runs south for 17km (10½ miles) following the Forest Emme (Waldemme) as this stretch of Little Emme is commonly called, through the hills along the Mariental valley to Flühli and the little climatic resort of **Sörenberg** (1,159m, 3,802ft), near which is a cable railway to the summit of the Brienzer Rothorn which gives an unrivalled prospect of Lake Brienz and beyond it the whole massif of the Bernese Oberland peaks. A postbus service operates on this route from Schüpfheim (Timetable No 460. 60) and continues beyond the Glaubenbuelen Pass (1,611m, 5,284ft), on a zigzag descent to Giswil, between the Lungern and Sarnen Lakes.

Road No 10 from Schüpfheim leads to another attractive village, **Escholzmatt**, still in canton Luzern although hereabout is the water-shed between the Entlebuch valley and the Emmental proper. In a further 3km (2 miles) the road reaches the hamlet of **Wiggen**. At this point motorists who wish to return to Bern at the end of this circular itinerary should continue forward on road No 10, reaching Trubschachen in 6km (4 miles), and Langnau-im-Emmental, the chief town of the district in 6km (4 miles) more.

Travellers making Thun their destination at the end of this circuit have an interesting option available to them. They too may choose to continue via Langnau. But they also have the possibility of taking a spectacular minor road which branches off to the left, ie south, at Wiggen. This road climbs moderately at first to **Marbach**, a well regarded unsophisticated winter sports resort with cablecar and skilifts to the Marbachegg sun-terrace (Timetable No 1500). Thereafter there is a steeper ascent to **Schangnau**, 10km (6 miles) south of Wiggen, a farming village which also caters for winter sports. From Wiggen there is a postbus service to Marbach and Schangnau (Official Timetable No 460. 50) and this also continues along the road which turns off sharply left at Schangnau, leading along the bank of the Emme to Bumbach and Kemmeriboden. Between these two villages lies a favoured cross-country ski area. But for Thun keep forward at Schangnau, dipping down to cross the Emme and tackling the ascent to the Schallenberg Pass (1,167m, 3,828ft). From the serpentine turns of the road magnificent views are obtained of the long sierra ridge of the 2,199m (7,213ft) high Hohgant, pride of the Emmental region. From the Schallenberg the road descends in the course of 15km (9 miles) via Oberei and Schwarzenegg to Steffisburg, which in modern times has become something of a dormitory suburb to 4km- ($2^1/_2$ miles-) distant Thun. **Steffisburg** has in its historic centre some buildings of considerable character: a church, rebuilt in the late seventeenth century but with a Romanesque tower that has a wooden belfry and spire; and two adjacent buildings known as the Hochhüser, the larger of which is transitional between the Bernese farmhouse and the country mansion styles and has a hipped roof on a really magnificent scale.

Travelling on from Wiggen on road 10, **Trubschachen** is reached in 6km (4 miles). The village has many imposing merchant residences; and in the district are many of the typical timber-built, roofed bridges. Following now the Ilfis tributary of the Emme, the road arrives, 6km (4 miles) further on, at **Langnau**. The principal market town of the Emmental has some handsome squares, one of which, the Hirschenplatz, is considered to be one of the finest and most unspoilt in the Bern region. The church, a late seventeenth-century 'preaching hall' in the Reformed style, is handsomely furnished with a richly carved baroque pulpit and font. Attractive stone built houses in the centre of the town have decorated timber surfaces under the gables and half-hipped roofs. A sixteenth-century building with a high saddle-roof, the Chuechlihaus, houses the Heimatmuseum which has a collection of old Langnau pottery products; it also has exhibits to illustrate the products and tools of the several local timber trades and crafts, which is particularly appropriate in a district where forestry and timber trades are of such importance. In the course of the itinerary outlined above, for instance, travellers would come across a fair number of the fifty or so Emmental saw-mills, and from their observation of farms and farmland would be able to appreciate the force of the Emmental saying 'An Emmental farm without woodland is like a bed without a blanket'.

From Langnau, road No 10 climbs out of the Ilfis and Emme valleys and in 21km (13 miles) reaches **Worb**, a town of 11,000 inhabitants. It has a baronial castle which was rebuilt in the early sixteenth century after fire destruction. From Worb, Bern is reached in 10km (6 miles).

Although no public transport service precisely covers the above itinerary in that form, local public transport makes the main points accessible. The main railway service on the Emmental route from Bern to Luzern, Timetable No 460 (or Thun via Konolfingen to Luzern) has stations at Langnau, Trubschachen, Wiggen, Escholzmatt, Schüpfheim, Entlebuch, Wolhusen and Werthenstein. From Wolhusen, a service links with Willisau, Hüswil and Huttwil.

Murten

There is a broad swathe of Mittelland in the form of rolling plateau country which forms a wide corridor along which modern roads and railways find their fastest and easiest passage between the country's capital and the shores of Lake Geneva. In the past that same tract was often the corridor along which migrating peoples or invading armies found their route. So it is not surprising that the Mittelland overrides cantonal frontiers. One of the most interesting small towns of the Mittelland illustrates this. Murten does not lie in Bernese Mittelland today but in the neighbouring canton of Fribourg. But it was once Bernese. And for a period of centuries it was under the joint rule of Bern and Fribourg.

Murten is conveniently reached from Bern, whether by road or rail. Although the rail journey involves a change of trains, the time-table of services is so well co-ordinated that the change is no great inconvenience. The best route with a Bern-Murten rail ticket is to take, from Bern main station (*Hauptbahnhof*), a train on the frequent

The Berner Gate at Murten

Bern-Neuchatel service (Timetable No 220), alight at Kerzers and change platform for a train to Murten on the line to Payerne (Timetable No 251). By road take the motorway N1 heading west from Bern, taking care in 12km (7$^1/_2$ miles) not to take the exit for Kerzers and Neuchatel but to continue on the motorway as it curves south and becomes an ordinary national road a short distance from Murten. Murten lies beside the lake which bears its name, close to the linguistic frontier between French and German speech. (The French form of the name is Morat.) The little town was founded in its present form in the second half of the twelfth century by the Dukes of Zähringen. It has preserved to the present day its architectural setting and character, and its medieval town walls (twelfth and fifteenth century) are an exceptionally complete example of their period. They are well preserved and maintained and the rampart walks are accessible, giving interesting views into the town and out over the surrounding countryside. One of two original gates, the Berner Gate, survives in its eighteenth-century baroque form. The wide main street, which the Berner Gate bounds and which forms a market place, has sixteenth-century arcaded sidewalks and houses, with seventeenth- and eighteenth-century façades. It is a delightful place to stroll through, as it is sufficiently small (with a population of under 5,000) for a visitor readily to come to terms with its layout.

Murten has considerable significance in Swiss history, as it gave its name to a critical battle fought close by in 1476. Just as the Central Swiss communities around the Vierwaldstättersee had to struggle for their independent rights against the Austrian Hapsburgs, their confederates to the west of Bern had to confront the might of the Burgundian realm. At Murten in 1476 the Confederates won their first victory over Charles the Bold's Burgundian army.

In the summer season an interesting boat excursion (Timetable No 2212) can be made from Murten, on the Lake of Murten and the Lake of Neuchatel (to which it is linked by canal), to Neuchatel, capital of the canton of the same name further west.

But perhaps the most interesting extension that can be made to a Murten visit is to make the very short journey of only 8km (5 miles) either by road No 1, or by rail on the same line as from Kerzers to Murten. The destination is the small town of **Avenches,** which stands on a hill just north of the bypassing main road No 1 which runs across the Mittelland plateau from Bern to Lausanne. Avenches illustrates the long history of settlement characteristic of Mittelland. Its name was once *Aventicum*, when in the first and second centuries AD it was the large and prosperous capital of the Roman province (before which it had been the hill town tribal capital of the Helvetii). It never quite recovered from its destruction by Germanic tribesmen in the third century AD and in the medieval period the extensive Roman town remains were used as a quarry-source of building material. Even so, the existing remains are remarkable, and include one of the best preserved Roman amphitheatres (accommodating 12,000

The Roman Amphitheatre at Avenches

spectators). There are also remains of baths, a theatre and many parts of the Roman walls, with gates and towers preserved. Next to the amphitheatre is an eleventh-century fortified tower, no doubt once part of the medieval town defences; well maintained, it now serves as a Roman Museum.

Apart from the Roman remains, Avenches preserves interesting buildings from the medieval period. In the market place stands the *château*, formerly the bishop's residence, which was enlarged in Renaissance style in the sixteenth century by the governor who ruled the town after it had become subject to Bern in 1536. In short, Avenches, lying aside a little from the bypassing main road from Bern to Lausanne, offers a new perspective on the Swiss Mittelland for the visitor who may only until then have known the ski or climatic resorts of the mountain regions.

Further Information
— Bernese Mittelland —

Entertainment

Gunten
Folklore evenings.

Interlaken
Dancing at Kursaal/casino; Horse-drawn coach trips; folklore evenings; evening cruises on the lake.

Schangnau
Trips by horse-drawn carts. Details from Verkehrsbüro.

Sigriswil
Folklore evenings in unique village square.

Thun
Dancing nightly in Kursaal/casino; also games of chance; folklore evenings; evening cruises on the lake.

Museums and Other Places of Interest

Burgdorf
Schloss Burgdorf Museum
Open: April to October, 2-5pm.
☎ 034/21 61 31
Exhibits illustrate Emmental culture, including ceramics, weapons, musical instruments etc.

Heiligenschwendi
Forest nature-study trail.
Details from Verkehrsbüro.

Langnau
Chüechlihus Heimatmuseum (Emmental Museum)
Open: Tuesday to Sunday 9-11.30am and 1.30-6pm. Closed December and public holidays. Includes an alpine cheese dairy and utensils.

Lützelflüh
Brandis nature-study trail.
Information from Verkehrsbüro.

Cultural centre in Kulturmühle.
Information from Verkehrsbüro.

Murten
Historical Museum
Opening times from Verkehrsbüro.

Oberhofen
Historical Museum in castle on
lake front
Open: mid-May to mid-October
10am-12noon and 2-5pm, except
Monday mornings.

Thun
Historic Castle Museum
Open: April, May, October 10am-
5pm; June, July, August, September 9am-6pm.
☎ 033/23 20 01
Exhibits include weapons, ceramics, folk art.

Sport and Recreational Activities

Gunten
Instruction in sailing, water-skiing
and windsurfing available from:
Sailing School Rasmus, Postfach 3,
CH-3654 Gunten
☎ 033/51 31 77 or 033/51 19 35

Water-ski School Gunten,
☎ 033/51 22 66

Windsurfing School Gunten, CH-
3653 Oberhofen ☎ 033/43 29 77

Interlaken
Information obtainable from
Verkehrsbüro on: Sailing and
Surfing School; eighteen-hole golf

course; tennis; archery; clay-pigeon
shooting.

Langnau
Indoor swimming school; sport
centre.

Lützelflüh
Heated open-air swimming pool.

Marbach
Winter sports; summer rambling
and hiking; cabin aerial railway to
Marbachegg run by: Sportbahnen
Marbachegg A.G Official Time-
table 1500. ☎ 035/6 33 88

Murten
Swimming pools, both indoor and
open-air.

Oberhofen
Indoor swimming pool combined
with regional 'Fitness Centre'
Open: 10am-9pm; Saturday and
Sunday 10am-6pm.

Sigriswil
Walking, horse-riding, mini-golf.

Sörenberg
Winter sports; summer hill-walk-
ing and climbing; cabin aerial
railway from Sörenberg-Schöner-
boden runs to Brienzer Rothorn
summit.Official Timetable 1505.
☎ 041/78 15 60

Thun
Swimming from biggest lake-
strand in Switzerland, with heated
inner pool; horse-riding (including
indoor provision); curling and ice-

skating indoor rinks; 'Fitness' trail; windsurfing school beside the lake strand-bathing station; Thun Rowing Club, ☎ 033/22 82 47; Windsurf Club Thun, ☎ 033/22 82 82; Swiss Sailing Schools, Thunersee: contact Sekretariat Verkehrsbüro.

Worb
Open-air swimming pool.

Hiking and Rambling
Among the Swiss the Mittelland regions are renowned for rambling and walking facilities, with well laid out and signposted paths. Useful information and maps available from: Sekretariat, Berner Wanderwege, Postfach 263, CH-3000 Bern
☎ 031/42 37 66
The REKA ramblers' pass for use of public transport, described in the Central Switzerland chapter, is also available in the Emmental area. The transport network available for unlimited use of the pass fully covers (and indeed extends beyond) the area included in the Emmental circular excursion.

Tourist Information Offices

Regional offices:
Verkehrsverband Thunersee
c/o Verkehrsverein Thun
Bahnhofplatz
CH-3600 Thun
☎ 033/22 23 40

Verkehrsverband Berner Mittelland
Geschäftsstelle Verkehrsbüro Bern
Im Bahnhof
Postfach 2700

CH-3001 Bern
☎ 031/22 12 12

Verkehrsverband Emmental
Geschaftsstelle Mühlegässli 2
CH-3550 Langnau im Emmental
☎ 035/2 42 52

For the places in canton Luzern which are included in the Emmental excursion:
Verkehrsverband Zentralschweiz
Alpenstrasse 1
CH-6002 Luzern
☎ 041/51 18 91

Local Offices
Avenches
Office du Tourisme
Place de l'Eglise 3
CH-1580 Avenches
☎ 037/75 11 59

Bern City
Offizielles Verkehrsbüro
Im Bahnhof
CH 3001 Bern
☎ 031/22 76 76

Burgdorf
Verkehrsbüro
CH 3400 Burgdorf
☎ 034/22 24 45

Dürrenroth
Verkehrsverein
CH 3465 Dürrenroth
☎ 063/74 14 50

Entlebuch
Verkehrsverein
Bahnhof
CH-6162 Entlebuch
☎ 041/82 13 25

Escholzmatt
Verkehrsverein
CH-6182 Escholzmatt
☎ 041/77 11 15

Giswil
Verkehrsverein
Brunigstrasse 80
CH-6074 Giswil
☎ 041/68 17 60

Goldiwil
Verkehrsbüro
CH-3624 Goldiwil-ob-Thun
☎ 033/42 12 89

Gunten
Verkehrsbüro
CH-3654 Gunten
☎ 033/51 11 46

Hasle
Verkehrsbüro
CH-3415 Hasle
☎ 034/61 12 36

Heiligenschwendi
Verkehrsverein
CH-3625 Heiligenschwendi
☎ 033/43 16 26; if not answering, try
033/43 15 03

Huttwil
Verkehrsbüro
CH-4950 Huttwil
☎ 063/72 12 89

Interlaken
Verkehrsbüro
CH-3800 Interlaken
☎ 036/22 21 21

Langnau
Verkehrsbüro
CH-3550 Langnau im Emmental
☎ 035 2 34 34

Lützelflüh
Verkehrsverein
CH-3432 Lützelflüh
☎ 034/61 36 23

Marbach
Verkehrsbüro
CH-6196 Marbach
☎ 035/6 38 04

Merligen
Verkehrsbüro
CH-3658 Merligen
☎ 033/51 11 42

Murten
Verkehrsbüro
Hauptgasse 6
CH-3280 Murten
☎ 037/71 51 12

Neuchatel
Office Neuchatelois du Tourisme
Place Numa-Droz 1
CH-2001 Neuchatel
☎ 038/25 42 42

Oberhofen
Verkehrsbüro
CH-3653 Oberhofen
☎ 033/43 14 19

Schangnau
Verkehrsbüro
CH-6197 Schangnau
☎ 035/6 37 87

Schüpfheim
Verkehrsverein
CH-6170 Schüpfheim-Dorf
☎041/76 23 23

Sigriswil
Verkehrsbüro
CH-3655 Sigriswil
☎ 033/51 12 35

Sörenberg
Rothorn-Center
CH-6174 Sörenberg
☎ 041/78 11 85

Sumiswald
Verkehrsbüro
CH-3455 Sumiswald
☎ 034/71 15 39

Thun
Verkehrsbüro
Bahnhofplatz
CH-3600 Thun
☎ 033/22 23 40

Trubschachen
Verkehrsverein
CH-3555 Trubschachen
☎ 035/6 52 05

Wiggen
Verkehrsverein
CH-6192 Wiggen
☎ 041/77 11 28

Willisau
Verkehrsbüro
Bahnhof VHB
CH-6130 Willisau
☎ 045/81 26 66

Wolhusen
Information from
Willisau tourist office.

Worb
Verkehrsbüro
CH-3078 Worb
☎ 031/83 07 83

6 • Bernese Oberland

The Bernese Oberland is the southern, alpine part of the canton of Bern, comprising around 4,500sq km (about 1,800sq miles) of country bordered by the high alpine chain to the south and the Thunersee and Brienzersee (lakes), and the Simmental (valley) to the north. Within this area there are a small number of mostly very well known valleys that lie north-south, penetrating, but never bridging the alpine chain. In addition there are a small number of towns, the best known being Interlaken, the sub-canton's capital.

The Oberland was 'discovered' as soon as the idea of travelling unaccompanied and for pleasure became popular, that is within the last two or three centuries. Rousseau is accepted by many as the first to have seen the scenery of the area for what it truly is — magnificent, and he was followed by the cream of Parisian society. The nineteenth century saw the English arrive — Byron, Ruskin and Thackeray as well as other literary giants — seeking solace or inspiration. Mark Twain devoted a now famous section of his travel book to the area, and Goethe was inspired to produce some of his more classical work. The area attracted musicians like Brahms and Mendelssohn, and, perhaps least surprisingly, painters.

Visitors still come to look with wonder at the scenery, now 'opened up' with cablecars and rack railways, and with the phenomenal increase in interest in winter sports the area now has a year-long season. The Lauberhorn race (at Wengen) is the classic of the downhill world championship, a fitting reminder that the first ever world skiing championships were held in the area, at Mürren, in 1931. Ironically it was the British who established the idea, the first races having been held, also at Mürren, in 1922 under the direction of Sir Arnold Lunn.

The Oberland's peaks have long attracted climbers, the attraction being both their height and their difficulty. The north wall of the Eiger is notorious, probably the only alpine climb that can be readily called to mind by the layman. The climb's reputation was built in part on its technical severity, but in the main on its position. The Eiger's north face grows, almost literally, straight out of the alpine meadows. This ready accessibility (the casual observer at Kleine Scheidegg has a grandstand position at any drama) meant that all such dramas were played out in publicity's full glare. But the face's position — the first major alpine face — also meant that it attracted a lot of bad weather, and this was the major character in most of the dramas played out on the peak.

Most visitors have no desire to climb the Eiger's north wall, but to go off the beaten track in the area it is usually necessary to do some walking. However, since the High Alps — that is high meadow, not jagged peak, ice and snow — is no great place to be in bad weather and with poor equipment, the walks will keep to waymarked or very obvious paths. It goes without saying that anyone contemplating a day or even a half-day in the outdoors in the Oberland should have reasonable clothing, and should keep one eye on the weather.

The Western Oberland

Thunersee

The tour begins at **Thun**, just about the lowest point in the Oberland, and long held to be the 'Gateway to the Oberland' because of its position at the head of the Thunersee and between two gatepost-like peaks. Today the town is rarely visited. The motorway from Bern towards Interlaken bypasses Thun, allowing Oberland visitors to pass the town without even noticing it and, despite being much bigger than Interlaken, it has less than 10 per cent of the latter town's visitor accommodation, and nothing to compare with its array of tourist traps.

The town's name derives from the Celtic word for a fortified hill, but that hill was neither of the two gateposts on the way to the Oberland, but the 30m (100ft) high, right bank of the Aare river as it leaves Thunersee. As the river leaves the lake it splits into two arms, the Innere Aare and the Aussere Aare, that flow around an island of central Thun before rejoining a couple of hundred metres downstream. From the time of the first Celtic fortress, Thun has a continuous history. The lords of the area had a later castle here, the remains of which probably support the present castle, which was started in the late twelfth century. To reach it, start from Marktgasse, which crosses the second road bridge over the Innere Aare, near where that arm of the river joins the Aussere Aare. An early right turn takes the

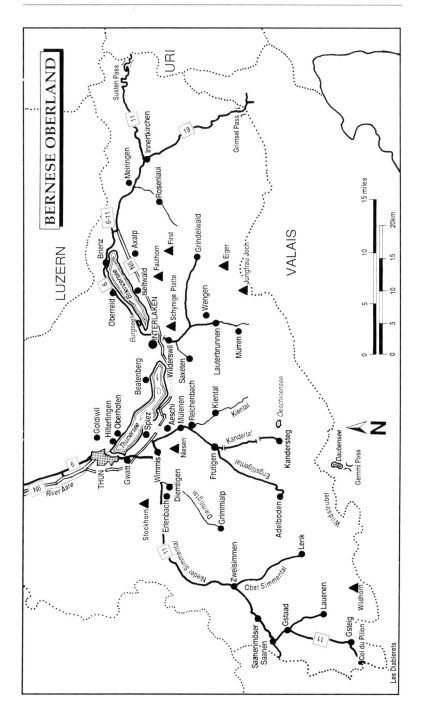

The Eiger from the Kleine Scheidegg

visitor to Rathausplatz, the Town Hall Square. This is the centre of old Thun, the town hall itself dating from the early sixteenth century. It is a magnificent building, elegantly tiled, with a fine pair of dormer windows, one each side of a clock tower with external bells. Even this building, municipal rather than private, is set off with marvellous splashes of colour in each window box, and do notice the left hand of the two carved lions on the coat-of-arms: that whiskered face is surely more human than leonine. Elsewhere in the square there is much of interest. In the west corner is Thun's oldest building, the Casa Barba or Velschenhaus, a fourteenth-century building with good windows which open inwards, as do most windows — perhaps so as not to knock the window box flower heads. The police headquarters was built in the late eighteenth century and served as an orphanage and school before being taken over as the *Stadtpoliza*.

Leave the square along Hauptgasse, in the diagonally opposite corner from where you entered it, and go gently uphill. Here, only the walkway rises, the street staying level to give a curious double

The castle at Thun

tier of shops. Look out for a sign pointing, in symbols, to church and castle and take this covered stairway upwards. Towards the top several other, uncovered, walkways meet at a small 'temple' built only in 1820 and with a frescoed ceiling completed by the Italian artist Tschabold in 1959. At the top of the steps go left for the castle. The castle is a fairy-tale building, a tall square keep with a wedge shaped, tiled roof and four circular corner turrets, conically roofed. To dispel the image somewhat, a smaller turret is known as Hangman's Tower. Entrance is through a gate-tower, where there was once a drawbridge and where remnants of the moat can still be seen, into an elegant courtyard. Today the castle houses, in part, the law courts, and also the town's museum. Here, be sure to see a somewhat static, but rather appealing, representation of William Tell and his apple-clutching son, in Heimberg pottery, dating from 1864; two very old and precious altar fronts, one from the mid-fifteenth century, the other from around 1300 showing St Maurice, the town's patron saint, surrounded by a fine array of mythical creatures; and a good collection of medieval weaponry.

Instead of going left at the top of the covered stairway, go right to reach the town church, a fine building from the eighteenth century, though built on a much earlier base. The original church — perhaps as early as the tenth century — stood inside the early town's wall that stretched all round this high ridge. From the outside, the church, with its porched spire, looks as though it should have a memorable interior. What is found comes as a surprise even to those expecting the austerity of German-Swiss churches. Inside there is an assembly of new pine pews, an organ gallery, an old, rope-tied, crucifix and nothing more.

The town is proud of its artistic heritage, particularly the fact that Brahms spent three summers here from 1886 to 1888 and entitled one of his pieces the *Thuner Sonata*. It is equally proud, and rightly so, of the *Wocher Panorama*, a remarkable view of Thun as it was in 1810, painted by Marquard Wocher, a Swabian engraver working in Bern. The panorama, whose production almost bankrupted Wocher, measures 39 by 7.5m (128 by 25ft) and is so faithful that many of the buildings represented can still be seen. It is not so much for that representation that the visit is worthwhile however, but more to wonder at the effort, and to admire the detail. Look for the little family group shyly looking out of the attic window, almost as though they are looking at the artist himself, and also for the cat quietly licking its paw while sitting on the stick-supported sill of another attic. The *Panorama* is housed in a special building in the delightful Schadau Park — go lakewards from the railway station.

Also worth a visit is Kriebers, a book shop on the corner of Freienhergasse and Bölliz, on the island between the two arms of Aare. There, on the first floor, is a superb series of engravings of the town.

Leaving Thun, go down the northern shoreline of Lake Thun, from where the view back to Thun across the water is excellent. Near Hilterfingen there is a small children's playground near the lakeside, and even with this the Swiss flair for imaginative invention — usually more obvious in their watch design — has come to the fore. The wooden rocking horses and the log-and-chain arrangement, are great.

Also at **Hilterfingen**, is another castle, and yet another stands at nearby Oberhofen. Each is very good, and both are rarely visited by the English. Hilterfingen's castle (Castle Hünegg) was built only a little over a century ago, the design being more elaborate than Thun's war-engine building, and less pleasing as a result, but it is beautifully set off by the trees of its own fine parkland, and by those of the hill slopes that form a backdrop to the village. Inside, the original furnishings of the castle have been maintained, so that it is a museum to the interior design concepts of the last half of the nineteenth century. Hilterfingen was the site of Switzerland's first ever sailing school, and there is a school here still. With the views and the safety of lake, as opposed to sea, sailing, there can be few better places at which to learn.

By contrast to Hilterfingen's castle, the castle at **Oberhofen** (once the baronial home of a local aristocratic family with a wonderful Germanic name — who could resist an invitation from Baron von Scharnachtal) is medieval, though it is still more mansion than fortress. It houses a fine museum of overflow material from Bern's Historical Museum, including weaponry, toys and musical instruments. The chief joy however, is the castle's parkland, with an excellent alpine garden and a fine view over the lake to the Stockhorn and the Niesen. As a complete departure from history and sightseeing, Oberhofen also has a swimming pool — the *Hallenbad* in the park that stands, complete with a statue of Sir Winston Churchill, beside the castle — with a 67m (220ft) water chute.

Both Oberhofen and Hilterfingen have good marked walks in the woodland behind the villages, but the better views are obtained from walking near **Goldiwil**, a village closer to, but well above, Thun. Two very fine walks, that are well signed, take the visitor from Obermatt, just to the east of Goldiwil, down to Heiligenschwendi through some very pretty meadowland, and from Melli, between Goldiwil and Obermatt, up the Schwendibach towards Steffisburg. The view from above the village extends from the Stockhorn, right along the alpine wall to the peaks of the Jungfrau, and the northern end of the Thunersee can also be seen. (See also Bernese Mitteland chapter.)

Good views are also available further along the lake, but first do take a look at the huge array of concrete 'things' marching up the hill at Merligen. The notice promises dire penalties for anyone daring to photograph this military installation.

Beatenberg, an extremely pretty village almost secretly positioned between stands of conifer, is reached from the lakeside road, or by a rack railway from Beatenbucht on the lakeshore itself, and is an off the beaten track winter sports centre. There is a chairlift (and, further into the mountains, a project to build a cablecar) reaching some gentle slopes; there are some very good *Langlauf* runs in the

Goldiwil

wooded valley slopes, and an ice-rink. In summer the lifts can be used to gain the summit of the Niederhorn, a 1,950m (6,400ft) peak from which a very fine ridge walk leads to the Burgfeldstand and on to Gemmenalphorn (2,082m, 6,830ft), a distance of about 4.5km (3 miles). The views from this ridge, of the higher Oberland peaks and the lake, are breathtaking.

Beyond Beatenbucht are the caves of St Beatus, a fine series of limestone caves that can be explored along laid out pathways. The caves are lit to enhance the natural beauty of the stalagmites and stalactites. Thankfully the number of fanciful names given to the various formations is limited. The caves are the reputed home of St Beatus himself, a sixth-century Irish Christian teacher, who arrived to preach to the heathen locals and established a home in the cave, having first expelled the dragon who lived there. There are small tableaux to the monk, and to known Stone Age inhabitants, and a small museum of the geology, biology and exploration of the caves.

For some time now there has been a project to create a continuous footpath around the shoreline of Thunersee, and though this is not yet complete, one section that does exist cannot be too highly recommended: that from Thun to Gwatt. Actually it is easier to go in the opposite direction as the starting point is then obvious. This pathway goes through some really exquisite woodland, with equally good marshland sections at the lakeside, and fine outlooks through the woods to the Stockhorn chain, and across the lake.

Alternative walks can be made on the pyramidal peak of the Niesen, 2,362m (7,750ft), that commands the entrance to the Kandertal, the valley that leads to Kandersteg and Adelboden. A rack railway climbs the mountain from **Mülenen**, and it is worth taking that, as the walks down the mountain are preferable to those up it, for view as well as for energy input. At the summit is a hotel, and the morning view of the Oberland peaks from the Wetterhorn to way past the Breithorn, of Titlis, beyond the Oberland, and also the French-Swiss Jura, must be worth the price of a room. The routes down blend high meadow with conifer, but usually have a fine long view as a backdrop. It takes about $3\frac{1}{2}$ hours to reach the bottom. If that is too long, a fine excursion is to walk back to the intermediate station — the only intermediate station — at Schwandegg, which takes about $1\frac{1}{2}$ hours.

Back at the lakeside the small town of **Spiez** is worth some time. There is another fine castle, basically medieval, but much modified in the eighteenth century to act as a manorial home. Inside the furnishings vary across the centuries of use, and the grounds command fine views of the lake, particularly of the small lake bay which is dominated by the town. The nearby church, in fine Romanesque style, contains some good, though occasionally poorly preserved, eleventh-century murals.

Near to Spiez are two good villages. **Krattigen**, further down the lake shore towards Interlaken, is a small, rarely visited village. The well spread chalets are set among quiet meadows covered, at the right time of year, with alpine flowers. In many respects villages such as Krattigen, well off the beaten track, are the essence of the old Swiss alpine chalet village, and for that reason alone they are worth the visit. In addition, there is a good collection of local crystals on show here. Inland slightly is **Aeschi**, another very fine village with a delightful church, its typical spire set slightly up from its square tower base by a series of little arches. At night, when it is floodlit, the church is a rare sight, particularly if its lower roofs carry the winter's snow. Behind the village a small valley cutting back into the prealpine hills carries a stream crossed by rustic bridges, and holds a waterfall (the Pochtenfall) every bit as delightful, if not as large and powerful, as its more noted neighbours.

Frutigenland

In this section the main Kander valley is visited: the Kandertal, with Kandersteg at its head; the Engstligental, with Adelboden at its head, these two valleys joining near the town of Frutigen; and the Kiental, which joins the Kander near Reichenbach, the next village up valley from Mülenen at the base of the Niesen.

Adelboden, the main village and almost at the head of the Eng-stligental, is a famous ski resort, but does not have the intimacy of Zermatt and the villages in the Lauterbrunnen valley, or the vitality of Grindelwald. While not being as manufactured as Crans-Montana in the Valais, it is nevertheless very much a winter resort, lacking that special something in the summer months. The church, however, is a fine building with an organ loft, some excellent stained glass and a fine sixteenth-century fresco of the Last Judgement. The gates to the churchyard were presented by Allied servicemen who, having been interned in Switzerland, were sent to the village.

Adelboden is, however, a great starting point for walking tours in some of the finest high country in the area, with some really good trips, including a crossing of the Gemmi Pass for a fleeting visit to the Valais.

Most people will rightly want to visit the Cholerenschlucht, the Choleren gorge that lies further down the Engstligental, but the best way to do this is to walk. A walk from the valley end of the village, via Ausserschwand and Schönbühl, takes about 3 hours, and has the advantage of being excellent from the outset, and also fairly easy, so that any who are having difficulties can turn back without having to overcome any formidable obstacles again. Also available directly from the village is a visit to a cheese making dairy, a trip usually reserved for those who understand German — the trip uses a guide from the tourist office — but which is fascinating for everyone, and has the distinct advantage of getting the visitor in touch with the real country. Also available, and very good except again, and more noticeably, for difficulties with the language, are organised botanical trips. It really is astonishing how the guides find so many varieties of alpine flower.

Those organising their own alpine flower show should go to the High Alp of Engstligenalp. This is reached by taking the minibus from the Adelboden coach station to Unter dem Birg, and then taking the cablecar up. The trip has the distinct advantage of a 'full frontal' view of the Engstligen waterfall, a Swiss national monument since 1948, and one of the country's most striking falls. At the cablecar top station, there is a hotel which must vie with that on the Niesen as the one with the grandest breakfast view, and a huge plateau of grass and alpine flowers that allows walks of any length and duration to be made, all the way to the last of winter's shrinking snows in the gullies of the Tierhörnli. This plateau is the realm of the marmot and the ibex, and the patient (and lucky!) visitor might see several. The more energetic visitor can cross the Chindbetti Pass at around 2,350m (7,710ft) to reach either Schwarenbach, where there is a restaurant, at the head of the Kandertal, beyond Kandersteg, or to reach Lake Tälliseeli. Each trip takes about $4^1/_2$ hours. The even more energetic could make a day of continuing to the Gemmi Pass where there is also a restaurant, as well as a marvellous view into the Valais and across it to the Matterhorn and Monte Rosa. The trip, which includes a visit to the dark and possibly frozen mountain lake of Daubensee at 2,206m (7,240ft), takes about 6 hours.

Another fine walk, taking about 4 hours, follows the valley leading back towards the Albristhorn and Seewlenhorn peaks, to the west of Adelboden, and lying to the left — when viewed from the village — of the ridge of Schwandfälspitz which the cablecar runs up. A well marked circular route follows this valley, taking in several little restaurants en route, and some very fine scenery, both to distant peaks and ridges, and, much closer, of stream and meadows.

In returning towards Frutigen to reach the road for Kandersteg, pause for a few moments in **Achseten**, surely one of the prettiest hamlets in the whole Oberland.

From the village a winding, uphill road leads off eastwards towards the high ridge separating the Engstligental from the Kandertal. At the road's end is Elsigback, and a cablecar that leads up to Elsigenalp. From there a gentle and well marked path leads up to the summit of the Elsighorn at 2,340m (7,675ft) which, being the last peak in the ridge between the valleys, offers a superb view northward. A fine alternative is to follow a much shorter path to the small lake of Elsigseelein. This good route, meandering between hummocks of flower-stream meadows, maintains its interest all the way — it is only half an hour's leisurely stroll — and the lake, a conifer-banked, transparent, emerald sheet of water, is a delight. For a really memorable day, take along your own barbecue lunch — wood is free to all visitors at an open-air barbecue beside the lake.

For the dedicated climber rather than walker, the steep cliffs of Senggi just north of, and obvious from, the top lift station, offer excellent, high-quality rock climbing in glorious surroundings.

Kandersteg is well known to anyone who has used the railway to

Kandersteg

ship his or her car from the Oberland to the Valais, or on through the Simplon tunnel towards Italy, as it is here that the motorist joins the train. Even if you are not intending to use the motorail service be sure to watch the railway as you drive towards the village, and to marvel at the engineering feat of its spiral loops as it climbs up the valley. Kandersteg is a straggling village which has one remarkable feature — a dry-ski-slope ski jump.

From Kandersteg there are many very fine walks, some starting from the village itself, and others utilising the very good trio of cableways that lift the visitor up onto the surrounding alps. One excellent 'village' walk is to visit the fine waterfalls on the Kander river, reached by going up and right from the lower station of the Stock cablecar. The falls are impressive, but equally good is the walk up through the woods, the stream either a pretty bubbling mass, or an impressive white foaming mass depending upon yesterday's weather. Another good thing to do, though having nothing to com- pare to the Kander waterfalls, is to explore the woodland and river banks of the Öeschiwald, that lie to the east of the village — take the road beside the Hotel Victoria. The area lies to the south, but only a few hundred metres, from the lower station of the Öeschinen chairlift, and, in passing, those camping in the area could do very much worse than use the camp site near the lift station, exploring the fine woodland of the Öeschiwald in the evening light, and taking advantage of the cableway for an early start to a good day from its top.

But this is jumping ahead, because one last walk allows the Kandersteg visitor to visit a couple of sites, one not really off the beaten track, the other more so. The footpath follows the left bank of the Kander, leaving the river, but staying on the left side of the valley to Blausee, the Blue Lake. The lake is indeed blue, and transparently clear, with a good surrounding of trees and shady gorges, and a trout farm. But there are also St Bernard dog's pulling carts and so on, all a bit twee for the purposes of this book. So go on instead to Riegelsee, where there is the alpine wildlife park. While there is ample oppor- tunity to see the real thing on a visit to the Alps, the wild animals do not always perform to order, and it is good to see Switzerland's native fauna for future reference. In addition, the animals are well kept in natural surroundings with — apparently — ample room.

Back at Kandersteg each of the cableways allows access to very good countryside, with ample opportunity to take in the scenery in peace and isolation. The best walk is from the top of Öeschinensee chairlift, where an easy and very attractive walk leads to Öesch- inensee itself, a beautiful, and beautifully positioned lake, deeply blue or blue-green depending upon the sun's position and cradled on its eastern side by high, snow-capped peaks. Both sides of the lake have easily followed footpaths — there are two, one at the lakeside, one higher up, on the northern side — though these only reach about half-way around the lake. A full circuit runs into some very serious and specialised country, and should not be attempted. But do not be put off. To visit the lake at all is worthwhile and is one of the highlights of the journey.

The more enthusiastic and experienced walker can, of course, extend the route. One good trip is to cross the Hohtürlipass (at around 2,750m, 9,000ft) and to go on to Griesalp in the Kiental. But it is also a long trip, certainly needing a full day, as well as some thought as to how a return to Kandersteg can be made.

From the southern end of the village two cablecars have their lower lift stations separated by about 1,200m (around ³/₄ mile). The first is the lift to Allmenalp, at 1,730m (5,680ft) allowing access to a delightful piece of high alp where cheesemaking can be seen at most times during the summer months. The lift takes a long time, giving a very good ride as the car only holds eight people. The high alpine meadow away from the upper lift station is very good for flowers, and the view into the Kandertal is excellent. The view can be dramatically expanded by climbing to the summits of the First or the Bonderspitz, both 2,550m (8,360ft) peaks behind the upper station, but neither climb should be undertaken lightly. The ascent involves over 800m (2,600ft) of climbing, with some gullies being snow-filled even in summer.

The last cableway, a cablecar from the lower station to Stock, and then a chairlift to Sunnbühl allows the experienced walker to gain relatively easy paths that lead to the Daubensee and, beyond that, the Gemmi Pass. An easier walk, however, goes only about 1¹/₂km (1 mile) — and that gently downhill, at least on the way out! — to the marshy land of Spittelmatte, and the small lake of Arvensseli. The marsh, with its patches of clear water and marvellous collection of mainly yellow bog plants, is beautiful, a botanist's paradise, while the lake, more deserving, perhaps, of being called a tarn, is another stretch of transparent emerald water ringed by conifers, a delightful spot in which to sit on the shoreline rocks, to drink in the view, and to contemplate.

The Engstligen and Kander valleys join at **Frutigen**, a pleasant, old town, some of its typical mountain houses dating from the sixteenth century. There are a number of old crafts still carried on in and near the town, including the ancient craft of wood chip carving which can be seen, during normal shop hours — but not weekends — in the workshop at Wengi, on the road to Reichenbach.

Frutigen straggles across the dying ridge that separates the two valleys, and at its extreme end in Kandertal are the ruins of the Tellenburg castle, well sited on a round, flat-topped hill. This is a rarely visited site, and though it has little to offer the serious viewer of medieval remains, it does offer easily accessible and surprisingly extensive views over the lower Kander valley, as well as giving a romantic insight into the old valley life. Before modern roads and snow clearing devices, draught excluders and central heating, this must have been a harsh place in winter. Even the lush and warm summers must have been filled with the labour of preparing for the winter to come.

The village of **Wengi** can also be reached by a walk from Reichenbach, a railway village at the junction of the Kiental and the Kandertal. The village has two interesting, and quite diverse, features. Firstly there is a small crystal museum and shop in the market place; secondly, there is a small airport near the village from which the company Fluggruppe offer flights over the Alps to visitors. The flights take in the Oberland peaks, Eiger, Monch and Jungfrau, or the Matterhorn, and even Mont Blanc. They are not cheap, but on a clear day they do give a unique view of the High Alps.

The Kiental is a small, secluded valley, less well known because it is not as exploited in the winter, than its two large neighbours. For that reason alone it is worth visiting. From Kiental village a chairlift takes the visitor to a fine piece of high alpine meadow, but the best walk is further up the valley from the Tschingelsee, or from nearby Griesalp. A round trip, of about 3 hours — the Barenpfad, taking in Garnern, Tschingelsee, Hexenkessel, the Pochten waterfall and Griesalp and well signed throughout — passes many of the best natural features the valley has to offer. Throughout its length the walk is excellent, the scenery varied. The Pochtenfälle is a fine waterfall, but much of the beauty comes from the less spectacular: the flower-filled meadows cut by streams of clear water, and a backdrop of snow-covered hills.

From Griesalp there are more exacting walks, the reverse of the trip suggested from Kandersteg across the Hohtürlipass being among them. In general, though, the country at the head of the Kiental is very wild and rugged, and can only be recommended to those with some experience. One less exacting, but still arduous trip, which is said to be excellent, and uncluttered by too many people, is via Steineberg, Sefinenfurgge and Poganggen to Mürren. Sefinenfurgge is at 2,610m (8,560ft) so it can be readily seen that the walk is no trivial undertaking. The time it takes, around 7 or 8 hours, also means that it should not be attempted by the ill-equipped or the unprepared. Nevertheless, the thought of emerging in the Jungfrau region by foot has a distinct appeal.

Simmental

The valley of the Simme is divided into two distinct sections: the Nieder Simmental, a usually broad, well trodden valley along which travels the main road from Gstaad to Thunersee, and the Ober Simmental, starting at Zweisimmen on the main road, and reaching back to the river's source in the wild country of the Wildstrubel

Zweisimmen

beyond Lenk.

The first village reached on a journey up valley is **Wimmis**, near the end of the small section of the N6 motorway that heads towards Gstaad. It is a pleasant spot with, below, the remains of the fifteenth-century castle, a fine church in tenth-century Romanseque style, built on foundations at least two centuries older and with some good fourteenth- and fifteenth-century murals. Beyond Wimmis the valley becomes very restricted for a short section, one side being closed by a huge wall of rock. Unfortunately this valley section also has some industrial sites which do not add to the attraction, and by the time they are passed, so too is the restricted, secretive section. It is still a good journey, however, through a fine series of villages that each have their points of interest.

Go south at Latterbach to the Diemtigtal, a magnificent and

*The Aletsch
glacier in the
upper Rhône
valley, Valais*

*The Aletsch
Forest, Valais*

The Mässersee, a lake in the high Binntal, Valais

The Grimselpass and Rhône glacier, Valais

almost always empty valley leading up to the hamlet of Grimmialp. The journey is about 12km (7$^{1}/_{2}$ miles), but it feels further, the road being occasionally narrow and, at one point, quite steep. The compensations are the views over pastureland and towards high hills, a bubbling stream and an air of peaceful seclusion. When the little valley hamlets are passed, it is easy to see why the Diemtigtal was awarded, in 1986, the Swiss Wakker Prize for architectural heritage. **Diemtigen** has an interesting vicarage, its balcony supported by wooden columns, and the Grosshaus, an early nineteenth-century house that is the largest private dwelling in Simmental. Grimmialp is surrounded by peaks, though these are lower than those seen in the Kandertal. The walking is excellent, but the peaks themselves, though low, are not easy to climb and it is best just to stroll on the lower slopes. The hamlet is named for the Grimmi Pass, 1,970m (5,560ft) to the south-west and about 950m (3,100ft) above the village. A very fine walk crosses the pass and descends the equally green and pastoral Fermeltal to the Ober Simmental at Matten.

At Erlenbach a cablecar rises to the Stockhorn, a distinctive peak, only 2,190m (7,180ft), but with a remarkable panorama including virtually all of Thunersee. The ride, on the second leg from Chrindi to the top, also passes over a beautifully set mountain lake, the Hinterstockensee. At this point it is easy to go off the beaten track, for there is a fine walking route from the Chrindi station past Hinterstockensee and along to Oberstockensee, another finely set lake. This walk on the high alp, and a continuation of it towards the summit of the Stockhorn — allow half a day for a full circuit, though much less if the Chrindi-Stockhorn section of the cableway is used in one direction — is renowned for its flowers. Rightly so, for the whole area is virtually a botanical garden: those with a particular interest in flowers are advised to take both an identification guide and a camera.

Zweisimmen, at the junction of the upper and lower valleys, is the valley's main village and has a good collection of finely worked wooden houses. There is also a museum of the local crafts and culture, at the Kirchstalden. Because of the town's position, there is fine walking in the area, and the local tourist office offers a walker's badge — the Zweisimmen boot — to visitors who complete a number of the year's newly opened paths. A very nice souvenir. But do not let enthusiasm for the boot deprive you of the great joy of a couple of Zweisimmen's better walks. The first to try is that from the village to the secluded Schwarzsee, set among the trees on the hillside northwest of the village. This walk, via Sali and Schauenegg, returning by

Walking near Lauenen

bus from Sparenmoos, where there is a restaurant, takes about 4 hours, is nowhere severe, and is delightful all the way. Another equally good trip is to use the cablecar to reach Rinderberg, from where a track can be followed back down to the village, or the south-going ridge can be followed to reach the valley running back down towards Zweisimmen, through Chaltebrunne. In addition there is a fine path at the edge of the Mühliport forest, only about 1km (just over half a mile) long, where many of the local trees and shrubs are named.

For the more adventurous, Zweisimmen is also a centre for trips on the river Simme. Canoeing is allowed, but the river is fast and strong — particularly early in the season when the snows are melting and after heavy rain — and canoeists need to be expert. Better, for the beginner or the complete novice, is river-rafting where the visitor joins a small party — about five or six people — in a strong inflatable raft with a couple of experts, for a wild and wet trip down the faster moving stretches of water. The trips — there are two, on the Simme from Boltigen about 8km (5 miles) down valley from Zweisimmen to Erlenbach, and on the Saane from Gstaad to Les Moulins, over the canton boundary — are not for the faint-hearted. Even with lifejacket and crash helmet as supplied it is not without its dangers, but is a fantastic experience. The river sections chosen tend to be high-rock sided and scenically very attractive, but it can be a bit difficult to concentrate on the view! Each trip lasts about 2 hours.

From Zweisimmen, the Ober Simmental leads southward, another fine valley, better known than the Diemtigtal, but no less lovely. Like that valley, the walking from its head — from **Lenk**, a very pretty village, once more famous as a spa, and **Oberreid**, a mountain-shrouded hamlet — is not easy. There are long routes, to the summits of the mountains of the chain to the south, and over the Hahnenmoos to Adelboden, but the walking is tiring, and the views though good, are not exceptional. This area is perhaps better suited to the more leisurely stroll. Above Oberreid the Simmenfälle is a fine waterfall, well endowed with viewing points, and the source of the Simme — at the Sieben Brunnen — can also be reached. Everywhere there are fine, clear streams, often crossed by insecure-looking bridges, an abundance of meadows, alpine flowers and clean air.

Around Gstaad

With the ski resort of Gstaad — the 'G' is not pronounced, but used to make the 'S' more gutteral in sound — obtaining the royal seal of approval it has, but perhaps only temporarily, these things having a habit of going in cycles, become very popular with the jet-setters. However, the area around the village is still, in places, little explored in comparison to, for example, that near Interlaken, and is worth a visit. Enter Saanenland, as the area is sometimes known, at **Saanenmöser**, a small village that sits on the low-level and green watershed between the Simmental and the land drained by the Saane river. Saanenmöser is a good centre for exploring the wooded land to the north, while from nearby Schönried, a cablecar reaches the Horneggli, at 1,770m (5,900ft) from where one of the very best walks in the area actually circles the Hornfluh (1,949m, (6,390ft). Another good walk descends to Gstaad itself, this journey making a long half-day if the postbus is used to reach the lower lift station at Schönried.

Beyond Schönried the main road hugs the side of the Rollerligrat as it descends, giving incomparable views, forward to the narrow valley of the Saane in Vaud canton, and to the left over the wide valley of the river with, behind, the fine chain of alpine peaks from the Wildhorn towards Les Diablerets.

Saanen is a pretty village, too often bypassed except by those looking for the best Vacherin cheese, or those attending the famous concerts organised by Yehudi Menuhin, and held in St Maurice's church. The church is, even out of the concert season, worth a visit. Set among delightful wooden houses, it is a fifteenth-century building — partially rebuilt after a disastrous fire in 1942 — which has a fine barrel-vaulted roof, and some restored medieval frescoes.

Gstaad is famous for hosting the Swiss Open Tennis Championships, and also hosts some of the concerts during the Yehudi Menuhin Festival. The chapel of St Nicholas is worth a visit, a small, austere, but dignified, building in the long high street that is almost all that the village possesses.

From Gstaad there is fine walking, very good paths lying along the valley floor, towards Feutersoey and Lauenen, and along the high ridges, reached by the cableways, to the peaks of Wasserngrat, Wispile and Eggli.

From the top station of the Wasserngrat chairlift a well marked path climbs to the summit itself at 2,203m (7,225ft) — it is around 275m (900ft) above the chairlift top station — and then descends southwards before turning west past Hinder Trütlisberg and Rütschli to Lauenen. This trip (the return to Gstaad can be made by postbus) takes about 5 hours and is over open high alpine meadow all the way, with excellent views of the Wildhorn massif. **Lauenen** itself is a pretty village, with a stylish sixteenth-century church and one house, dated 1765, that is a brilliant example of the local woodcraft, and worth coming many a mile to see. The village is also the start for another fine journey, southward towards the Wildhorn. There, nestling below the trees and rocks, is the Lauenensee, as fine a mountain lake as will be seen anywhere in the Oberland. Its occasionally reedy foreshore is a delight, its clear waters and mountain backdrop equally as good. South-east from the lake, there is the nature reserve of the Geltental, a wild landscape softened by alpine flowers. At the head of this small valley are the Geltenschuss, a pair of beautiful waterfalls, each of which can be easily approached. Approach to the first is over the aptly named 'Spraying Bridge'. The second fall, dropping into a secluded hollow, is the bigger of the pair and is an excellent crash of water.

Also from Lauenen, a fine walking path crosses the Krinnen Pass to the south-west and reaches Gsteig. On this walk the views are of Les Diablerets, and the more local alpine meadows. The walk takes about 3 hours. A postbus from Gsteig returns to Gstaad.

As mentioned previously there is a good valley floor walk in the Saane valley, starting from Feutersoey or from Gsteig. A well marked path follows the river downstream through meadowland, passing Saali, Feutersoey, Grund and the Eggli cableway bottom station. The going is never more than easy, and, as the walk can be comfortably completed in $2^1/_2$ hours, it can be thoroughly recommended for families, or for the less athletic, but equally natureloving, walker.

Beyond Gsteig, from Reusch or (just over the canton border into Vaud), the Col du Pillon, there are cablecars to the Glacier des Diablerets, a summer skiing resort in Vaud. Most visitors will want to go to the top, but there is excellent walking to be had from Oldenegg, at the end of the first stage of the three stage lift. A 'small' mountain hollow immediately behind the stage station — do not get your bearings wrong, the other side of the station has an imposing drop! — is a joy to visit, and you can be assured of being entirely alone.

From the Col du Pillon a fine walk rapidly re-enters Bern canton, going north to the tree-shrouded, quiet Lac de Retaud, and on, circling the the peak of La Palette to the left or right, to reach the Vore Pass. Beyond is Seeberg alp and beyond that a fabulous view of Arnensee, a blue lake sitting among trees. The descent to the lake is steep, but the path on the left side of the lake is soon gained and followed to Feutersoey.

The last walk in this area is very good, but can be difficult to arrange transport for. Although the postbus reaches both ends of the walk, it still requires the train to complete the round trip, unless the walk is to be made in both directions. The walk starts from Gsteig and crosses the Sanetsch Pass and in doing so crosses from Bern canton to the Valais. In the early stages, through Innergsteig, the walk follows the Saane, reaching the fine Sanetschfälle below the pass itself. Those not wishing to 'waste' time regaining their start point from the Valais, can return from here. This is not a bad idea, as there is always something new to look at on the retraced path.

The Eastern Oberland

Interlaken and the Jungfrau Region

At the opposite end of Thunersee from Thun is **Interlaken**, named for its positions between the two lakes of Thunersee and Brienzersee. The town is the capital of the Oberland area of Bern canton, and is a

Unterseen, Interlaken

thriving tourist centre, so given over to tourism that little now remains of the small village that attracted English tourists to come, in the late nineteenth century, and set up base here, content to stand in the parkland of the still-preserved Höhenmatte, and to stare in wonder at the Jungfrau.

On the north side of the Aare river, which traverses the town, is Unterseen, a small, quiet square of old houses, a fine church in one corner and a gateway with a wooden portcullis, which although bearing the date 1296 is modern. There it is still possible to escape the bustle on the Höhenweg, but only just possible. A walk through the old village sites of Unterseen, to the north-west, near Thunersee, or through Matten in the south-east, is also worthwhile for a view of how the town might have looked a century ago. Further afield it is also still possible to be alone with a view if you go walking from the top of the Harder Kulm rack railway that goes up the mountain to the north of the village. There are ibex here — only semi-wild ones it's true, but still as majestic — and innumerable species of tree and shrub. The view, to be snatched occasionally between the trees if you are off the beaten track, as only the top station offers a true panorama, extends from the Stockhorn beyond Thun, to peaks near the Grimsel Pass. The main peaks of the Eiger, Monch and Jungfrau are there too, though the Schynige Platte does impede the view.

Lastly, if you have children, consider a trip to Heimwehfluh. It

Unterseen, Interlaken

can be a bit crowded, and some of the attractions are a little 'touristy', but the model railway is certainly worth a look.

The Schynige Platte is itself ascended by a longish, but interesting, rail journey from Wilderswil, close to Interlaken. Again the view is the chief reason for the journey, the relatively short distance from Harder Kulm to here producing a quite impressive change in the

Stechelberg Falls

view of the larger mountains. But be sure to visit the Alpine Garden, with over 500 species of plant growing, a true botanical delight, and a great help in the later identification of the more common specimens on the high alpine meadows. The walk from the upper station (at 2,100m, 7,890ft) to the Faulhorn (2,681m, 8,800ft) and 8km (5 miles) distant, is a fine one — allow 3 hours — and the view from the

Faulhorn — the name really does mean 'foul' although rotten, from the nature of the underlying rock, is a better translation — is acknowledged as about the best of the Bernese Alps. Continuing to First — about 3 hours further — past the delightful Bachalpsee, and taking the chairlift down to Grindelwald, makes a complete day, and this walk is the best in the area. It may be preferable (to reduce — though not by a great deal — the uphill slogging) if the walk is accomplished in the reverse direction, using the chairlift to gain First, and visiting the Alpine Garden last, perhaps even waiting to watch the setting sun turn the high Oberland peaks pink before going down.

Wilderswil, the small village at the bottom of the Schynige Platte railway, has a fine seventeenth-century church reached by taking the covered bridge over the Lütschine and the ruins of an old sixteenth-century castle, the Unspunnen, set romantically in the trees, and traditionally the castle of Byron's *'Manfred'*. Here too is a very good crystal museum and shop (H. Dorn, Sydach) which includes a phenomenal smoky quartz crystal, the largest in the world, that is 1.6m (5ft 3in) tall, and weighs 1 ton.

From the village there are several fine walks, though the best is actually better completed by finishing rather than starting at Wilderswil. The start point is Saxeten, perhaps the only village in the Jungfrau region that can be termed off the beaten track. The Saxetental, at the head of which the unknown village lies, runs south-west from Wilderswil, cutting into the Bernese pre-Alps. Behind the village, a pretty spot at 1,100m (3,600ft), is a tremendous amphitheatre of peaks. The walk leaves the village downhill, following and crossing the river, and traversing the excellent conifer forest of Sytiwald. In the lower reaches of the valley the walk recrosses the river, near to an old mill. This walk, taking about $1^1/_2$ hours — use the postbus to reach Saxeten — makes the most of what little genuinely off the beaten track land there is in the Oberland, and is strongly recommended for a quiet day. Elsewhere in the area some better-known villages will be visited, with an attempt to pick a way between the honey pots.

One such way can be picked from Lauterbrunnen to Stechelberg. Lauterbrunnen is the starting point for trips to the Jungfraujoch, and site of the Staubbach, one of the most famous of all alpine waterfalls. The walk follows the Lütschine river back up its valley. Early in the walk there is a fine view of the Staubbach: at Buchen, a bridge crosses the river giving access to the beautiful Trümmelbachfälle, while a later bridge gives access to the lower lift station of the Mürren-

Mürren

Schilthorn cableway. To the right here is another waterfall, less spectacular than the Staubbach perhaps, but very grand. The water-fall is easily approached, indeed you can go right up to the cold shower level. On from the falls, the path to Stechelberg goes through some delightful alder and beech woods. And there are several other waterfalls in the valley: not for nothing is it called 'Lauterbrunnen' — 'with many fountains'.

Most people will want to take the cableway to the Piz Gloria on the Schilthorn — James Bond and all that. But the upper station can be horribly crowded, as indeed can the cable cabins themselves, a high price to pay for the view, even if the alpine choughs do compensate with their clowning. Make a resolution to walk down to the interme-diate station, Birg, or stay there to admire the view before walking down to Mürren.

Grindelwald

Mürren is a good place to go in summer, as is Wengen. In summer most people are passing through on the way to higher spots, and you can quietly absorb the delights of their characteristic chalet houses, resplendent with colourful window boxes. In **Mürren** go to the Hotel Eiger. Throughout your travels in Switzerland you will have seen little fire hydrants with double-cone bodies and symmetric short outlet arms. For all the world the hydrants look like daleks, or small knights in armour. Finally, someone painted one as a little man — and he stands in front of the hotel.

Grindelwald suffers from the same problem as the Lauterbrunnen valley — being too well known. As a winter sports centre it is justly famous, and even in summer the tourists come, drawn by the lure of the First chairlift (Europe's longest), the trip to the Männlichen to view the Eiger's north wall, (Europe's longest cablecar ride), and the railway up to Kleine Scheidegg. Grindelwald is also a start-ing point, as Lauterbrunnen is, for trips to the Jungfraujoch, Europe's highest railway station. But there are things to see which are missed by the village-bound visitor, and very good things too.

Grindelwald, the 'glacier village' lies between two glaciers, the lower or Unterer flowing down from near the Eismeer station of the Jungfraujoch railway (through the station window it is the top of this glacier that is seen) and the upper, Oberer, glacier that flows down from the hollow between the Wetterhorn and the Schreckhorn. The closeness of the glaciers to the village and, therefore, to the visitor, made Grindelwald famous as early as the eighteenth century. Goethe stood on the Oberer in 1779, one of many of the great and the good who came. Since that time the glaciers have retreated from the village, although they are now moving down valley again — by nearly 700m (2,300ft) since 1965 in the case of the Oberer. Doubtless in time the glaciers will retreat again, as is the natural order of things. Not that you could have persuaded the villagers of that when, in the early eighteenth century, they brought in an exorcist to halt the advance of the Oberer.

The glaciers are still the best local attraction, and can still be viewed at very close quarters, particularly the upper, which can be touched. But go to see it along a less well-beaten track. From the Upper Pfingstegg cableway station there is a series of seven way-marked geological trails that explore the geology of the strata be-neath the scenery. A leaflet is available from the tourist office in Grindelwald, and is absolutely necessary to an understanding of the trails. Trail I goes from Pfingstegg to the Milchbach restaurant above the Oberer glacier, the walk taking about an hour. An easy descent from here takes the visitor to the ice caves where the glacier can be experienced at first hand. Trail II, signed to 'Bäregg', (refreshment hut) climbs to the Stieregg restaurant above the Unterer glacier. This walk — also about an hour — is more spectacular than that on Trail I, but the end point does not allow actual contact with the ice.

From **Pfingstegg** there is also a fine walk to Grindelwald's glacier gorge, the wonderfully named Gletscherschlucht. The route goes via the village's old marble quarries, from which were extracted stone for the parliament and university buildings in Bern, amongst others. The gorge is about 15 minutes beyond the quarry, and is a fine, if busy, place. A wooden walkway is needed for a full penetration of some 800m ($^1/_2$ mile) of the gorge, which is incredibly high and steeply sided in places, the limestone walls polished as smooth as the quarry's marble by the river Lütschine. Later, another glacier gorge that is distinctly less busy will be visited.

The walk from Pfingstegg to Grindelwald, via quarry and gorge, takes a couple of hours with stops to admire the scenery, so a combination of the three walks, with breaks at the restaurants, offers a magnificent day away from the bustle of mainstream Grindelwald.

Brienzersee

The Brienzersee is, by scientific study, the cleanest of Switzerland's large lakes, and so the first conclusion to be drawn is that in the villages of its shore the visitor should eat the fish. The second conclusion is that the area should be rich in animal and plant life, and so it is. The first place to go is a nature reserve, but pause on the main road from Interlaken that follows the lake's northern shore to view the Gasthaus Schöenegg, a new lodge built with such woodcraft that it denies the suggestion that all craftsmen are long dead.

Beyond is the Burgseeli nature reserve, though the lake of the reserve is not actually connected to the main body of the Brienzersee. It does, however, share its cleanliness and is a haven for water lilies and reeds, frogs, fish and ducks. In summer it warms to an astonishing 77°F, and swimming is allowed, with certain regulations on air beds etc to protect the wildlife. No local swimming pool can possibly compete with the lake.

The nearby twin villages of Goldswil and Ringgenberg have several old ruins of great interest and romantic beauty. **Goldswil** has a ruined Romanesque church , while the one at **Ringgenberg** is seventeenth century and set within the ruins of a thirteenth-century castle. The ruins point to an historic past, Ringgenberg having once been home to an important family, one of whose number was renowned in the early fourteenth century as the ablest of politicians and the best of minstrels, which seems a remarkably unlikely combination.

The lake road towards Brienz offers good views towards the Faulhorn, and passes a couple of pretty villages before **Brienz** itself is reached. This, the lake's largest village, is famous for woodcarving and the making of violins. Today much of the woodcarving is very specifically for the tourist trade, and somewhat the worse for that, but it is still possible to find the odd corner where the traditional skill is being put to the more traditionally designed work. In addition, Brienz's houses, each alive with colour from its window box, are a joy, and make a walk around particularly worthwhile. But do not keep both eyes on the woodwork. Brienz has some very narrow

The Aare gorge at Meiringen

sections in its main street and it is easy to find yourself near a piece
of road that seems to be not quite wide enough for vehicles to pass,
just as a coach reaches it too. One of the best views in Brienz is near
such a 'death-trap', where a side street away from the lake opens up
straight at the Brienzer Rothorn, framing the peak between two rows
of particularly beautiful houses.

A good place to visit further east is the Swiss Open-Air Museum
at **Ballenberg**. The museum is justly famous, but is still missed by too
many visitors who believe that large museums are as dry as dust and
form no part of a holiday. It consists of 50ha (about 130 acres) of
farmland dotted through with over fifty buildings representing the
traditional design and construction methods for farmhouses and
outbuildings throughout Switzerland's cantons. Each farm is beautifully set, against a wooded hillside, and the layout roughly corre-

Brienz

Rosenlaui

sponds to a map of Switzerland. Each building is also furnished in the traditional way, and there are exhibits of traditional crafts, including many live exhibits. The museum is spread along the side of the main road to Luzern, from Hofstetten to Brünig — right up to the cantonal boundary — and is a very different, but very worthwhile trip. There is adequate parking, good refreshment facilities and information in English is available.

On the southern side of Brienzersee there is no continuous road, though there soon will be when the section of the Luzern-Bern motorway which will run along that shore is open. It is possible, with a car, to reach Iseltwald, about halfway along the lake, and also to reach Axalp at the eastern end. A magnificent walk links these two, starting from **Iseltwald** to keep the best to last. Iseltwald is *the* place, if you are intending to try local lake fish, because there are still a

Stalden, in the Vispa valley, Valais

Summer in the Saasental, Valais

Lötschental, a relatively undeveloped valley between the Bernese and Valais Alps

Lötschental

A view from the top of the Susten Pass

handful of professional fishermen living in the village, supplying the
local restaurants with fish that is just about as fresh as is possible.

The highlight of the walk is the Giessbachfälle, a fine, foaming
waterfall that drains the Axalp district into the lake close to its eastern
end. The falls are the better for being right at the end of the river's
course, as all the water drops over the narrowed cascade, and there

is only the lake to catch it. **Axalp,** above the falls and readily reached by road through a couple of small mountain hamlets, is developing as a ski resort. At present it is quiet, with limited facilities, but its intention is to maximise use of the excellent wooded slopes leading back up to mountains close to Grindelwald's First. Go there now before the cableways provide access for too many. In the high alpine meadow behind the village there is good, safe strolling off the beaten track. But be sure to visit Hinterburgsee, another secluded, tree-shrouded and mountain-enveloped lake.

Meiringen and the Mountain Passes

Meiringen is reached along the wide, flat-bottomed valley of the Aare. The valley seems almost to have been cut by some gigantic earth mover, a channel rather than a true valley, not even remotely U- or V-shaped. To the left, going from Brienzersee to Meiringen, the rock of the square cut wall is curiously folded, while to the right there is a series of waterfalls tumbling down the steep side. One, near Unterbach, is the Oltschibachfälle, the very aptly named Mare's Tail.

Meiringen itself is wider and airier than Brienz, less quaint, though no less endearing. It is said to be the home of the meringue, the story being that Napoleon, while staying here, had the first ever concoction of sugar and egg-white and was so captivated that he named it after the village. Others say that meringue derives from the Latin for 'between meals', which has nothing like the same romance.

The village is an excellent starting point for walks in the hills that lie to the north, and whose high ridge forms the border between the Bern and Luzern cantons. The best approach is to use the cableway to Planplatten — at 2,245m (7,360ft) and with an impressive view towards both the Bernese Alps and the snow-capped peaks from Titlis to the Sustenhorn — but not to complete the journey, stopping at Reuti for high meadow walks, or at Mägisalp for more rugged country. From Reuti the Panoramaweg leads off towards the lower station of the Wasswendl-Käserstatt cableway, reaching it after about an hour. The route then descends through Hasliberg to the Brunig Pass. A better continuation is to use the cableway to reach Käserstatt and from there to follow the Murmeliweg to Mägisalp for a cable ride back to Meiringen. That last walk also takes about an hour. Coupled with a trip to Planplatten, this makes for a very enjoyable long half-day in this relatively unspoilt and uncrowded area.

Close to Meiringen are the Reichenbach Falls, well known, as a bronze tablet at the bottom states, for being the scene of the last fight between Sherlock Holmes and Professor Moriarty, and a very worthwhile trip. A small rack railway takes the visitor close to the most spectacular part of the falls, and they really are very good.

Near the falls is the Aareschlucht, a spectacular 1.5m-long (1 mile) narrow, high-sided (200m, 650ft) gorge with a continuous walkway through it, that can be reached from both ends. The gorge is excellent, but perhaps a little too well known — though less so with the English — so go instead up a road that is not for the faint-hearted, from near the Reichenbach Falls, to Rosenlaui. As compensation, it does offer great views. Look too, for the water trough hewn from a single trunk on the way up. High up on this road is the Rosenlaui Gletscherschlucht, another fine glacier-wrought gorge, with spectacular water plumes and gloriously sculptured rocks. The trip through, or rather up into, the gorge takes about 45 minutes. Though not quite as impressive as the Aareschlucht, it is very good, and much less crowded.

On from the small and pretty village of **Rosenlaui** the road cannot be passed by the ordinary tourist, and it is necessary to walk — a postbus visits this spot — crossing the Grosse Scheidegg Pass and continuing down to Grindelwald. This is one of the great pass walks and is well trodden, but a reasonable and less well trodden alternative is to branch off and maintain height from the pass, going to Oberlager, over Alp Grindel to the top station of the First chairlift which is then used to descend to Grindelwald. This spectacular walk takes about 4 hours.

At Innertkirchen, just beyond the second entrance to the Aareschlucht, roads branch off to two passes out of the Oberland, the Susten into Uri, and the Grimsel into the Valais. The Susten is a straightforward pass in approach, with fine views all the way. At the restaurant just below the top of the pass, a limited access road can be followed, on foot, to a hands-on meeting with a fine glacier descending from the Sustenhorn. The visitor here is almost invariably alone, and provided sensible precautions are taken with the ice — ie. don't go on it if you have no glacier experience — then it is a fine off the beaten track place to visit.

The Grimsel Pass is a much more spectacular route, one with a long history, the Bernese having come this way several times when they invaded the Valais. The road passes, in its lower section at Guttannen, a good crystal museum, but the real interest starts higher.

As the real uphill work starts, watch for the statue of a man with a pneumatic drill. It is nice to see a memorial to the construction worker rather than to the architect or chief engineer. Beyond is a series of lakes feeding a hydro-electric power station. The lakes themselves look very odd, more painted than real, with all the appearance of being of putty rather than water. Among them, set on a high pinnacle of rock, is a hotel, the Grimsel Hospiz, which must be one of the strangest places to stay. The views are certainly spectacular, but the whole area has an eerie feel, a mad jumble of frost-shattered and ice-smoothed rocks. From the pass top the road falls in spectacular style, dropping down into the Valais.

Further Information
— Bernese Oberland —

Museums and Other Places of Interest

Ballenberg
Swiss Open-Air Museum
Open: daily April, May, October 10am-5pm; June to September 9.30am-5.30pm.

Beatenbucht (near)
St Beatus Cave
Open: daily Palm Sunday to October 9.30am-5.30pm. Guided tours every 30 minutes.
Information from: Beatuschöhlen Genossenschoft, CH-3301 Sundlauenen, ☎ 036/41 16 43

Grindelwald
Glacier Gorge
Open: daily June to October 9am-6pm.

Guttannen
Crystal Museum
Open: daily June to September 10am-12noon and 2-5pm.

Hilterfingen
Hünegg Castle
Open: daily June to October 2-5pm, Sunday 10am-12noon and 2-5pm.

Interlaken
Heimwehfluh
Open: daily mid-May to October 10am-6pm.

Kandersteg (near)
Blausee
Open: daily mid-May to mid-October 9am-6pm.

Meiringen
Aare Gorge
Open: daily Easter to October 9.30-6pm.

Oberhofen
Castle
Open: daily except Monday morning mid-May to mid-October 10am-12noon and 2-5pm.
Park open: 9.30am-12noon and 2-6pm.

Riegelsee
Alpine Wildlife Park
Open: daily 9am-6pm.

Rosenlaui Gorge
Open: daily June to mid-October
9.30am-6pm.

Thun
Castle and Museum
Open: daily June to September
9am-6pm; April, May and October
10am-5pm.

Wocher Panorama, Schadau Park
Open: daily except Monday morning April to October 10am-12noon
and 1.30-5pm.

Zweisimmen
Museum
Open: Wednesday, Saturday and
Sunday 10am-12noon and
2-4.30pm.

Tourist Information Offices

The main office for the whole
region is:

Bernese Oberland Tourist Office
Jungfraustrasse 38
CH-3800 Interlaken
☎ 036-222621

Adelboden
Verkehrsbüro
CH-3715 Adelboden
☎ 033-732252

Brienz
Verkehrsbüro Brienz am See
Bahnhofplatz
Postfach 59
CH-3855 Brienz
☎ 036-513242

Grindelwald
Verkehrsbüro
(Kurverein Grindelwald)
Sportzentrum
CH-3818 Grindelwald
☎ 036-513242

Gstaad
Verkehrsbüro
CH-3780 Gstaad
☎ 030-41055

Interlaken
Höheweg 37
CH-3800 Interlaken
☎ 036-222121

Kandersteg
Verkehrsbüro
CH-3718 Kandersteg
☎ 033-751234

Meiringen
Verkehrsbüro
CH-3860 Meiringen
☎ 036-714322

Mürren
Verkehrsbüro
CH-3825 Mürren
☎ 036-551616

Thunersee
Verkehrsbüro
Bahnhofplatz
CH-3600 Thun
☎033-222340

Spiez
Verkehrsbüro
CH-3700 Spiez
☎ 033 542138

Wengen
Verkehrsbüro
CH-3828 Wengen
☎ 036-551414

Zweisimmen
Verkehrsbüro
CH-3770 Zweisimmen
☎ 030-21133/22545

7 • The Valais

The top of the Grimsel Pass, in the Bernese Oberland, is almost, but not quite, at the eastern extremity of Valais, and the canton also extends to the top of the Furka Pass (reached from Gletsch, the first Valaisian village) and to the top of the obvious mountain ridge to the south, forming at first a border with Ticino canton and then with Italy. Many sources identify Valais (that title is French, the German word for the canton is Wallis) as deriving from the Latin *Vallis Poenina*, the upper Rhône valley, but not everyone agrees with this definition. When the Saxons were pushing the original Celtic British westward before them in their advance across what was to become England, the Celts collected in the country beyond the Severn which they called Cymru, the land of the fellow countrymen. To the Saxons the Celts were foreigners, and they gave them their name for foreigners, a name that derived from the Celtic tribe of *Velcae*, known to the Saxons from contacts on mainland Europe. They called the Celtic brotherhood the *Wallas*, the Welsh, and their land Wales. Elsewhere in Europe they gave the same name to other groups of 'foreigners' — *Walloons* in Belgium, *Vlachs* in Romania, *Velsch*, the German name for Italians and, quite possibly, gave the name *Wallis* to this secret valley full of odd foreigners.

The Valais is Switzerland's third biggest canton, covering just over 5,200sq km (2,000sq miles), compared to Bern's 6,000sq km (2,300sq miles) and 7,100sq km (2,730sq miles) for the Grisons, but with a population of less than 250,000 who are mostly gathered together into a few large urban areas in the centre. It is an L-shaped canton, covering the valley of the Rhône from source (the Rhône glacier lies wholly within the canton), to Lac Léman. That distance is only 120km (75 miles), but the river falls many hundreds of metres. It is therefore, a fast moving river and in times of heavy rain or fast thaw it can cause problems. As lately as 1987 villages in the upper valley were severely water damaged.

The Rhône valley is curiously shaped, a reasonably straight section from source to Martigny being followed by a quite distinct right-
angled turn as the water heads off north to the lake. This sharp turn
adds a dimension to a journey up the valley from Lac Léman, the
sudden appearance of the long upper valley as the corner is turned
coming as a surprise. Many streams flow into the Rhône, draining
the northern and southern retaining peaks, and as a result there are
several side valleys. The most well known is the Mattertal to Zermatt
and the highest Swiss peaks. The most famous peak is the Matterhorn which, as with the higher Monte Rosa, is shared with Italy. The
highest peak wholly within Switzerland, the 4,545m (14,900ft) Dom,
also lies in this valley.

The eastern, upper, end of the valley is German speaking, while
the Lac Léman end is French speaking, the interchange between the
two languages occuring around Sion where some locals talk in a
curious dialect which is part German and part French, but with an
Italian influence. In general the lower and middle valley dwellers are
bilingual, and many of the towns and villages in these areas —
particularly in the central valley section — have both German and
French names. This usually causes no problem as both are intelli-
gible. Brig and Brigue are obviously the same place. But the occasional town catches out the unwary: Visp is well known as the town
at the junction of the main valley and the Mattertal, but the French
name for the town is Viege.

The Upper Rhône Valley

From the Grimsel Pass the road falls like a helter-skelter to Gletsch.
From about half way the eye is naturally drawn to the Rhône glacier,
and it is the glacier that dominates the road beyond Gletsch up to the
Furka Pass. The Furka, named from the fork-like ridges of hills it
divides, is, at 2,431m (7,975ft) one of Europe's highest passes, and
one of the first to close when the winter snows begin. Just before the
top of the pass is reached, the Hotel Belvedere, off to the left, can be
visited. The hotel commands a magnificent view of the glacier, which
at 11km long (about 7 miles) and up to 3km wide (2 miles), is not as
big as the Aletsch glacier further down the valley, but at these very
close quarters is more impressive, seeming almost to hang in space.
Near the Belvedere is an ice grotto, an oddly permanent feature in
this world of shifting ice.

Gletsch is an odd village, a place on the way to other places, with
an air about it which would probably have been familiar to travellers

The Rhône glacier

in the Old West. Leave down the helter-skelter again, to the more gradually falling valley floor. There, as soon as the ground feels flat, stop to look back up towards the pass. Gletsch is no longer visible now, and all that reminds you of human presence is the switchback of road-retaining walls against the hillside. At this point, with the Rhône quieter, though still lively, with conifers and rocks, there is ample time to explore a little visited part of the valley, a secret world of flowers, butterflies and animals.

At **Oberwald**, the first valley village, is the entrance to the Furka rail tunnel, the world's longest narrow-gauge tunnel (14.5km, 9 miles, long) which carries both people and cars to Andermatt when the pass is closed. Note too the fine baroque church. The next village, **Obergestein**, is very different from the other valley villages, being mostly of stone, the difference dating from 1868 when the original chalet village was burnt to the ground in a disastrous fire. Look in the little streets for the barns and stables, which offer a fine mixture of wood and stone. At **Ulrichen**, a village famous in the proud history of the Valaisians as the site of two battles, in 1211 and 1419, in which the valley dwellers successfully defeated invading Bernese armies that had crossed the Grimsel Pass, the Nufenen Pass road branches off. The Nufenen, slightly higher at 2,475m (8,120ft) than the Furka, but much less frequented, links the Valais with Ticino, but from it — the top represents the boundary between the two cantons — a fine

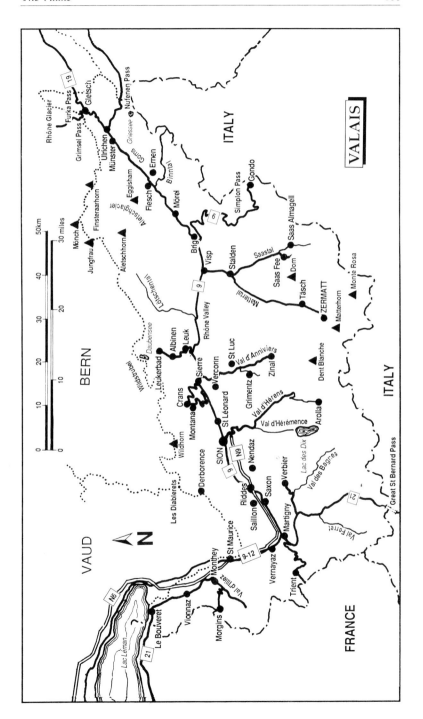

The Grimsel Pass

walk past the large mountain lake of Griessee leads to the Gries Pass beyond. The Gries is at 2,479m (8,130ft), so there is little uphill work involved. On the other side of the pass is a fine view into Italy, the Val Formazza to be precise, where the river Toce (which flows into Lake Maggiore) rises.

Beyond Ulrichen, in a part of the valley known as Goms (and where, incidentally, the Rhône is known as the Rotten) are a number of villages, each of which can be used as a start for walks along the valley floor, or up into the hills on either side. The walks are all excellent — high meadowland, stands of conifers, clear streams and good views — and no particular one stands out. As a rule, walk on the northern side of the valley, because the alpine chain to the south is the most impressive of possible backdrops, and stay on the ridges of the hills coming down from the northern Alps, to increase the view. There are exceptions: the valley leading north from Münster (*not* the one into which the cableway goes) offers a very fine walk, but leave it to follow a path to the Galmihütte to gain a descent route through the trees offering great views southwards; the Schreckhorn mountain, rising above, but well back from Münster, is a beautifully shaped peak as is its jagged neighbour, the Finsteraarhorn — each of these peaks is best viewed by going onto the ridges to the south.

Elsewhere, **Münster** has much to interest the visitor who is willing to spend time and energy looking around. Find the two old water

The Aletsch glacier

wheels that ran an ancient mill, and the late Middle Ages houses, distinguished by a carved cross below the gables. Look inside the elegant white church to see a fine early sixteenth-century triptych, part of an elaborate pulpit. The ceiling is excellent, and the altar — from the early sixteenth century — is considered to be the finest late Gothic carving in the country. The *curé* (parish priest) will also allow the interested visitor to see a small ecclesiastical museum attached to the church. In Münster, and in several of the other upper valley villages, some of the chalet outbuildings are set on staddle stones — here known as *planes* — to keep out rodents and damp, a strange link with, for instance, the English Cotswolds.

Also in Münster, ask in the tourist office, (the Verkehrsverein), if you are adventurous enough to try river-rafting. Trips in rubber

The Tellenhaus at Ernen

inflatables are organised from the village, the trip taking the visitor down 14km (9 miles) of the Rhône. The trip is in the charge of an expert, and equipment — life jackets, crash helmets and insurance — is all included, as is the bus back from the finish at Fiesch. The trips last about 3 hours, can be arranged for families or parties, and are an exciting way of seeing the scenery, less thrilling, perhaps, than the corresponding Oberland trips, but still a fine adventure.

At **Reckingen**, the next large village down the valley, there is a poignant reminder of how terrible these lovely looking mountains can be, a monument to those lost in an avalanche disaster in 1970. Here too is the first onion-domed church, which will become an occasional feature of the journey to Brig.

Fiesch lies at the entrance to a valley which is of great interest to anyone keen on geology, because the retreating Fiescher glacier, flowing down from the sharp Finsteraarhorn, has blocked the valley with the detritus known as terminal moraine, and it is a fascinating glimpse into the world of glaciation to walk up the valley (follow the stream) to see the moraine hummocks. Frequently in the ice-sculptured regions of Britain the phrase terminal moraine is invoked, to explain lake formation or particularly fertile land areas, but this site is real, not projected back to a distant, invisible Ice Age: an outdoor geography lesson.

Most tourists will want to take the Fiesch cableway to the shoul-

George & the Dragon at Ernen

der of the Eggishorn, from where an easy and distinctly well trodden, path leads up to the summit and a truly fantastic view of the Aletsch glacier, Europe's longest at 27km (17 miles). The view is definitely worthwhile, giving a greater awareness of the size of the ice flow — it covers around 115sq km (45sq miles) — than is obtainable from the Jungfraujoch. But the real off the beaten track trip is to leave the cableway at its first stop, Kühboden, and to walk down to the glacier, to experience it at first hand. The path that goes to the east (right) of the Eggishorn offers the better walk, passing the Märjelensee en route for the ice. The round trip takes about 4 hours and great caution should be exercised when the glacier is reached. A glacier is no casual playground, and the inexperienced should limit their ambitions. The very enthusiastic can take a path back down to Fiesch instead of using the cablecar, but this offers more exercise than scenery and cannot be recommended in preference to the glacier walk.

Either way, when you reach the lower cableway station, visit the enclosures on the hill behind, where there is a small zoo, but a completely free and usually overlooked one, of the local fauna. The cages are not ideal — which ones are? — but they do offer visitors a chance to see what they may otherwise be unlucky enough to spend their entire holiday searching for and failing to find.

Below Fiesch, take a side road off the main valley road, to visit

Ernen and Binntal. **Ernen** is spectacularly picturesque, a small square with a statue of a local bishop surrounded by fine, richly dark brown houses that are so characteristically Valaisian, so obviously not from the Bernese Oberland. The village is rarely visited, as few venture so far from the main valley, a point driven home by the local tourist office which is infrequently open. The building that houses it is very good, however, with excellent external frescoes of agricultural scenes. Another fine fresco — which has recently been restored — can be seen on the outside of the Tellenhaus, Tell's house. The house is not so named because William Tell was born, or lived, or died in it, but because the fresco is the earliest known representation of the legend, dating from the last quarter of the sixteenth century. All the ingredients of the story are there: Tell with crossbow, son with apple, in typical medieval style, stilted yet vibrant. Another representation of a legend adorns the St George restaurant, a very fine woodcarving of the saint slaying the dragon. This is a copy, the original being in the church, where it forms part of a three-dimensional work, standing in front of a fresco of a walled city beside a lake. In this original the saint's lance breaks as it strikes the dragon.

From Ernen, or better, from the close-by hamlet of **Mühlebach**, a very fine walk goes up the Rappetal, the valley of the stream above which Mühlebach sits. This valley, turning through a sharp right-angle after a couple of kilometres, is almost invariably empty and very wild, a splendid off the beaten track place where any length of time from an hour to a half-day can be spent exploring. A far prettier and more interesting valley, though somewhat less empty, is the Binntal, which winds up from Ernen itself. This is the equal of any of the more famous Valaisian side valleys, and is superior to most. So good is its collection of wild flowers that part of it has been made into a nature reserve, an area that includes forest with as deep and varied a moss floor as it is possible to see. Several paths can be used to explore the woodland and some of these break out on the higher, more broken mountain slopes, which are equally interesting, holding just about the finest and most easily discoverable rock crystals in Switzerland. So good are the slopes that the last of the country's professional crystal hunters make a living from the fine village of Binn and the collection of hamlets further up the valley. **Binn** has a small museum that includes many good specimens of the local crystals for the visitor with limited time or limited luck.

Closer to Brig there are two sets of villages set on each side of the valley that encloses the Aletsch glacier. First is the group that includes Riederalp, Bettmeralp, Mörel and Breiten, the last of which

Brig

has statistics to prove that it averages three hundred sunny days annually, which must be close to a record for a mountain resort and worth considering when choosing a site from which to explore the upper Valais. In addition **Breiten** is a spa, which, even if you do not suffer from rheumatism, obesity, heart or gynaecological problems, might be of interest because the facilities include an indoor salt water swimming pool at the incredible temperature of 33 °C (91 °F, about 10 °F higher than the average British swimming pool. Any of the villages, and the cableways that link them, can be used as a base to explore the Aletsch forest, a beautiful piece of woodland full of butterflies, birds and animals, the high lakes of Blausee and Bettmersee, and the high ridges that allow a magnificent view of the Aletsch glacier itself.

Riederalp has a small but very fine museum, a mountain chalet furnished in authentic seventeenth-century style, and is also the start of a most enjoyable (but care is needed) walk across the terminal moraine of the glacier to the village of **Belalp** on the other side of the valley. Ask at the small tourist office in Belalp for details of two very interesting expeditions from the village. The first uses guides to trek out onto the glacier itself — this is the *only* way for the inexperienced to walk on a glacier — while the second uses donkeys to trek over the high ridges which offer great views of the glacier.

Brig, the largest town of the upper valley and the point where the upper reach can be said to end, has long been an important town because of its position, at the point where the road over the Simplon Pass reached the Rhône valley. Because of modern developments, that importance has been increased: the Simplon rail tunnel starts at Brig, the Lötschberg rail tunnel is only a few kilometres away, and new work on the Simplon road makes the pass a very attractive way into Italy. Unlike Martigny, in the lower valley, Brig has not yet been bypassed by the N9 motorway and so receives its share of visitors who are re-stocking before crossing the alps. It cannot therefore strictly be seen as an off the beaten track town, but there are still places that are usually beyond the gaze of most visitors. In the main tourists are anxious to be off to the Simplon, or into the Rhône valley, so that only those who use the town as a base for exploration see much of it. The Stockalper castle, more realistically called a palace, is Switzerland's largest, a magnificent building completed over a twenty year period from the mid-seventeenth century. The three towers with their onion-shaped domes take the eye, but look too at the triple-arcaded courtyard that stands between them, and be sure to visit the museum on the first floor, with its local history collection.

Elsewhere, find the Heart of Jesus church (the Herz-Jesu-Kirche) built only twenty years ago and having contemporary sculptures and stained glass by local artists. Another fine church, well worth the visit, stands in Glis, the part of the town to the south-west near where the main valley road leads off, a large building and a very important pilgrim church with many interesting features. Find too the Gamsner Wall, a section of the mid-fourteenth century defensive wall, built here where the valley narrowed, which still has one round tower and is thought to be Switzerland's best such structure.

The Simplon Pass runs south from Brig, a pass that until the turn of the eighteenth century was used only by merchants from Italy, a use on which Brig grew rich and influential. Then, after the battle of Marengo, Napoleon decided that the pass should be brought up to the standard of a military highway and up to 30,000 men laboured for several years to construct the earliest road. Lately there have been considerable improvements, widening, galleries etc, though the (relative) difficulty of reaching Brig means the Simplon will never be as popular as the other alpine passes, which is a pity for two reasons: firstly because it leads directly to Lake Maggiore; and secondly because it goes through the Gondo gorge, and some of the most spectacular scenery on any alpine pass. And this fine scenery is in Switzerland, as the Simplon is also unusual in having the frontier well down beyond the top of the pass. The country is equally good

Stalden gorge

for walking, in the area to the west of the pass road, up to the ridge that is the frontier with Italy. From **Gabi** the Laggintal offers walks from half an hour up to several hours, back up towards the bottom of the Weissmies glacier, while a right turn at Gondo, near the Italian border, leads to **Zwischbergen**, from where the Zwischbergental leads off towards a high (walking) pass to Italy beside the Balmahorn. The walk up the valley is through Valais' largest beech wood and passes the ruins of an old gold mine.

Around Visp

Visp stands at the junction of the Rhône valley and the valley of the Vispa. The town has a long history which includes a century of Italian rule, and still has a very fine old section, the Gräfinbiel, where narrow, winding streets run between fine old buildings. Elsewhere there is an interesting juxtaposition of Valaisian dark wood chalets, and stone houses. Across the valley from Visp, the village of **Eggerberg** has a fascinating wine museum with an eighteenth-century press.

From the town, the first stop is **Visperterminen**, a high-set village to the south-east, on the spur of upland that separates the Rhône from the first of two tributaries of the Vispa, the Saasen Vispa. It is a beautiful village, a mixture of dark Valaisian chalets and white houses, and the local wine is grown from Switzerland's highest vineyards. The wine is called *Heidenwein*, which literally translated is 'Heathen's Wine'. From the village a superb walk starts at Giw at the top of the Gebidem cableway. From there it goes up to the Gebidem Pass, with a fine view of the Gebidemsee, over it and into the Gemsital where the river drains down to the Rhône through a marvellously tight gorge. The path continues to Bististafel and goes up and over the Bistine Pass. From there, still with superb views in all directions, the path descends to the hospice on the Simplon Pass road. This fine walk is a day-long trek — probably 6 hours of walking time — and uses the postbus to return to Visperterminen.

Further up the Vispa, stop at **Stalden**. Do not be put off, as it is easy to be, by the electricity sub-station at the entrance to the village, or by the closeness of the Saas valley and Zermatt. It is worth spending some time here. The cableway to Staldenreid and Gspon crosses the road and, incidentally, gives a great view into the valleys of the Saasen and Matter Vispas. This comes as a surprise when first viewed, adding a truly alpine air to the village on its steep hill, with the high-sided gorge of the Matter Vispa just beyond. The gorge is beautiful, and the view from the road bridge to the rail bridge high above the river is magnificent.

The Matterhorn

Saas Fee

At Stalden the visitor is spoilt for choice. The left valley, of the Saasen Vispa, leads to the Saas villages and the fine scenery of Monte Rosa, while to the right, the Mattertal runs up to Zermatt. The Saas villages are well set. **Saas Balen**, one of the early ones, has a very pretty early fifteenth-century church, while the most famous, **Saas Fee**, is set high on the side of the Saas Grat, the rugged ridge that divides the Saasental from the Mattertal. There are fine walks and excursions in the area. The Mattmarksee reservoir is easily reached, another curiously coloured stretch of water, and one with a sad history — during the construction of the dam in 1965 a section of the Allalin glacier collapsed onto a workmen's camp killing eighty-eight workers. It is the start of several walks into the surrounding mountains. The best head for the two passes, south to the one beside Monte Moro — a pass used since at least the twelfth century — and east to the Antrona Pass. Mattmarksee is at 2,117m (6,945ft) while the Monte

Moro Pass is at 2,868m (9,410ft): this walk up takes about 5 hours from the reservoir dam, and offers the interesting possibility of a cablecar descent into Macugnaga in Italy, but take your passport! The Antrona Pass, at 2,842m (9,320ft), offers an equally good view, but no cableway.

A very different walk is to follow the chapel path from Saas Fee to Saas Grund. It starts along a pilgrim track to the pilgrimage chapel of Höhen Stiege, the High Staircase, from where it descends past fifteen small, white chapels which represent the fifteen secrets of the rosary. This walk, which takes only an hour, offers excellent views of the Saasental.

Beyond Stalden the Mattertal is a bit overcrowded at first, a long builder's yard, but it soon becomes very scenic. A road leads off left to **Grächen**, a very fine Valaisian mountain village which is worth considering for off the beaten track skiing. Further on, the road reaches **Täsch**, the starting point for the romantic entry into Zermatt. It seems little more than a car park and railway station, an annoying place en route for those who see little romance in waiting for a train to Zermatt. It would be nice, therefore, to be able to say lots of nice things about the village, but it is not easy. There are walks in the forest of Schalenabi over the river to the west of the village, but the crooked finger of the Matterhorn beckons, and it is difficult to resist. If you catch the train to Zermatt, sit on the left side of the carriage, and watch the fields about two-thirds of the way along. In an obvious large meadow, with a couple of not well hidden holes surrounded by bare earth, live a colony of marmots, and though it cannot be guaranteed that the visitor will see them, they are frequently above ground.

In **Zermatt** be sure to visit — many visitors do not — the Alpine Museum, which includes not only exhibits on the history of the area, but a fascinating history of the attempts to climb the Matterhorn and the tragedy of the eventual conquest in 1865. The museum even has the rope that broke, allowing four of the first seven successful climbers to fall to their deaths. The grave of one of those that died, the Reverend Charles Hudson, lies in the town's English church. Hudson's body was re-interred in the church, having been first buried in the local churchyard, along with those of Douglas Hadow — later re-buried in England — and Michel-Auguste Croz. The fourth member of the party who died, Lord Francis Douglas, was never found.

Not much else around Zermatt can be classified as off the beaten track, so here are just a few suggestions about the less well known.

About ten times each summer, that is July to September, the Gorner-grat railway runs a very early service (between 4.30 and 5.30am depending on the date) that allows visitors to watch the sunrise from the top station at 3,130m (10,265ft). Breakfast is available at the station hotel. The railway can also be used to reach the best view of the Matterhorn, though this is hardly unknown. Set down at Rot-boden station and walk to the Riffelsee. On calm days the peak is beautifully reflected in the water. The Kleine Matterhorn cableway may well give access to Europe's highest cable station, and hence to the mountain's summit at 3,885m (12,746ft), but the trip is not cheap and the height reached is irrelevant if the visibility is awful. On good days Mont Blanc and Italy's Gran Paradiso are visible, as well as the local big mountains, but on less good days it's best to go elsewhere. If you are just going for the summer skiing, ignore this advice. An impressive view of the Matterhorn, when something of the true scale of the peak can be gained, is that from the base of the Hornli ridge — the ridge of the first ascent — which can be reached in a walk of about 2 hours from the Schwarzsee cable station. Helicopter flights around the Matterhorn and the other high peaks leave from Zermatt. The service is not cheap, but group hiring of the helicopter reduces the individual fare, and could be worth considering for a once-in-a-lifetime trip. Finally, the tourist office has a map that shows the most likely places to see ibex, chamois, marmot, eagles and the other rarer alpine creatures. This can be used to construct excellent walks in the area. For example, the walk up the beautiful valley to Trift from Zermatt itself passes chamois and eagle haunts — allow about 4 hours for the round trip — and the excellent walk to the old hamlet of Zmutt passes some very old oak and fir woods that hold several species of alpine bird, as well as being overflown by eagles. Here, allow about $2\frac{1}{2}$ hours for the round trip.

Down the main valley from Visp, and beyond the fine half-avenue of trees that line the main road, is the impressive gash of the Lötschental, the only valley, apart from the main one, that runs east-west, and one whose off-set position actually places it between the Bernese and Valais Alps. Until the rail tunnel from Kandersteg to Goppersten was bored, around 1910, the valley was virtually im-penetrable, its folk a relatively backward and insular race. Even today their carnivals, at which traditional costumes are worn and the 'Tschaeggaettae' (men dressed in furs and with frightening wood-carved masks) run through the villages, are peculiarly individualis-tic. But times change, communications improve and with character-istic Swiss efficiency the valley is being opened up as a ski centre. So go now, while the feel of the valley is still (just) as it was, the villages still only of dark, almost black, houses with no hotel blocks yet. The scenery will not change, but at present it is particularly untouched by metalwork. Lötschental is a place to be savoured.

Around Sion and Sierre

Along the main valley from the entrance to the Lötschental, the receivers of the Swiss PTT Earth Satellite Station stand like giant woks on the hillside to the right. A permanent exhibition on the site details the purposes and design of the station, but a knowledge of German is a requirement to gain most from it. Next is **Leuk**, a delightful village. The Bishop's Castle, a fine building commanding an excellent view of the middle section of the Valais, is being renovated at the time of writing, but will soon be open and will hold a local museum when work is completed. In the steep town square, up a steep road from the castle, the magnificent church, rebuilt in the late fifteenth century but with its original Romanesque tower, is high set, giving extra height to its already tall construction. In front of it a brilliantly conceived, wrought-iron knight, larger than life, holds a standard that bears a dragon carrying a sword, the town's motif, which is repeated on the church tower and also on more minor objects, such as the town's water trough.

Beyond Leuk, the valley road runs precariously up to **Leukerbad**, a famous *bad* or spa, set below the Gemmi Pass at 2,350m (7,710ft). The walk up to the pass — allow about 3 hours — is exciting, with a fixed wire rope handrail on occasions to help negotiate the tricky bits. Astonishingly, this path used to be followed by visitors to the baths on mules. Less astonishingly, a plaque at one point commemorates one team of mule and rider who disappeared down the imposing cliff towards Leukerbad. Needless to say, no amount of healing water was likely to revive either of them.

The pass can also be reached by cablecar, a preferable option for those who like their walking a little flatter. From the pass the walk to Daubensee (also reached by a walk from Kandersteg, see the Bernese Oberland chapter) is straightforward. The more adventurous can visit Lämmernsee, the Lamb's Lake, set among 3,000m (9,840ft) peaks.

Another cablecar reaches the Rinderhütte, set high (2,340m, 7,680ft), on the flank of the Torrenthorn (2,997m, 9,830 feet). The walk up the peak is straightforward, and the high alp is carpeted with flowers.

A final, and again adventurous, outing is to take the Leitern, the

The Leuk swordsman

Leukerbad

Ladder, path to **Albinen**. This is a small, pretty village, nicely set on the flank of the valley to Leukerbad, now reached by an upper road from the PTT satellite station. Formerly it had no such luxury, and was reached only from the lower, valley, road by a series of ladders set up against the near vertical valley side. Today the same approach can be used, and even though the original rough, wooden ladders have been replaced by stronger, newer ones, the journey is still adventurous.

The Val d'Anniviers — note the abrupt change of language on maps from German to French at this point, just east of Sierre — offers an equally adventurous drive in its early stage. At first the road is on the hill flank, with superb views down into the Valais, but then it becomes confined, with steep cliffs on one side, equally steep drops on the other, and the road on a (sometimes crumbling) ledge between the two. But it is all quite safe, though dramatic, and the scenery — especially the rock architecture of pinnacles and towers — is excellent. Zinal is the last village in the valley, and it is usually the last that gives best access to the hills, but in this case it is better to go to St Luc or Grimentz. **St Luc** has a cableway giving access to numerous walks on the flank of the Rothorn, but the tops are all a little far off and difficult to reach, and it is more a place to stroll than to walk with great purpose. Legend has it that small flames in the shape of humans can be seen here in bad weather, the souls of sinners unable to find peace. Only if a squirrel buries a nut of the Cembra pine, the tree grows, is felled and turned into a cradle, a baby lies in the cradle, grows to become a priest and reads his first mass, will a flame go out. At **Grimentz**, just walk around the village. It is a tight collection of dark Valaisian chalets, their sombre colours offset by window boxes and the occasional white stone of the lower storey. It is, quite simply, an exquisite spot. Further on from it the Lac de Moiry is set among beautiful hill scenery, flower-topped meadows giving rise, by degrees, to snow-sprinkled peaks.

Another fine, well preserved village is **Salgesch**, close to Sierre. **Sierre** itself has a twelfth-century monastery, the Monastère des Bernardines, at Géronde in the south of the town; a fine fourteenth-century church, Notre Dame des Marais, north of the information office; a seventeenth-century town hall, near the information office; and, on the other side of the office, the Château Vidômes. What it does not have is that special air of intimacy that Sion, the Valaisian capital a few kilometres further west, most assuredly does have.

Above the village is **Crans-Montana**, a created winter sports centre, now famed for having staged the world skiing championships. But the creation of such a complex, almost out of thin air, seems to produce a sterile centre, devoid of character. In summer the hotels seem forlorn — you almost expect to meet tumbleweed blowing along the road. The only positive virtue seems to be that the cableways allow access to fine high-ridge country where the visitor can comfortably escape the arid modernity.

By contrast, go to **Vercorin** on the opposite side of the valley. Here there is a real village, a real community. The famed Valaisian poet Rainer-Maria Rilke — whose grave, incidentally, can be seen at Raron, a small village between Visp and the mouth of the Lötschental — said that Vercorin seemed to hang between heaven and earth. And from that enchanted vantage point, the view of earth, the Rhône valley, is heavenly. A very fine walk links Vercorin with the village of Nax above Sion. It is nowhere difficult, 3 hours is ample time, and has a satisfying mixture of meadow and forest paths.

Near Nax, at **St Léonard**, is a most interesting spot, a huge underground lake, which can be explored by boat. The trip, with the water

Château Valère, Sion

reflecting the rock formations, is an unforgettable experience. For the more adventurous, a company in **Chamoson** runs a spelaeological centre, organising trips into local limestone caves, all equipment supplied. Those who take up this challenge will find that, unlike St Léonard which is beautifully lit and where the boat does all the work, these caves are seen by carried lamp, with movement by leg power.

Sion, the Valaisian capital, is a nicely positioned city which has retained a sense of wholeness in its older quarter despite the modern development which has sprung up around it. From a distance the town is dominated by the castles of Valère and Tourbillon on twin hills above the eastern approach to the city. Because the N9 motorway ends short of the city, visitors do still have to visit Sion, but too many just use the circling road en route to the upper valley. But the old town, with its distinctly Italian touches, is worth an afternoon — at the very least — of anyone's time. Start at the cathedral, in the centre of the old town, a fifteenth-century building, part Gothic, part Romanesque but with a tenth-century belfry below the spire. Unfortunately the interior of the cathedral has been poorly 'restored', making it of less interest than the nearby church of St Théodule, a very good sixteenth-century building with several very interesting features.

East from the churches is the tight, steep Rue des Châteaux at the base of which is the town hall, a mid-seventeenth-century building with an early seventeenth-century astronomical clock on its tower, marvellously carved doors and panelled rooms. Be sure to see the earliest Christian inscription known in Switzerland, dating from 377 and found among a collection of Roman inscriptions.

Rue des Châteaux has two museums, the Cantonal Archaeological Museum, and the Cantonal Art Gallery housed in the hugely restored sixteenth-century Bishop's Palace, but continue to the top where paths go left and right: there is also a car park here for those brave enough to drive up.

To the left is the romantic ruin of the castle of Tourbillon, built in the late thirteenth century, but destroyed by fire in the late eighteenth. The view from the ruins (reached by a difficult path complete with, and needing, a handrail) both of town and valley is excellent. To the right is the fourteenth-century chapel of the Château Valère, reached by a quick, steep walk above. This castle is the earlier, dating from the twelfth century and contains the church of Notre-Dame, once the city's cathedral. The church is interesting, being built on the site of a Roman temple, and having a tenth-century section, ie, it precedes the castle building. Inside, there are fine medieval frescoes, but be sure to look out for the carved capitals and the fourteenth-century organ, one of oldest in existence, and actually the world's oldest playable organ since concerts are occasionally given. The castle also contains the Cantonal History Museum, a very fine setting for the collection. One room, its beamed ceiling elegantly held aloft by a heavy wooden Y-beam, holds a beautifully displayed collection of medieval weaponry. There is also a fine collection of early religious art.

Elsewhere in Sion, in the Avenue de la Gare (in the north-west of the town) is the Cantonal Natural History Museum, an odd collection, originally started to preserve oddities. The 'Monster of the Valais', for instance, is a huge wolf from Eischoll.

South of Sion is the Val d'Hérens — called with all due modesty the valley of the true Valais — with a side valley, the Val d'Hérémence. Each is pleasant, though why the fertile Val d'Hérens should carry its particular claim is unclear. Is it really more Valaisian than the Val d'Anniviers? Be that as it may, there are good walks passing many of the most interesting spots in the valleys. For the first spot however, it is not necessary to get out of the car, for the road cuts through the Pyramids of Euseigne. These are eroded pillars of morainic earth, some capped by a flat stone or boulder, that look like giant termite nests, but, because of the capstones, have a distinct other-worldliness about them. Though there are better pillars elsewhere in Europe, most notably those above Lago d'Iseo, one of Italy's

Tourbillon

large northern lakes, there are none that are quite so accessible.

Val d'Hérens continues through a fine series of villages to Arolla, set high up underneath the massive Mont Collon. It is finely positioned, the surrounding area being a favourite haunt of marmots, and is at the start of a very fine walk. This heads off along the forest edge towards the Pas de Chèvres, which is climbed with the assistance of fixed ladders. Beyond, there is a glacier, the Cheilon, to cross before a descent to La Dixence is made past the reservoir of Grand Dixence. The dam of this reservoir is the world's highest, a monstrous concrete wall, 284m (932ft) high, 75m (246ft) wide and over 20m (66ft) thick at the bottom. The wall holds back 400 million cu m (90,000 million gallons) of water. Indeed the dam wall is worth a look in its own right. This 6 hour walk is for very experienced walkers only, the climb to the Pas de Chèvres is exciting and the crossing of the Cheilon glacier requires both experience and equipment. The walk cannot be recommended to the inexperienced or to walkers of modest accomplishments. They should cross the Col de la Meina, reached from Evolène by way of Lana, Flanmayens, a magnificent larch wood, Baran and La Meina. Beyond the col the route loops down to Pralong. This route is also 6 hours long. Those wanting something less ambitious can try paths along the streams in each valley, or can venture into the high meadows above Arolla.

A more reasonable walk follows the Gorge de la Lizerne, that lies west of Sion on the other side of the Rhône from the Val d'Hérens. The walk starts from **Derborence**, a very quiet village beside a finely set lake. The path leads off into the Ecorcha forest, crossing the Lizerne river. At the road, cross the Lizerne again and re-enter the forest. Soon the gorge of the Lizerne is reached, and the path goes high above it with fine views into it. Cross another forest section, the Vaye Basse forest, to reach the village of Ardon. Walking time is about 4 hours, and the postbus can be used to regain Sion.

From Ardon, the high village of **Ovronnaz** can be reached, an ideal spot for strollers, with magnificent views to huge rock walls, the High Alps and the Rhône valley.

Around Martigny

South of Sion the famous Mont d'Or vineyards dominate the road, and very attractive they are. Those keen to try the wine produced here can buy it from numerous roadside stalls where, in season, apricots are also sold. To the left the Val de Nendaz leads off to Monte Fort where there is summer skiing reached by cableway either from this side, or from Verbier. The valley also has several hundred kilometres of marked paths through forest, over meadows and past streams.

At **Saillon** the valley is dominated by the fine ruins of the thirteenth-century castle of Peter of Savoy. Despite being ruinous, it is still the best preserved castle of that age in Switzerland. To see the effect that this fortress, and the one at Saxon on the other side of the Rhône, had on the valley it is really necessary to approach from Martigny rather than from Sion. From the N9 it is obvious that whoever controlled the castles controlled the Valais. At the nearby village of **St Pierre-de-Clages** the church, with an octagonal tower and a spire, is one of the finest twelfth-century Romanesque churches in the country, and is rightly held to be a national monument.

Then, just as the N9 is reached, go left to Mayens de Riddes, Iserables and La Tzoumaz set high on the valley side beneath Mont-Gelé — literally, the 'Frozen Mountain'. In summer this area is a magnificent land of yellow and red flowers, water, conifers, pretty villages and views, and should on no account be missed.

Martigny is the town that lies at the elbow of the Valais, noticed, if at all, by the driver on the N9 for its wind-generator power station and its ruined castle set on a conical hill, and by the traveller to the Great St Bernard Pass as the annoying town with the hold-ups. In

Martigny

truth it is a fascinating place, with both a long history and modern shops. The site was always an important one, as the Great St Bernard is a time-honoured route, and there are Roman remains here, including a Roman milestone beside the parish church. Here too is the Gianadda Museum, a very fine cultural centre. The museum was founded by Pierre Gianadda as recently as 1978 in memory of his brother Léonard, killed in an air crash. Within the elegant modern building are the remains of a Roman temple — probably dedicated to Mercury — which was excavated and then left *in situ*. Around the excavated site are Roman remains — or replicas of them — found at Martigny, together with some Gallo-Roman remains. Of these, notice particularly a three-horned bull. The central horn is missing, but the bull still possesses the savagery so familiar in Celtic art. The museum also has some contemporary art work, and a superb collection of vintage cars. The Gianadda Foundation also sponsors an annual music festival.

Between Martigny-Ville and Martigny-Bourg, the Roman amphitheatre is still in the process of excavation. It was built around the end of the fourth century and held, it is estimated, 5,000 people. The castle of La Bâtiaz was built in 1260 by Peter of Savoy, but was destroyed in the mid-sixteenth century. It is a fine looking ruin, well positioned, and is worth a visit. Also worth a visit is the zoo of Swiss fauna at Les Marécottes, a few kilometres to the west.

From Martigny the main road leads to the Great St Bernard Pass, one of great passes of European folklore, home of big dogs with brandy casks and so on. But few of those who cross the pass visit the hospice's fine museum, which houses, in superb surroundings, exhibits on the natural history of the area, and on the history of the hospice itself. In addition, on the way to the pass, there are several places of interest and some fine scenery. Perhaps it is best to visit the area when you are not going to cross the pass, so that there is no rush to be over and into Italy. Then the elegant village of **Bourg St Pierre** can be savoured — a Roman milestone beside the church notes that it is 24 (miles) from Octodorus Martigny — or the walking and scenery of the country around Lac de Toules can be better appreciated.

From the main valley to the Great St Bernard, several smaller valleys are accessible. The first is the Val Champex from which the Gorges du Dumond can be visited, a narrow cleft almost filled with a roaring stream and reached by a series of walkways. Definitely worth the effort. The village of **Champex** itself, beside a small, reed-enclosed lake is excellent.

The next valley leads off towards **Verbier**, a well known ski resort, less manufactured than Crans-Montana, but not as authentic as Zermatt or Grindelwald. From Verbier or, rather, from the top of the Ruinettes cablecar, a really excellent walk leads over the Col de Termin to Fionnay further up the Val des Bagnes. The path leads to the Monte Fort mountain hut where the night can be passed. This section of the walk takes about $1\frac{1}{2}$ hours, leaving a 5 hour section for the following day, so it is worth considering the overnight stay to avoid a long day on an exacting route. From the hut the path — called the Sentiers des Chamois, the Chamois Path — leads to the Col de Termin, beyond which the beautiful Lac Louvie is found. From there the descent to Fionnay is made. From Fionnay the Val des Bagnes is a protected nature reserve, a haven for flowers, animals and birds.

The last valley is the Val Ferret, joined at Orsières, a fine valley with excellent views to the Grand Jorasses and other peaks of the French Alps above Chamonix.

Chamonix can be reached from Martigny by crossing the Col de la Forclaz. From the col, wholly within Switzerland, a fine walk leads up to the Buvette du Glacier, the bottom of the Trient glacier from where ice was taken and shipped to many of the largest towns of France and Switzerland, Paris included. The walk, up and back, takes about 3 hours. From the glacier, the Trient river runs down its own valley to the Rhône. Near the river junction, at Vernayaz, the

St Maurice abbey

river is confined into a fabulous gorge, and pours over a most picturesque waterfall with the unlikely name of Pissevache.

From St Maurice to Lac Léman

St Maurice is said to derive its name from the leader of a Roman legion massacred to the last man at this spot, in AD287, either for refusing to fight against fellow Christians in Gaul or for refusing to worship pagan gods. Supporting evidence is wholly lacking, though it is certainly true that there was a Roman presence in the area, and the Rhône bridge is strongly believed to rest on Roman foundations. A chapel is said to have been built in the fourth century on the site of St Maurice's tomb, and a monastery was founded here in 515. Since 1128 the monastery has been Augustinian, although it has not been lucky with the forces of nature. It was almost completely destroyed by fire in 1560, and by landslide in 1611. By the early twentieth century, little but the tower remained of the early buildings, and that, of the twelfth century on a tenth-century base, was badly damaged by a rock fall in 1942. What is now seen is elegant rather than magnificent, but go inside to see the stained glass windows, which are savage and vibrant in their depiction of martyrdom and massacre. Even the colours, rich primaries, seem to have been chosen to amplify the effect. Also inside, but not often open and then only with a monk as guide, is the abbey treasury, hidden behind a door that would grace any strongroom. Here there is a gold Byzantine ewer once given to Charlemagne, and an engraved Roman vase as a reliquary. There are other fine objects too, and a collection of interesting bits brought back from Tibet. Beside the treasury is a delightful, and peaceful, small cloister.

Just outside the town on the road to Monthey, the old castle holds the Cantonal Military Museum and here the visitor can also visit the Fairy Grotto, an illuminated natural cave with a lake and waterfall.

Monthey is a pleasant town with a beautiful wooden covered bridge across its river. That river flows down from two valleys, the Val d'Illiez below the Col de Coux, not crossed by road, and the valley of the Pas de Morgins where the visitor can cross into France. The Val d'Illiez is a fine valley, with an equally good village of wooden chalets, **Champery**, at its head. The chalets here are much more elaborately carved than the normal Valaisian houses, looking much closer to those of the Bernese Oberland. From Champery the view is dominated by rocky peaks, and the Dents du Midi, though outcrops of rock feature also in lowland walks laid out from the village.

Morgins, a village on the road to France, and **Torgon**, the last hill-set Valaisian village as the Valais Alps fall finally into Lac Léman, are worth considering for a quiet, peaceful skiing holiday.

Finally the lake is reached, and for those who want to escape the hills with a quiet lake swim, **Le Bouveret** is the place, its unique sand bank offering safe bathing.

And as a final trip off the beaten track, check locally for the times of the steam trains that operate in summer from here to Evian-les-Bains in France.

Further Information
— The Valais —

Activities

Münster
River rafting
See tourist office for full details.
July, August: 3 trips daily 9am, 1pm, 4.30pm; September, October: first 2 trips only. Weather dependent.

Museums and other Places of Interest

Binn
Museum
Open: summer months only, Monday and Thursday only, 4-5pm.

Chamoson
Centre de Spéléologie
5 Rue Chez Moren
1915 Chamoson
Details from tourist office at Ovronnaz, ☎ 027-864293

Eggerberg
Wine Museum
Open: by request.

Leuk
Bishop's Castle
Being renovated. Ask at tourist office for details.

Les Marécottes
Swiss Fauna Zoo
Hours under review. Enquire at tourist office.

Martigny
Gianadda Museum
Open: daily except Mondays April to October 10am-12noon and 1.30-6pm; November to March 1.30-6pm.
During special exhibitions the museum also opens on Mondays.

Riederalp
Chalet Museum
Open: June to mid-October, Tuesday, Thursday and Sunday only, 2-5pm.

St Léonard
Underground Lake
Open: daily March to October 9am-7pm.

St Maurice
Abbey Treasury
Open: July and August, daily tours at 9.30, 10.30am, 2.30, 3.30 and 4.30pm; May, June, September and October, daily tours at 10.30am, 3 and 4.30pm; November to April, daily tours at 3 and 4.30pm.

Castle and Military Museum
Open: daily except Monday 10am-
12noon and 2-5pm (6pm from June
to September).

Fairy Grotto
Open: daily 9am-6pm.

Sion
Cantonal Museums

Archaeological
Open: daily except Monday 10am-
12noon and 2-6pm. Open Mondays
(same times) in July and August.

Art Gallery
Open: daily except Monday May to
October 10am-12noon and 2-6pm.

History
Valère Castle
Open: November to April 10am-
12noon and 2-5pm. Open Mondays
(same times) in July and August.

Natural History
Open: Sundays all year 10am-
12noon and 2-6pm; daily mid-July
to August 2-6pm.

Zermatt
Alpine Museum
Open: daily 10am-12noon and
4-6pm.

Tourist Information Offices
Main Office:
Union Valaisanne du Tourisme
(Walliser Verkehrsverband)
Case Postale
CH-1951 Sion
☎ 027-223161

Local Offices
Brig am Simplon
Kur-und Verkehrsverein
CH-3900 Brig am Simplon
☎ 028-231901

Martigny
Office Régional du Tourisme
Place Centrale 9
CH-1920 Martigny
☎ 026-21018/23213

Sierre
Verkehrsbüro
Max-Huber 2
CH-3960 Sierre
☎ 027-558535

Sion
Office du Tourisme de Sion et
environs
Rue de Lausanne
CH-1950 Sion
☎ 027-228586

Zermatt
Offizielles Verkehrsbüro
CH-3920 Zermatt
☎ 028-661181

8 • Ticino

T he Ticino (its German and French name is spelled Tessin) is the only Swiss canton that lies wholly on the south side of the Alps, and this position gives it a unique character. Its climate, its flora and fauna reflect this, especially in the southern section; yet having its highest point at over 3,400m (11,152ft) above sea level and its lowest at less than 200m (650ft), it exhibits considerable extremes.

On the map the canton has a shape roughly resembling that of a Stone Age arrowhead, with the point to the south towards the Mediterranean. In that there is a kind of symbolism. For the Ticino has a key position on historic trade and cultural transit routes across the Alps. For centuries the St Gotthard route (and neighbouring alternatives) have used the valley of the river Ticino (for the canton is named after its main river) to link the Mediterranean world not merely with northern Switzerland but with much of northern Europe.

The Ticinesi are Italian-speaking and share with Lombardy not only their language but also much of their cultural heritage and their daily customs and ways of living. Indeed, up to the thirteenth century the Ticino shared its history with the rest of Lombardy. When the Gotthard Pass was re-opened to use about the mid-twelfth century, the Central Swiss developed trade contacts with their southern neighbours. And from the earliest days of the independent Confederation of the original Forest Cantons the route across the Alps as a corridor to the world of Mediterranean trade and culture was a magnet for the Confederates. The 'Gotthard policy' was one they pursued with great tenacity. It led in three stages to the incorporation into the Swiss state firstly of the region as far as Bellinzona, then of the Locarno area and finally the area, beyond the barrier of Monte Ceneri, which lies north and south of Lake Lugano. (This apparently easy 'annexation' of a population of Lombard race and language is not so paradoxical as it first seems. In the sixteenth century when it took place, Lombardy was strife-riven by French, Spanish and

Austrian claimants for dominion compared to whom the Swiss might, to many, seem welcome.) After a long period under dominion of the northern cantons, the Ticino finally, in 1803, became a constituent canton of the Swiss Confederation.

The river Ticino rises high up in the Alps not so far from where the Rhône and the Rhine also rise; it cuts its way with turbulent force through granite and gneiss in a very rapid descent over a comparatively short distance on its upper course and ultimately flows into Lake Maggiore near Locarno. The region is particularly interesting to botanists because in many places alpine plants coexist with Mediterranean ones. The streams have brought alpine flora down to the foothills of the lake districts where they flourish alongside Mediterranean flora, which can survive there because of the mild winters. Hours of sunshine are much greater throughout the year than in the zones immediately north or south, especially in winter. Rainfall is in aggregate higher than in these neighbouring zones, but the number of rainy days is notably fewer than on the north side of the Alps.

One of the most dramatic climatic experiences for a traveller in Europe is to pass, whether by road or rail, through the Gotthard tunnel after climbing up the valley of the Reuss from Central Switzerland on, say, an overcast spring day when snow is piling high in Göschenen. Twenty minutes later, you emerge into sunlight, blue skies and a landscape where workers are in shirt sleeves and where bedding is hanging out on wooden balconies to air in the sun. (Once in a while the reverse can happen, when the warm, moisture-laden wind from the Mediterranean is precipitating rain south of the alpine barrier — but it reaches Central Switzerland as the strange wind they call the *Föhn*, that brings almost unseasonable warmth and great clarity to the horizons.)

Today a majority of those travelling south over the Gotthard are heading either for the popular lakeside resorts on Lakes Maggiore and Lugano, or beyond that into Italy and other Mediterranean lands. So the paradox exists that although no main road (or rail) can more truly be called a 'beaten track' than the one which follows the valley of the Ticino, one needs do no more than turn for a few kilometres into its side valleys to find oneself truly 'off the beaten track'. Indeed, now that (since 1986) the old 'Gotthard road' has been supplanted so far as through traffic is concerned by the completed Basel-Chiasso motor expressway (E9,N2), even many towns and villages on the former road can be rated as 'off the beaten track'. In 1988 this was recognised by Swiss Federal Railways' promotion of

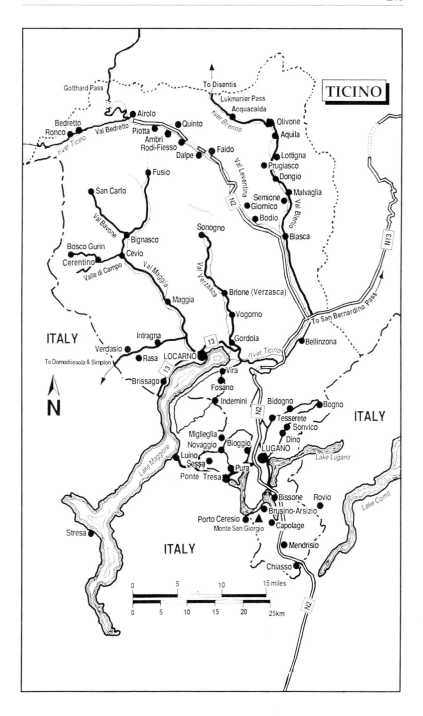

the stretch of former 'Gotthard road' between Airolo and Biasca as one suitably traffic-free for those who seek to combine touring with the pursuit of 'fitness' (the English word has been taken over into Swiss-German) by cycling!

Although it is quite practicable to travel to the Ticino via Milan, the great majority of English-speaking visitors prefer the traditional route used by travellers from northern Europe, and enter Switzerland via Zürich (by plane) or via Basel (by road or rail). For the railway or road journey from northern Switzerland through Central Switzerland and over the Gotthard is not only a direct route but is also one of the most interesting and spectacular journeys in Europe.

It often surprises travellers to find that the southern side of the alpine crossing involves an even more headlong descent and precipitous rocky surroundings than the northern. And the human habitations and settlements merge into this landscape, as the typical Central Swiss wood-framed 'chalet' gives place in the valley to grey stone houses, roofed with stone slabs. Gardens and land plots are bounded neither with fencing nor hedging, but with up-ended split slabs of granite set edge to edge. The Ticino has been called a land of gneiss and granite! Villages are characteristically set wherever terraces or ledges offer a bit of level ground, however high, above the channel carved by the river Ticino. Roads branch off from the main road to zigzag up to the inhabited terraces at many levels. Often the first obvious sign of human settlement is a glimpse of the slim square stone tower with tent-shaped stone roof which is the campanile of the village church.

Airolo is the first town in the Ticino which travellers meet when they emerge from the 16km-long (10 mile-) Gotthard rail or road tunnel from the north. It stands 1,154m (3,786ft) above sea level, and, set in a ring of mountain scenery, is an important winter and summer resort and starting point for excursions — particularly high pass walks and ski tours. As well as being gateway to the south, it is also gateway to the upper valley of the river Ticino. That river's upper course flows from the west down what is called the Bedretto valley until it reaches Airolo, where it swings round into its course southwards in the Val Leventina, which runs the 37km (23 miles) from Airolo to Biasca.

Before heading south all too few travellers think to turn west from Airolo up the short but impressive Val Bedretto. It is sparsely inhabited, given over to pastureland and coniferous woodlands, dominated to the north by the peaks of the Pizzo Lucendra and Pizzo Rotondo chain, and to the south by the Cristallina group, and it leads

The Nufenen Pass, the highest alpine crossing entirely on Swiss territory

in 14km (9 miles) to Switzerland's second highest mountain road
pass (first opened in 1969). First villages of the valley are Fontana
(where the road is very narrow) and Ossasco. The road then crosses
to the north bank and climbs to **Villa** where the church bell-tower
appears to be five-sided, having in fact an acute angled buttress to
deflect avalanches. The next village, **Bedretto**, is picturesque with its
Gotthard-style wooden houses. In the background over the river to
the south rises the ridge which is the frontier with a salient of Italian

territory. (A pack road over it, the Gries Pass, used to be known as the Wine Pass!) The Val Bedretto road soon passes through the last of the all-year-round inhabited places, **Ronco**, near the mouth of the valley of the same name, which is notorious for its avalanches, and shortly thereafter the summer pasture settlement All'Acqua, where the road formerly ended. Now the road continues and crosses the Nufenen Pass (2,478m, 8,130ft) soon leading down in 13km (8 miles) to Ulrichen on the High Rhône valley road between Brig and Andermatt, if the traveller should wish to do a round trip. (Note: The Nufenen Pass is only open in summer. And also from late June until early October it is possible to do the Airolo-Nufenen Pass-Ulrichen excursion by Swiss postbus, Line 600. 51.)

Six kilometres (4 miles) south of Airolo on the 'old' road lie two villages in an open space in the valley, **Piotta** and **Ambri**, sharing the railway station Ambri-Piotta. On the left hand, beyond the motorway and the river, is a large electric power station which supplies current for the railway. Close by it is the valley station of a funicular railway, the country's steepest, rising 785m (2,575ft) in 23 minutes. The funicular serves three destinations: a cantonal sanatorium, the village of Altanca, and the uppermost station, Piora, from which it is a 15-20 minute walk to Lake Ritóm, an artificial lake supplying the hydro-electric station at Piotta below.

Piora (and Altanca) can also be reached by motorists with their own transport. Either leave the 'old' No 2 road just before Piotta, turning left and crossing both motorway and river, then taking the steep climb by zigzags up to Altanca. Or, if travelling by motorway N2 from Airolo, use the exit for Quinto and take the longer snaking ascent to Altanca and Piora. Do not omit to stop in **Quinto** for a look at the church of St Peter and Paul. The six-storey Romanesque campanile that survives from the predecessor church of the twelfth century is particularly fine. (It is again to be noted that a postbus service operates from Ambri-Piotta railway station to the power station and funicular, Line 600. 55, and another to Quinto and Altanca, 600. 56.)

Lake Ritóm, destination of this deviation from the main valley and dominated by mountains to the north, has on its south flank the canton's most extensive area of pasture land, the Piora Alpine Park, famed for its alpine flora which is reckoned to exceed five hundred varieties. The area has numerous marked trails, including routes through to the neighbouring Blenio valley.

The most spectacular part of the Valle Leventina for travellers either by road or rail lies between the villages of Rodi (railway station

The village of Quinto in the Leventina valley

Rodi-Fiesso) and Giornico. The river Ticino bursts its passage down through two narrow gorges involving a huge drop in the valley floor. To cope with this drop the railway uses four spiral tunnels boring into the rock faces of the gorges in order to climb down. In this section there are also some striking glimpses of waterfalls.

In the Valle Leventina there are many interesting options for 'off the beaten track' tours and excursions by motorists who leave the modern expressway and take to the older cantonal road which passes through towns and villages, now free of through traffic. And in most cases similar opportunities are open to those who travel by public transport, by leaving the train (or long-distance bus) at a main valley stop and then using the ubiquitous Swiss postbus services which penetrate to even the most remote villages. A case in point would be the narrow mountain road that goes off just after Rodi-Fiesso to the right and ascends through hill grazings to the little village of **Prato Leventina** where the baroque church at the cemetery has kept its fine, tall Romanesque bell-tower. The road, an old pack road that circumvents the gorge of Piottino continues in bends through larches and firs before coming out into high pastureland again with magnificent views of, among other peaks, Campo Tencia, the Ticino's highest peak at 3,073m (10,082ft), and ultimately reaching the pleasant village of **Dalpe** (with overnight possibilities), favourite starting point for high climbs. Prato and Dalpe are also served by postbus from Rodi-Fiesso (Line 600. 58).

Returning to the junction with the cantonal road south of Rodi-Fiesso, it plunges into the spectacular gorge that the old pack road to Prato had avoided and thereafter reaches **Faido**, principal town of Valle Leventina, at the much lower level of 725m (2,379ft). Faido is picturesque, for alongside the typical Ticinese stone houses it has conserved some handsome sixteenth-century wooden residences with decorative carvings. For more than three centuries this was the seat of the north Swiss representative governors of the valley, and an important transit centre for Gotthard trade. It is here, too, that the first definite signs of a 'southern landscape' manifest themselves — at 725m or 2,379ft above sea level — in the form of vines, mulberries and sweet chestnuts. To the west, facing the village, is an impressive view of three waterfalls of the river Piumogna as it drops to join the Ticino.

Other waterfalls can be seen from the cantonal road in the course of the 11km (7 miles) between Faido and Giornico. Halfway, the road enters the last of the great 'steps' downward of the valley floor, the Biaschina gorge, dropping 225m (738ft) in 5.5km (3.4 miles), just before reaching Giornico. (The rate of headlong descent of the Leventina valley floor — a total fall of 974m in the 37km from Airolo to Biasca, or 3,196ft in 23 miles — is unique in all Europe).

The village of **Giornico** lies on both sides of the river. Indeed it owed its early importance to the fact that there the historic pack road of Gotthard trade crossed over to the other side of the valley; a lovely old arched bridge is said to mark the place. It is a handsome village and has what is regarded as the finest Romanesque ecclesiastical building in a canton which abounds in architectural treasures. The twelfth-century church of St Nicolao is reached in 5 minutes from the railway station by crossing the river bridge. Epitomising pure Lombardy-Romanesque style, it probably belonged originally to a monastery. Sculptured beasts guard the portal, and uniquely carved

The twelfth-century church of San Nicolao, Giornico

capitals adorn the columns in the crypt. A 15 minute walk uphill to the site of a former castle leads to another church, the chapel of St Maria of the Castle, noted for its fifteenth-century wall paintings. Back across the river in the other part of the village is the Casa Stanga, sixteenth-century residence of a noble family, with exterior walls bearing painted coats of arms of its period; for a long time an inn, it now houses the Folk Museum of the Leventina valley. Just at the northern entrance of the village, on the left, is the memorial to a decisive battle in the year 1478 when a small force of Swiss Confederates defeated a well equipped Milanese army of the house of Sforza.

On the right, leaving Giornico, is another beautiful waterfall, and within 5km (3 miles) the road reaches **Bodio**, a smallish village in an important complex of metallurgical and chemical engineering industry fuelled by the valley's hydro-electric power. Four kilometres ($2^1/_2$ miles) farther on is **Biasca**, town of 6,000 inhabitants (which will be described in more detail later) where the valley has opened out into a broad, fertile basin which stretches almost to Bellinzona, the cantonal capital 17km ($10^1/_2$ miles) farther south; this wide valley floor is known as the Riviera. At Biasca the river Ticino has been joined from the left (north-east) by the river Brenno which flows down the Blenio valley. Biasca has an important industry in its gneiss stone quarries. Its fertile soil also produces mulberries, vines, figs and walnuts. Historically it has been a place of strategic and commercial importance as the gateway to two of the medieval pass routes: the Gotthard route coming down the Leventina valley, and the Lukmanier (Lucomagno) Pass route down the Blenio.

The Blenio Valley

The Blenio valley makes a striking contrast to the near parallel Leventina, valley of the river Ticino, which it joins at Biasca. Compared to the rocky, precipitate, 'shut in' aspects of the Leventina, the Blenio is wider, sunnier and more kindly. Because it is more open, the sun's rays seem to penetrate every corner, while its neighbour has many zones of all-year shadow beneath lowering mountains. The Blenio has a long history of settlement, and a long history of providing a through route between north and south. There is evidence that the Lukmanier Pass — which is the lowest of the alpine passes and more flat in contour than the Gotthard — was favoured by the Romans. It was also an invasion route into Italy of early medieval German Emperors such as Otto I and the great Barbarossa. It was known as the Emperors' Pass as well as the Passo del Sole — 'The Sunny Pass'. However, the nineteenth- and twentieth-century rail and road engineers applied themselves to the more direct, if more challenging, route by the Gotthard. So nowadays the Lukmanier-Blenio route has no railway, no motorway, and so escapes the full flood of modern tourism. Yet it has many treasures that make it well worth exploring. And for those without independent transport, it is well served by the splendid Swiss postbus services.

The village of Olivone seen from the Lukmanier Pass road

For motorists who are already acquainted with the Gotthard road from the north via Airolo, the Val Blenio provides a fascinating alternative. Coming from the north on the new N2 motorway, instead of taking the Gotthard tunnel to Airolo, take the exit for Andermatt. For this is where the great alpine crossroads occur, where the north-south valley route cuts the west-east valley route. Take the road for Chur which zigzags towards the north-east to cross the Oberalp Pass (2,044m, 6,706ft high), the boundary between the Uri and the Grisons cantons. A second series of zigzags leads the descent into the uppermost valley of the Vorder-rhein. The great Rhine is, here, but a small mountain torrent. The road descends further to **Disentis** (nowadays also named Mustér in Switzerland's fourth national language — the Romansch spoken in the Grisons, descended from the vernacular Latin spoken in Rome's province of *Rhaetia*.) From Disentis — which is rather dominated by its extensive, imposing and historic monastery — take the road going off right for Biasca. This climbs through a wooded ravine with the romantic name of Hell's Gorge (Höllenschlucht) and some straggling villages. After a bit the surroundings become wilder, as the road steadily climbs parallel to the Medelser Rhein. Where the sombre Val Cristallina opens to the left the spectacular 30m- high (98ft) Fumatsch falls are seen on the right. Soon the ascent mounts to a great expanse of bleak, poor pastureland between the dark smoke-grey mass of Monte Scopi (3,199m, 10,493ft) in the east and Pizzo Rondadura (3,016m, 9,892ft) to the west. An artificially dammed lake comes into view down on the right, below the road level, taking its name, Lake Santa Maria, from a former hospice on the old road to the pass. A moderate ascent now leads to the pass. A large modern statue of the Madonna marks this rather unspectacular watershed between the catchments of the Ticino and the Rhine, and between the cantons of Ticino and Grisons.

Beyond the pass the road, first in rocky surroundings then in high pastureland, reaches in about 5km (3 miles) an attractive belt of pine woodland at Acquacalda. Soon it picks up the water course of the river Brenno (there is a fine waterfall here) flowing down from the west, and follows it, at first high above, on the north slopes of the valley, later crossing and recrossing until, after passing Camperio on its level pastures, it suddenly swings over the river and executes a long tight loop to the south and then back north to effect its descent to Olivone. In the course of this loop it presents magnificent panoramas of the Val Blenio and of the snow-clad peaks of the Adula alpine range which forms the north-south boundary between Ticino and Grisons and of which the Rheinwaldhorn (3,402, 11,159ft) is the highest peak. A striking view of **Olivone** itself, with its impressive background of the great pyramid mass of Sosto, is had on the final descent to the village, nowadays a favourite summer holiday centre, particularly for hill walkers and climbers. It has an unexpectedly mild climate and is situated among fruit and nut orchards. Olivone's village church, with a fine Romanesque bell-tower, gives a hint of its long history as a key transit station on the pass route. As late as the mid-nineteenth century tolls for passage were still exacted here. There is a local museum in the former prebendary house at the church (Ca da Rivoi) which holds historical and ecclesiastical exhibits, including *ex voto* items, also costumes and agricultural items representative of the upper Blenio. The key may be borrowed at the parsonage.

The next stretch of road is lonely and wooded, following the left bank of the Brenno on the valley floor. At **Aquila**, about 5km (3 miles) on, there is the opportunity of taking a secondary road across to the right (west) bank. This adds a few kilometres to the route, but allows visits to places of unique interest on western terraces of the valley. Before leaving Aquila, however, it is worth recalling its contribution to social and dietary history. Inhabitants of the pretty village were

Underground cave, St Léonard, Valais

La Bâtiaz, Martigny, Valais

Sion, dominated by the castles of Valère and Tourbillon, Valais

The church of San Carlo, Negrentino

famed as manufacturers of chocolate. As early as the turn of the seventeenth century one emigrant passed on this craft to the Spaniards, and in the nineteenth century emigrants set up factories in England and France and even, it is believed, in Constantinople. Chocolate is no longer manufactured in the valley, the last establishment — in Dangio — having closed down in 1966. But locals believe the valley's reputation contributed to the high regard in which Swiss chocolate is held.

About 5km (3 miles) along the narrow right-bank road lies **Prugiasco**, which has one of the attractive parish churches for which the Ticino valleys are famed. But high above the village, on an alpine pasture called Negrentino, is another, which is one of the most important Romanesque buildings, not merely in Switzerland but in all Europe, the church of San Carlo. The Negrentino meadow can be reached in about 30 minutes walk from Prugiasco on a clearly defined footpath. Alternatively, by driving up a corkscrew road on the immediate right to **Leontica** village, it is possible to use the large car park at the Leontica chairlift station and walk over the meadows to San Carlo in 5 minutes. There is a bus service to Leontica four or five times a day from Acquarossa, the next village south of Prugiasco on the valley road (Line No 600. 75) operated by the postbus concessionaries in the valley, Autolinee Bleniesi.

The first record of San Carlo church, originally dedicated to St Ambrose, dates back to 1214. It consists of two aisles, each having a semicircular apse; the larger, northern aisle dates from the eleventh century, and the smaller from the thirteenth. The self-standing tower — which is characteristic of the region — dates from the turn of the twelfth and thirteenth centuries. The interior possesses notable wall paintings, some Romanesque (one eleventh-century fresco showing Byzantine influences), some Gothic. The Negrentino alpine meadow where the church stands offers splendid views over the whole Blenio valley. Keys to the church are available at all restaurants in Leontica and Prugiasco.

The Leontica chairlift mentioned above is associated with winter sports use. Its upper station is near the col below the Bassa di Nara (2,123m, 6,963ft) which in turn provides a way into the Valle Leventina for high-level walkers.

The west bank secondary road from Aquila rejoins the more direct east bank road at Acquarossa, which as its name may suggest was once a mineral spa resort. By taking the west bank road however, one village on the other road has been missed which might warrant a short backtrack on the east bank. **Lottigna**, once the principal village of the Blenio, has a picturesque site on an eminence with, nearby, magnificent views of the valley in both directions — including, to the north, Sosto's dramatic pyramid in the distance. The handsome sixteenth-century Casa dei Landvogti or Governors' Residence — sometimes also described as the Palazzo del Pretorio or old Police Headquarters — was once the headquarters of the Swiss Confederation's representative governor or bailiff in this valley. From the fifteenth to eighteenth centuries governors appointed by the Swiss Confederation administered Ticino. Their old residences are prominent in the valleys, and the one at Lottigna, probably built early in the sixteenth century and converted to the administrative centre of the governors, was later their seat. As is frequently the case, the façade is adorned with appropriate coats-of-arms. Today the building houses an interesting museum of local history (including items on emigration, chocolate making and weaponry).

By this stage of descent into the valley, lush vegetation shows southern, near Mediterranean climatic influences, with mulberries, walnuts, chestnuts and vines. **Dongio** is surrounded by fruit gardens, orchards, vineyards and *grotti*.

The *grotto* is a great institution in the Ticino valleys. Originally the word meant simply a storage place dug out in a rock face in which to keep wine and cheeses at a cellar temperature. They were mostly

A view of Dangio in the Blenio valley between Lottigna and Aquila

just outside the village in the shade of trees, and became favourite spots for the men of the village to meet on Sundays or holidays to play a game or two of *boccia* (bowls) and to talk over a glass of local wine; often someone cooked up a snack of some local dish, perhaps game shot locally, setting up a granite slab as a rough table. This caught on. Some *grotti* became favourite rendezvous for wider circles and began to cater as a regular enterprise for local customers and even for visitors or strangers of the right sort. Nowadays some places are called *grotti* that are simply ordinary eating places. But if you can be fortunate enough to learn the favourite *grotto* of a local Ticinese citizen, that is where to find homely local food and wine — often with entertainment, too.

Some 6km (4 miles) south of Lottigna at Motto, a minor road again makes it possible to cross to the right bank and so pass the ruined twelfth- to fourteenth-century castle of Seravalle, erected for the control of this strategic part of the 'Imperial Route' into Italy. Here Barbarossa rested his imperial army for some days before leading them to defeat at the battle of Legnano in 1176 — a defeat which led to a siege of Seravalle Castle by local peasants in the first stirrings of the sense of independence which revealed itself in the taking of the solemn Oath of Torre (a pretty little village north of Lottigna where the village church has a plaque on its façade with extracts from the Oath.) The village nearest the castle, **Semione**, has a museum of fossils and minerals, some 25,000 specimens.

The main road, on the opposite side of the valley, has a slip-road into **Malvaglia**, a large village at the mouth of the valley of the same name. Here too is a beautiful church of Romanesque origin. Its belltower is the tallest and considered the most beautifully proportioned in the Ticino.

South of Malvaglia the valley broadens. Tumbled rocks on the valley floor prepare the traveller for, shortly before Biasca, the notorious Buzza di Biasca, remains of a cataclysmic landslide of the year 1512 when a great mass of the 2,328m (7,636ft) high Pizzo Magno collapsed into the valley below, damming it into a lake which gave way 2 years later with devastating effects as far as Lake Maggiore.

Biasca is the main town of the mountain region of the Three Valleys — Leventina, Blenio and the Riviera, the latter being the luxuriant, fertile section of the river Ticino's valley between the junctions of the river Brenno from Lukmanier Pass and the river Moesa from San Bernardino Pass. This region is also the centre of the Ticino's stone quarrying industry, for in this region the natural stone is a slatey gneiss which cleaves readily — witness the roof covering of typical Tessin houses and the formidable boundary walls of fields and gardens. **Biasca** itself has a modern look, and a variety of industries which originated with the coming of the Gotthard railway last century. But it is also a long established ecclesiastical centre, and the collegiate church of San Pietro e Paulo has a dominating site. It is a Romanesque basilica, probably of the twelfth century, restored in the mid-twentieth century and has an art treasure of thirteenth- to seventeenth-century frescoes.

Thanks to the Autolinee Bleniesi bus services (enquiry office in Biasca, ☎ 092 72 31 72), the places of interest in Val Blenio can be reached by public transport, even to beyond the Lukmanier Pass. Regular services run all year to Olivone from Biasca railway station via Malvaglia, Acquarossa etc (Line 600. 72). During the months of June to September two services a day go onward to Lukmanier and Disentis (Line 600. 73). All postbus services, however remote, and whether run by the PTT's own staff and vehicles or contracted out to concessionary operators, are included in volume 2 (yellow cover) of the annual Swiss 'Official Timetable' — which can also be purchased in principal offices abroad of the Swiss National Tourist Office.

The villages of Dongio and Acquarossa might be considered

A game of boccia *being played in a shaded* grotto

suitable localities to stay for sightseeing in the middle Blenio valley.

For keen walkers or ramblers the round tour on foot from Acqua-rossa to Prugiasco, the church at Negrentino and return via Leontica would involve about $2^{1}/_{2}$ hours walking; For experienced and ade-quately shod hill walkers a longer and more strenuous programme could take the chairlift from Leontica to the Bassa di Nara for a high-level walk via the col to the first village in the neighbouring Leventina valley, **Molare**, thence downhill to Faido FFS railway station on foot, or by postbus service from Molare (Line 600. 61), taking 30 minutes) to Faido FFS, returning by rail to Biasca. The necessary walking maps are readily available in bookshops and tourist offices.

Very experienced and equipped mountain walkers might be interested in a more ambitious summer (June to September) round trip which links the two valleys, beginning on a section of the High

Alpine Trail of the Blenio. It starts from the FFS railway station Piotta-Ambri south of Airolo. Walk or take the bus to Piotta Centrale (power station) over the river. From there the steep cablecar runs to Piora, from which top station it is a 15 minute walk to the Lake Ritóm reservoir. A passable road runs along the north side of the lake and passes between it and the smaller Lake Cadagno. (There is a mountain hut refuge at Cadagno, 1,986m, 6,514ft). From there the route is via the Piora high pasture plateau, then an easy rise to the Passo del Sole (Sun Pass) at 2,376m (7,793ft), from which a fine view opens out to the Adula Alps to the east (prominent being the Rheinwaldhorn 3,402m, 11,159ft), and backwards to the Valais' Alps. The track then leads down more steeply by Stabbio Nuovo over meadows past Frodalera, where a track breaks off on the right towards the Bareta Pass (a further section of the Blenio High Trail). Continuing downwards however, towards the floor of the Santa Maria valley coming from the Lukmanier Pass, this is reached near Pian Segno (1,660m, 5,445ft). The trail then continues on the broad valley floor, for some of the way on the old Roman road, to Camperio. At the Camperio hospice bus stop on the main road to Biasca a bus passes twice daily during the mid-June to September season (Line 600. 73). Olivone, the main head of valley village with a more frequent all-year bus service is 7km (4 miles) on from Camperio on the Biasca road. (Total excursion time to Camperio is estimated at 5 hours. Detailed sheets on this and longer trail sections can be obtained from the tourist office: Ente Turistico Blenio, CH-6716 Acquarossa, ☎ 092/78 17 65).

Before leaving Biasca and the Valle Leventina it is worth noting an interesting initiative there promoted by Swiss Rail, (known in German by the initials SBB, in Italian FFS). The completion of the Basel-Chiasso motorway freed from through traffic the cantonal road down the valley, and among the activities which profit from this is cycling, which in Switzerland has become popular as part of the current movement for promoting 'fitness'. The SBB/FFS scheme provides a new and interesting way of exploring the historic towns and villages of the Leventina, and is based on Airolo and Biasca railway stations. At any time up to the day before travel, phone Airolo station and reserve a cycle for hire. On the day agreed, travel to Airolo by rail on a special round-journey ticket, take over the reserved hire cycle at Airolo, and set off on the journey of exploration downhill on the old cantonal road, taking as much time on the journey, with whatever halts and detours, as inclination dictates. At journey's end in Biasca, the cycle is returned to the FFS station and the round-ticket covers the return journey to home. A similar ar-

rangement exists on the north side of the Gotthard between Göschenen and Flüelen, and in other suitable regions. A variety of models
of cycle are available.

Only 17km (10$\frac{1}{2}$ miles) separate Biasca from the Ticino's cantonal
capital, Bellinzona, lying at the southern end of the Riviera. Before
reaching it the cantonal road crosses the N13 motorway coming in on
the left from the Mesolcina valley and San Bernardino Pass. It
bypasses the small town of Arbedo which gave its name to a battle
in 1422 when the Swiss Confederates suffered a disastrous defeat at
the hands of a greatly superior Milanese force in this key strategic
area.

Bellinzona, at once a modern industrial city, administrative and
route centre and historic cultural centre, has been for centuries a
strategic point. Here, three key routes from alpine passes, Gotthard,
Lukmanier and San Bernardino, meet together, along with two
routes to Italy and the south via Lakes Maggiore and Lugano. It is
ironical that such a city should feature in a book dealing with 'off the
beaten track' places. Yet, of the legions of tourists who annually pass
through Bellinzona by rail and road, the vast majority give it scarcely
more than a passing thought as a junction town.

The one time frontier fortress city, which controlled passage
between Lombardy and Central Switzerland, has three impressive
castles which, although they have other formal names are commonly
called after the three original Forest Cantons of Central Switzerland
which ultimately made the Ticino Swiss: Uri, Schwyz and Unterwalden. A city tour best starts at the FFS station, along Viale Stazione
to the Piazza Collegiata with its charming eighteenth-century baroque buildings. The picturesque heart of the 'old town', which has
retained its original character, is concentrated between this square
and its neighbour to the south, Piazza Nosetto, with the lovely
arcades in the Lombardy tradition. The Piazza Collegiata takes its
name from the very fine collegiate church of San Pietro e Stefano, a
building of the Renaissance period with baroque interior features.
Beside the church is the stepped pedestrian alley that climbs to
Castello Montebello (or Castle Schwyz) standing some 90m (295ft)
above the city, an impressive example of fortification techniques
with walls, towers and battlements. Today it houses the Civic
Museum — largely archaeological and historical. From its high keep
is a fine panorama of the city, with the Ticino valley and Lake
Maggiore in the distance.

Returning to the triangular Piazza Nosetto (where the tourist
information office can be found) a short walk leads through to the

Bellinzona market

eighteenth-century Palazzo del Governo, on the way to the avenue which ascends past vineyards to the Castello Grande (or Uri) dominated by its two thirteenth-century towers. The third castle, Sasso Corbaro, (or Unterwalden) lies further from the 'old town' centre. South-east of Castello Montebello, it is best reached either from there by the windings of the Via Artore past houses and vineyards, or by Via Lugano, Via Hospedale and then by serpentine Via Sasso Corbaro to its height above the city. This castle is said to have been built by the Milanese forces in only 6 months in 1479 after the Confederates' victory at Giornico to block further Swiss advance south.

About 3km (2 miles) south of Bellinzona is industrial Giubiasco (also a railway junction) where entrance may be gained to the motorway south to Lugano; or, remaining on the cantonal road, there is soon a choice between continuing south or turning east to Locarno and its valleys.

Castello Montebello

The Locarno Valleys

Locarno is beautifully situated on a bay near the head of Lake Maggiore, sheltered from the north. Along with its satellite resort, the one time fishing village of Ascona, it is one of the two main tourist centres in the Ticino, with a pronounced southern type of climate and character. Even so, it has a hinterland of 'off the beaten track' interest, particularly in the lateral valleys to the west which present a striking contrast to the large lakeside resorts. Because of the half-circle of towering mountains to the west of Locarno, these valleys are short and steep sided, with impetuous water-courses. Valley populations for centuries lived a hard life on grudging soil. Depopulation in the present century has been precipitate, and many specialised crafts — such as straw-weaving — have died out. Some villages have been partly re-populated by townspeople taking over or converting rural cottages into holiday homes, or, in the nearer areas, improved roads have brought commuter residents in their wake.

Of all the valleys, the most secluded, and the one which has largely kept its wild original character, is the Val Verzasca. Travelling on the cantonal road No 13 which runs along the west side of the Ticino valley, whether coming from Bellinzona or Locarno, Gordola

Corippo, a compact Ticino mountain village in the central Verzasca valley

is the point at which to turn west into the valley. The road to Sonogno is only 25km (15^1/$_2$ miles) in length but is both varied and picturesque. It climbs sharply through vineyards giving backward views of the plain of Magadino (through which the river Ticino flows in the final stretch to Lake Maggiore). In tight bends it rises steeply through the inhospitable valley towards the great dam of the Verzasca, the Vogorno Lake, which feeds a hydro-electric power station. The road runs on through the vineyards on the slope above the lake's north shore following the twists of the lateral valleys, often through tunnel galleries. On the far shore Mergoscia village is seen on its picturesque terrace site. After passing through two villages there comes a view across the valley of Corippo village, its houses apparently stacked tightly and clinging to the terrace at its valley mouth. Within a kilometre (just over half a mile) a country side road branching across

Lavertezzo

the valley to the left gives the chance of making a brief 1.5km (1 mile) detour in the form of an ascent to **Corippo**, a village once noted for its linen weaving, and so characteristic of traditional patterns of building on its terrace site as to be declared a national monument. (The few settlements hereabout are either on terrace ledges or on alluvial deposits. Tourist infrastructure is scant.) After another 2km (just over a mile) comes a defile leading to **Lavertezzo**, a highlight of the valley, with its elegant late medieval double-arched bridge, the Ponte dei Salti, resting on rock set in the Verzasca's tumbling green waters, a remarkable memorial to medieval builders. (Lavertezzo, being a good centre for walking excursions into side valleys, is also quite well provided with *grotti* for catering). The road, running here in the confined valley bottom, allows a near view of the fantastic rock forms sculptured by the erosive power of the waters. Shortly after crossing to the other bank, the road climbs again to reach **Brione-Verzasca**, the main village of the valley, known for its granite quarries. The valley's most important parish church is here, St Maria Assunta, which is thirteenth century with later extensions. The façade has a larger than life fresco of St Cristoforo, the interior some fourteenth- to fifteenth-century frescoes in the Giotto style. On the square stands an imposing seventeenth-century fortified residence with corner towers and wall, and an interesting interior now accessible as a restaurant. Brione also offers rambles in the neighbour-

A spinner in Sonogno

hood, especially into the lonely Val d'Osola to the west, where many deserted *rustici* homes are witness to emigration from alpine husbandry. Seven kilometres (4 miles) further on, the post road ends at the mountain village of **Sonogno**, on level ground where the valley forks into two tributary branches, with well preserved, typical dry stone built valley houses. Here attempts have been made to arrest depopulation by reviving local handicrafts, including a home industry of wool spinning and knitting. A local museum exists in the Casa Genardini, open afternoons from July to September, which illustrates old-time valley life.

Val Maggia is a longer valley than its neighbour and differs from it by having a road of almost imperceptible gradient over its first 30km (18$^1/_2$ miles). Leaving Locarno to the west by the Via Vallemaggia, stay on the east bank at Ponte Brolla in 4km (2$^1/_2$ miles) (where

Cevio, at the entrance to the Campo valley

the Centovalli road crosses the bridge to the left). After a short defile the road enters the Maggia valley, wide but bounded by precipitous sides. In 9km (5$\frac{1}{2}$ miles), shortly before reaching **Maggia** village in its setting of meadows and vineyards, there is another famed Ticino church on the left, near a stone bridge. This is the chapel of St Maria della Grazia, with its painted wooden ceiling and interior frescoes from the sixteenth century as well as numerous *ex voto* offerings from the eighteenth. About halfway from Maggia to Cevio, the principal village of the valley, a most spectacular waterfall is to be seen across the river: the 91m-high (300ft) Soladino fall. The road crosses the river just where the beautiful Valle di Campo enters the Maggia from the left. **Cevio** has much of interest: as the valley administrative centre under Milanese rule and later under the Swiss Confederate governors (Landvogts), it has in the village square a three-storey Casa Pretorio (court house), showing the coats-of-arms of the Maggia villages and of Landvogts. Nearby is the former residence of the eighteenth-century governors, and many houses of prominent citizens of the same era, with wall paintings and fine gardens.

The picturesque Valle di Campo is a favourite excursion from the Maggia. The road into it corkscrews up in spectacular fashion from Cevio, and after some 5km (3 miles) reaches, at Cerentino, a road

Bosco-Gurin, Ticino's highest village

fork. The right hand branch climbs to the head of the tributary valley where the Ticino's highest village stands, at 1,503m (4,930ft), the road having climbed 915m (3,000ft) in 16km (10 miles). **Bosco Gurin's** inhabitants speak a German dialect (usually called Walser-deutsch), their thirteenth-century ancestors having crossed the mountains from canton Valais. As well as their language they have also preserved many customs and manners from the Valais. Their buildings too are reminiscent of canton Valais in style.

Bignasco, 3km (2 miles) upstream from Cevio, is sited where the Val Bavona joins the Maggia from the left, an attractive village with some quaint medieval corners. Even the right-hand valley now ceases to be known as Maggia and becomes Lavizzara, and the vines and chestnuts make way for alpine flora. For the next 16km (10 miles) the valley becomes wilder, narrower and steeper, finally zigzagging

The Froda di Foroglio waterfall in the Bavona valley

to where the mountain post road ends at Fusio, on a steep slope lying below the Lake Sambuco. **Fusio** shows a mixture of typical Ticino stone houses with outbuildings of timber, Gotthard style. It is a base from which climbers and mountain walkers taking the track past Lake Sambuco towards the Passo di Naret penetrate the mountain and lakeland plateau under the Cristallina massif, with the option of a round trip returning via the Robiei cablecar to San Carlo and the Val Bavona.

The Val Bavona is one of the most appealing alpine valleys, deep and wooded, and one of the few in which the settlements preserve an integrity of rural architecture. The modern road, constructed in connection with hydro-electric utilisation, has taken away a little of the romantic atmosphere. The road runs up it for 10km (6 miles) to the hamlet of **San Carlo** at its head, from which a cable railway runs to Robiei (2,000m, 6,560ft) between June and October. At the upper level are a subterranean hydro-electric station and a system of reservoir lakes.

For those without a car, these valleys can also be explored by the use of the Swiss postbus services (Official Timetable Nos 630. 60 for Verzasca; 630. 65, 630. 70 and 630. 72 for Maggia branches).

The Centovalli

The Val Centovalli differs from those already described in that it runs in the east-west direction. *Cento valli* means literally 'a hundred valleys' and the reference is to the numerous side valleys that run at right-angles into the valley of the river Melezza. It also differs by having a narrow-gauge electric railway running from Locarno up the valley, continuing beyond Camedo, the last Swiss station on the line, into Italy and ultimately to Domodossola, the main line station on the Milan-Stresa-Simplon line into Switzerland. (Locarno-Domodossola takes about $1^{3}/_{4}$ hours in a through train.) A road runs along the same valley all the way, providing motorists with an interesting link with the Simplon Pass road. However, a good sample of Centovalli landscape can be gained from an excursion without the use of a car:

Travel by the Centovalli train (avoiding the through train) from Locarno to the 'request stop' station of Verdasio, which takes about 35 minutes. From Verdasio a cablecar runs to Rasa, which lies on the shaded side of the valley which in summer is an advantage. From the cablecar station at Rasa turn left (ie east), leaving the village on the old mule track which leads down through a wooded stretch to an extensive clearing. The track reaches a steep, tree-clad ridge that drops down toward the river Melezza. On it you pass broad meadows, and then taking the exit from the glen find your way down to the Melezza at Corcapolo, a railway station further east, from where the footpath continues along the banks of the river — a particularly attractive walk — to Intragna. The walk takes about 2 hours. Each of the villages is worth a visit: **Rasa** has preserved unspoiled its charac-

River Melezza in the Centovalli, Ticino

Gandria, Lake Lugano

A view of the Sciora mountains from Soglio in the Bondasca valley

Intragna

ter of a Ticinese hill village with its almost monumental stone buildings and roofs, and **Intragna** is a charming old town in a particularly
romantic setting, surrounded by vineyards and having spectacular
bridges, gorges and rock tunnels. Not far from the village is a 91m
(300ft) span railway bridge at a height of 70m (230ft) above the river
Isorno. From Intragna return to Locarno by train.

The Gambarogno

It would be hard to find a greater contrast to the sophisticated resorts of Ascona/Locarno than the opposite, south shores of the head of Lake Maggiore. The Gambarogno district, lying between the mouth of the river Ticino and the Italian frontier, is a particularly unspoilt example of old-world Ticino — and its very name rarely occurs in English language guide books. The stretch along the lake shore is not particularly remarkable. The interest is in the hinterland and offers a suitable short excursion for motorists. It can also be covered by a postbus service (No 630. 80) from Locarno; and from Bellinzona by train on the Bellinzona-Luino regional line (Timetable 631) in under 20 minutes, to the Magadino-Vira station, and by bus from there.

From Locarno by car the route is by the regional road towards Bellinzona, but turning right at Gordola as if for the airport. After crossing the flat Magadino plain and the river Ticino, turn right onto the road which follows the south bank of the lake, through Magadino village (for centuries a transhipment point for trade goods crossing the Alps) to the village of **Vira** with its pleasant lake front and fishing haven. The countryside is lush and fertile with vineyards in abundance and cherries, apricots, peaches and figs testifying to the subtropical climate of the terraces on the gentle slopes of Monte Gambarogno. From Vira, leaving the shore off to the left, is a road that climbs to a village uniquely remote, though only 15km (9 miles) distant. The road first climbs steeply to **Fosano** with its little chapel and an incomparable viewpoint over the lake to Locarno and valleys. Then the zigzagging road (which is said to have 250 windings and thirty-seven hairpin bends), turns along Monte Gambarogno's flanks and winds over the Alpe di Neggia that lies between Monte Gambarogno (1,734m, 5,688ft) and Monte Tamaro (1,952m, 6,403ft) and finally winds downhill to **Indemini** which lies right on the Italian border at the head of the Veddasca valley. It is a good example of an unspoiled traditional Ticinese mountain village with houses of undressed stone and massive stone-slab roofs. The lie of the land would put the village geographically in the Veddasca valley belonging to Italy. In fact it has always been part of the Locarno district of Swiss Ticino. The road was only built during World War I, because with Italy a combatant the village had been cut off from the rest of Val Veddasca. More recently it has suffered sadly from depopulation.

Travellers using public transport might care to consider doing the final stage of the return journey to Locarno by lake steamer from Vira or Magadino (checking Official Timetable 2630), while those using

Vira, in the Gambarogno, facing Locarno, Lake Maggiore

private cars might think on the return journey of visiting the nature conservancy zone, beyond Magadino village, known as the Bolle di Magadino. It lies on the delta zone between the outfalls of the rivers Verzasca and Ticino and the plant and rare bird life on such a site and in such a climate is unique in Europe.

Lugano and its Lake

Lugano, and the lake which in English bears its name (though the locals know it as Ceresio), lie south of a natural barrier, Monte Ceneri, between them and the river Ticino's valley floor in which lie Bellinzona and Locarno. Through the ages a very clear distinction was made between the northern Ticino, or Sopra-Ceneri, as they call it, and the south, or Sotto-Ceneri. The barrier mass of Ceneri presents its steep rock face to the north and shows a more gradual slope taking the form of a long trough to the south — the Val Vedeggio — a zone that was for centuries outwith the full control of law, scene of tales of robber bands who preyed on wayfarers. (In the eighteenth century, when a famous market was sited at Lugano, the Ceneri Pass was posted with soldiers to protect the passage of traders during the market period). Today, although Lugano, one of Europe's most sophisticated small cities and a resort to which well-to-do northerners flock to find spring at its earliest, is the very antithesis of 'off the beaten track', it is nevertheless a centre from which to reach many places that take one back to the 'little old-style world' described in Fogazzaro's great Italian classic *Il Piccolo Mondo Antico*. This applies even to the valleys immediately south of Monte Ceneri through which tourists usually hasten to reach the lake.

An example is quite a short round trip that can be made from Tesserete, principal village of the Cassarate valley and situated about half way between Monte Ceneri summit and Lugano, but lying a few kilometres to the east of main road and rail. **Tesserete** itself, with some 1,300 inhabitants, is set among trees and meadows and is a popular excursion centre, with several hotels and holiday homes where accommodation is less expensive than in the lakeside city. From Lugano main station it can be reached by road via the picturesque villages of Vezio and Cureglia, normally turning right at the fork after the latter. On a sightseeing excursion, however, it would be well to go first straight on to **Ponte Capriasca**. Its sixteenth-to seventeenth-century parish church of St Ambrose is famed among art scholars as possessing the best preserved copy (better than the original) of Leonardo da Vinci's famous *Last Supper*. Tesserete's own church of St Stefano is one of the Ticino's rare examples of the Gothic

A view of Lugano and the Monte Salvatore from the Cassarate valley

style, only the seven-storey campanile surviving from its Romanesque predecessor. There are fine paintings and carvings in a richly decorated interior. Little more than a kilometre (half a mile) northwest lies a romantic little village with narrow, cobblestoned alleys — **Bigorio** — which has on the hill above it what may have been the first Capuchin monastery founded on Swiss soil. To the east of Tesserete opens up the entrance to the Val Colla, a narrow wooded valley, formerly one of the most inaccessible in the Sotto-Ceneri and only reached by road in 1950. The road to **Bidogno**, with its picturesque peasant houses often seemingly glued vertically to the precipice, keeps high up on the steep north hillside with a view at times down to Lugano and the lake. The steady climb continues, past hamlets clinging to the hillside, each with its baroque church, and after 13km (8 miles) of steep curves, rises in a more open valley to **Bogno**, a handful of houses and a *grotto* at the foot of steep Monte Garzirola. The return route twists along the south side of the valley, passing roads to tiny hamlets, until — nearly opposite Tesserete — **Sonvico** is reached. A substantial town of 1,300 inhabitants, in charming surroundings, this was once a place of some importance, where

Roman and medieval remains (including fortified walls) have been excavated. In the square there is a Governors' Residence (Casa dei Landvogti) with façade paintings of the imperial eagle and of cantonal arms. Its attractive neighbourhood makes it an excellent base for excursions, including mountain climbing. The return to Lugano is by way of Cadro and Dino. From **Dino** there is a splendid view over Lugano and the bay below.

The above tour can also be substantially carried out by the use of the postbus mountain road service, but would involve changing buses, ie, Lugano-to-Tesserete changing to Tesserete-to-Bogno, then Bogno via Maglio di Colla to Sonvico, after lunch at the *grotto* in Bogno (Official Timetable numbers 633. 28; 633. 30; 633. 33; 633. 35; 633. 37).

Incidentally, in the Val Capriasca area a simple 'family walk' of little more than an hour's duration can be recommended for its interest. It too can be reached from Lugano (and its suburbs) by postbus (Line 633. 28). Dismount at **Origlio Paese**, ie, the village stop. The picturesque village itself is well worth a walk around, its houses having typical loggias and inner courtyards, and it is only 5 minutes' walk to Lake Origlio, which is very unspoilt, surrounded by reeds and chestnut trees, and now a breeding place for rare birds. Keep to the right bank, following the good footpath — again lined with chestnut trees — through vineyards to Cureglia, where the same bus line can be caught for the return to Lugano.

Mendrisiotto

South-east of Lugano and its lake is the Mendrisiotto district which forms the 'tip' of the Ticino's 'arrowhead' map outline. A broad, fertile basin, it is at once the most industrialised region of Ticino and the most productive in agriculture. At one time the centre of mulberry culture for the silk industry, it now specialises in textiles, tobacco and food and is the great home of the Merlot wine-grape. In climate, architecture and vegetation it is already like a part of Lombardy. From Lugano it is approached by the route which carries the heaviest tourist traffic in the country — the great causeway (*ponte diga* they call it), first built in 1844-7, which now carries the main railway, national road and also motorway across Lake Lugano. (The national road leaves Lugano via the suburb of Paradiso for the causeway. The motorway, having bypassed the city to its west, tunnels under the ridge of Monte Salvatore — Lugano's southern 'sentinel' — to the causeway.) Roads and rail swing south after Bissone on the far bank.

Brusino Arsizio, between Lake Lugano and Monte San Giorgio

Bissone, despite such road and rail neighbours, has managed to preserve its stylish old arcaded centre and its showpiece patrician mansion, Tencalla, of AD1600, furnished in the style of its period, still lived in, but open in the afternoons to the public. From Bissone, 2km (just over a mile) uphill to the left on a terrace on the slopes of Monte Generoso, is **Rovio**, a hamlet in which time seems to have stood still: cobblestoned alleys, peasant houses with tiled roofs, fresco-decorated walls, and further uphill an eleventh-century chapel of art-historical importance.

Capolago is reached shortly, lying at the head of the south-east 'horn' of the lake. Here is the bottom station of the cog railway to Monte Generoso (1,701m, 5,579ft). A kilometre (just over half a mile) west of Capolago is **Riva San Vitale** which, just off its main square, possesses a unique treasure, Switzerland's oldest ecclesiastical building, an early Christian baptistery of around AD500; in the centre of the original floor is an octagonal basin for immersion. Turn north now along the lakeside, round the flanks of the wooded mass of Monte San Giorgio (1,100m, 3,608ft.) In 7km (4 miles) **Brusino Arsizio** is reached with an impressive view of Morcote on the opposite shore of the lake. Here is the starting point of a cablecar to **Serpiano**, a resort on a terrace (645m, 2,116ft) of Monte San Giorgio. It can also be reached by postbus from Mendrisio (Line 637.10, a 30 minute journey, and then the cablecar down to Brusino Arsizio can provide a round trip of considerable interest by public transport; for there is also a regular bus service between Brusino and Mendrisio via Riva San Vitale operated by Autolinea Mendrisiense (Line 637.18; for information ☎ 091 43 33 86).

There is yet another way of using the postbus service to Monte San Giorgio, so as to take in an interesting walk of some 4 hours duration. From **Mendrisio** (chief town of the district) take the bus only as far as **Meride**, a village well worth a visit. It is a conservancy area and a national heritage for its lovely setting and unspoiled village character with alleys, squares and houses with inner courtyards and loggias. In the middle of the village is a fossil museum with petrified specimens of prehistoric creatures and skeletons of saurians (of which Monte San Giorgio is considered one of the richest sources in the world). From Meride there is a nature trail on an easy and well marked ascent up Monte San Giorgio, with signposts at intervals giving information on the geology, plants and animals. At the best viewing points are panoramic charts; the peak provides a splendid view of Ceresio and Lugano.

Ceresio and Malcantone

Tourists who have reached Brusino Arsizio with private transport can continue further west round the shores of Lake Lugano provided they have passports with them, as the lake shores are in some places Italian, in others Swiss. A Swiss-Italian frontier is 2.5km (1½ miles) west of Brusino. And 2km (just over a mile) beyond that is **Porto Ceresio**, small resort on a bay at the foot of Monte Grumello, calling-place for lake steamers between Lugano and Ponte Tresa, and terminal of a regional railway to Varese and Milan. Trains on the Porto Ceresio line to Milan reach Varese, the administrative centre of the Italian province of that name, in 22 minutes. It makes an interesting excursion to travel by lake steamer from, say, Lugano to Porto Ceresio and take a regional train to Varese, a good town for shopping and sightseeing.

The pier at Porto Ceresio, looking across to Morcote

From Porto Ceresio the road passes the railway station (opposite the steamer-pier) keeping to the shore, with a good view over the lake to Morcote, dominated by its Madonna del Sasso church on the slopes of Monte Arbostora. The road continues in curves to **Brusimpiano**, a fishing village looking across to Figino on the Swiss shore. In the background are the hills of the Malcantone. Turning the promontory Punta della Fava, the gulf of Agno is opposite. Shortly, on the shore to the right, is Lavena, which lies on the narrow strait formed by the peninsula of Monte Caslano projecting from the Swiss side. The Italian and Swiss shores are only a stone's throw apart at this point, and it is fascinating to navigate the little strait aboard the lake steamer to and from Ponte Tresa.

Beyond these narrows there is enclosed a circular stretch of water about 1km (just over half a mile) in diameter, along the shore of which runs the road to **Ponte Tresa**, for long an important transit point. The river Tresa, leaving the basin of the lake, divides the town into two parts: the nucleus lying on the south, ie Italian side, linked to the Swiss side by a modern bridge which is an important customs station.

From Ponte Tresa two roads run west, one on the Italian, one on the Swiss bank of the river, to **Luino**, an Italian town on Lake Maggiore famed for its weekly Wednesday market which occupies

Cademario

virtually all the central part of the fairly large town.

Turning right however, the Swiss cantonal road from Ponte Tresa heads north towards the district known as the Malcantone, first cutting across the neck of the Caslano peninsula and in little more than 2km (just over a mile) reaching Magliasina. Turn off to the left here on the minor road for the Malcantone, held by many to be the most beautiful district in the canton in respect of the integrity of landscape, rural architecture and way of life. It occupies roughly the rectangle between the western arm of Lake Lugano and the mountain ridge which includes Monte Lema and forms the Italian boundary on the west. It has a complicated network of twisting and intersecting country roads; but perhaps the route best adopted to see the most interesting corners starts at **Pura**, 1km (just over half a mile) from the Magliasina turn off, a particularly pretty country resort with lots of attractive and easy walks and rare flowers to be seen. Next is **Novaggio**, with vineyards and typical loggias and porticos to the houses. Here a road goes off left for Astano, a hill-resort with many attractive country houses. (This was the birthplace of another Ticinese architect-builder, the Trezzini who in the early eighteenth century helped to build St Petersburg in the reign of Peter I). The same branch road (which is also a nature trail) drops down with many twists and contortions (near the Italian frontier) to **Sessa** which was once the chief town of the district and has many interesting things to see, such as a fifteenth-century winepress, a Governors' Residence in the square, and woodcarvings in the church.

Having made this detour to visit Sessa, it is worthwhile to return to Novaggio and continue on the road going north to **Miglieglia**. This pleasant village, interesting for the excellent condition of the late Gothic wall paintings in its upper church, is also the station for a chairlift to the peak of Monte Lema (1,621m, 5,317ft).

The top of Monte Lema is a wide grass-covered plateau — a good skiing area. Ticino's best viewpoint gives an impressive panorama of Valais, Bernese and Grisons Alps as well as Malcantone and the lakes of Lugano and Maggiore. A well laid and marked path leads walkers down to Miglieglia.

The road continues to Breno, where a right-hand fork twists down to cross the Magliasino river and climbs to **Cademario**, an important climatic health resort with a spa-hotel centre and botanic garden, open to non-residents. This has a good postbus service from Lugano (Line 633.15). From Cademario the road curves down to **Bioggio** (noted for good local wines) in the Val Vedeggio from which, on one or other of the main roads, a return is readily made to Lugano or any other base-resort.

Further Information
— Ticino —

Festivals

Bellinzona
Open-air risotto feast, August; Shrovetide carnival and procession, February.

Biasca
Carnival procession and risotto feast, Shrovetide Saturday; Choral Festival, May; Festival in *grotti* above village, June.

Museums and Other Places of Interest

Note: many of the places of interest 'off the beaten track' are villages of small population; consequently they do not always find it possible to man, for instance, local folk museums for the number of hours that would be taken for granted in a larger town. However, they usually take it as a compliment if visitors interested in their community's art treasures, village church or other places of interest take the trouble to enquire where keys, caretakers or a guide may be found. Even when opening hours are stated it is as well to check the hours by telephone if your visit involves travel.

Bellinzona
Castello Grande
Open: daily except Monday.

Castello di Montebello
Houses Civic Museum of History
and Archaeology.
Open: daily except Monday.

Castello di Sasso Corbaro
Houses Ticino Museum of Arts,
Crafts and Folk Traditions.
Open: March to October daily
9am-12noon and 2-5pm.

Bissone
Casa Tencalla
Museum showing patrician lifestyle in baroque period.
Open: daily 2-6pm.

Bolle di Magadino
Nature conservancy area on river
Ticino delta.
Guided boat trips Monday and
Thursday pm.
Details: Ente Turistico Gambarogno.

Bosco-Gurin
Museum Walserhaus
☎ 093//96 15 80
Lifestyle and history of unique
community.
Open: May to October daily except
Monday 9-11am and 2-5pm, Sundays 2-5pm

Cevio
Antica Casa Franzoni
Maggia Museum
Open: April to October, daily
except Monday 9.30am-12noon
and 2-6pm, Sundays 2-6pm.

Disentis
Benedictine Abbey

☎ 086/7 51 45
Culture-historical exhibition
Due to open 1989.

Giornico
Casa Stanga
Leventine Valley Museum
☎ (custodian) 092/74 24 01
Open: Easter Monday to end
October, Saturdays and holidays.

Leontica
San Carlo Church
Keys from restaurants in Leontica
and Prugiasco.

Lottigna
Casa dei Landvogti
Local History Museum of Blenio
Valley
Open: Easter to end October daily
except Monday 2-5pm, also 10am-
12noon Saturdays, Sundays and
holidays.

Meride
Town Hall (Municipo)
Fossil Museum
☎ 091/46 37 12
Collection of fossilised animals and
plants from local excavations on
Monte San Giorgio.
Open: daily 8am-6pm.

Olivone
Museum in typical Gotthard-style
house, Ca da Rivoi: traditions and
local lifestyle.
Open: Easter to end October daily
except Monday 2-5pm, also 10am-
12noon Saturdays, Sundays and
holidays.

Sonogno
Casa Genardini
Local Museum

☎ 093/31 85 46
Open: July to September 1.30-
4.30pm daily. Exhibits on local
crafts and agriculture, utensils,
costumes.

Sports

Airolo
Climbing, angling (permits from
local authority office), *boccia*,
winter sports. Starting point for
hiking and hill walking excursions
in Bedretto, Leventina and Blenio
valley. Details from Ente Turistico
Faido.

Special cycling project:
contact main line SBB-FFS station
for cycle hire between Airolo and
Biasca.
☎ 094/88 12 22

Bellinzona
Rock Climbing, fishing, tennis,
horseriding, ice-rink in winter.
Details from Ente Turistico Bellinzona.

Biasca
Fishing, horseriding, tennis, *boccia*,
canoeing: details from Ente Turistico Biasca; Riviera Gymkhana,
September.

Meride
Nature trail over Monte San Giorgio
(7km, 4 miles) begins at St Silvestro
parish church. Information boards
at ten different points.

Olivone
Hill walking, climbing, skiing.
Information from Ente Turistico
Blenio.

Tourist Information Offices

For general tourist information the
Swiss National Tourist Offices
(SNTO), whether at national,
cantonal or local level, are models
of efficiency and helpfulness.
Cantonal office:
Ente Ticinese per il Turismo
Villa Turrita
Casella Postale 1441
CH-6501 Bellinzona
☎ 092/25 70 56

District Tourist Boards:
Ente Turistico Bellinzona e dintorni
CH-6500 Bellinzona
☎ 092/25 21 31

Ente Turistico Biasca e Riviera
CH-6710 Biasca
☎ 092/72 33 27

Ente Turistico Blenio
CH-6716 Acquarossa
☎ 092/78 17 65

Ente Turistico Gambarogno
CH-6574 Vira
☎ 093/61 18 66

Ente Turistico Leventina
CH-6760 Faido
☎ 094/38 16 16

Ente Turistico Locarno e Valli
CH-6600 Locarno
☎ 093/31 86 33

Ente Turistico Lugano e dintorni
CH-6901 Lugano
☎ 091/21 46 64

Ente Turistico Malcantone
CH-6987 Caslano
☎ 091/71 29 86

Ente Turistico Mendrisiotto e B.
Ceresio
CH-6850 Mendrisio
☎ 091/46 57 61

Ente Turistico Tenero e Valle
Verzasca
CH-6598 Tenero
☎ 093/67 16 61

Ente Turistico Vallemaggia
CH-6673 Maggia
☎ 093/87 18 85

Ente Turistico Valli di Lugano
CH-6950 Tesserete
☎ 091/91 18 88

9 • Tours Over the Ticino Borders

L ake Lugano (Ceresio) is shared by Italy and Switzerland; of its surface area very slightly over half is Swiss, the rest Italian. It adds to the atmosphere of some cruises on board a boat of the Lake Navigation Company's fleet that customs officers board the vessel at the first landing stage after a border crossing. And any circular tour on dry land that takes in a fair circuit of the lake inevitably crosses frontiers. There is one of particular interest because of the great variety of landscapes and experiences it includes in an afternoon circuit:

Leave Lugano by way of Castagnola and the Via Riviera, climbing round the steep flank of Monte Bre (the eastern of Lugano's two sentinel hills), passing at a level above the former fishing village of **Gandria**, picturesquely built on terraces overhanging the lake. Very shortly the Swiss-Italian frontier is reached with its customs controls. A rock-cut galleried section of road follows, and then **Oria,** the first Italian hamlet, tightly grouped round the church. Near the church and facing the lake is the house where the classic Italian novelist Fogazzaro lived.

The first substantial village is **San Mamete,** in a fine position at the mouth of the Val Solda, with its pretty square open to the lake front and narrow alleyways running off it; the parish church is above, with its tall bell-tower and spire. (Mamete was head village of the Val Solda, which for long had independent status under the protection of the archbishops of Milan.) From here ascents can be made to the Denti della Vecchia peak (1,500m, 4,920ft). A pleasant stretch of olive trees and greenery follows, then a bare rocky one, before Porlezza is reached at the north-east head of the lake, sited on the delta of a seasonal stream, the Rezza. Across the basin of the lake, at the opening to the glen of the same name, Osteno can be seen. Take the road heading in that direction, turning off right. In 4km (2¹/₂ miles) is the site of the Rescia caves with stalactites and stalagmites and a fine waterfall, and another 2km (just over a mile) on is **Osteno**, an isolated village on the delta of the river Telo which flows from the plateau of the Val d'Intelvi.

After Osteno the road leaves the lake and rises in bends into the pleasant Val d'Osteno, soon reaching a crest which separates the catchment of the river Telo from that of the Livone. In a further 12km (7¹/₂ miles), is **Laino**, a little resort set among meadows and woods, with barely five hundred inhabitants. Its most famous son was one of the first architects of Milan cathedral and later of Como, (only one of the countless instances in this region of great building craftsmen, stucco-workers, stonemasons and architects making a name for themselves throughout Europe.)

Soon the road joins the one coming over from Argegno on Lake Como. At this junction a right turn leads to Pellio, and as the road continues beyond that village there is a view of Lake Lugano with Porlezza in the background. The road then crosses a seasonal torrent, the Mora, and (disregard the side road to the right) starts to climb again, passing below **Scaria d'Intelvi**, the home of another distinguished family of architects and sculptors, the Carlonis (to whom there is a local museum in the parish church, which also has examples of their work in frescoes and stucco-work). The climb continues to the plateau where Lanzo is situated, passing on the right the road leading in 3km (2 miles) to the funicular upper station for Santa Margherita where there is a fine panorama of the lake. **Lanzo d'Intelvi** is then reached in 2km (just over a mile). This is the main centre of the valley and a climatic resort of some importance, with many villas and well equipped with amenities, in its sheltered position on the tableland, girt with woodlands. The road to Monte Sighignola shortly goes off to the left, climbing through chestnut trees then beeches to the 1,302m (4,271ft) summit in 6km (4 miles), where at the Swiss-Italian border there is extensive open space, parking facilities, a restaurant and a sweeping panorama taking in Monte Generoso, the bays at Porto Ceresio and Ponte Tresa as well as Lugano and the nearer lake surrounds.

From the summit the return is by the same road as far as Pellio. There, instead of turning off left for Osteno (the outward route) remain on the road for Argegno on Lake Como. Within 2km (just over a mile) the watershed between Lake Lugano and Lake Como is met near San Fedele, another summer resort. Other hill resorts are passed on the way down the serpentine road that leads through a

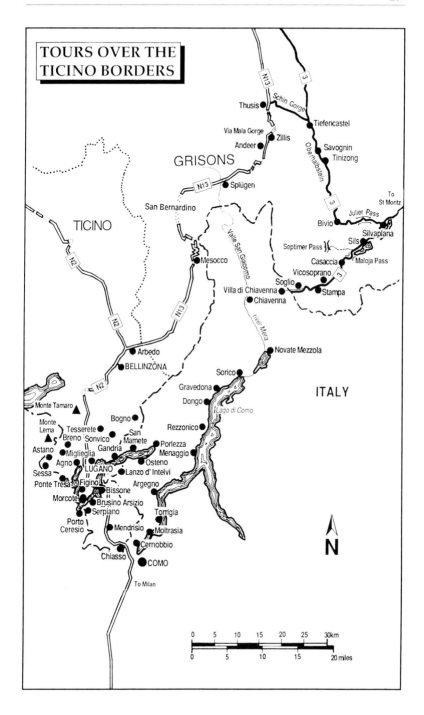

TOURS OVER THE
TICINO BORDERS

Gandria, typical old fishers' village on Lake Lugano

pleasant valley to reach Argegno, where it joins the National Road 340 (the Strada Regia) that runs along the fairly bare and sparsely inhabited west bank of Lake Como towards Cernobbio and the city of Como. In about 7km (4 miles) at Torrigia, near the lake's narrowest part, a twin-lane bypass alternative to the coast road branches off to run higher up the hillside, cut into the rock face. It gives panoramic views of the lake, while the old road is boxed in by villas and garden walls. The two roads reunite north of Cernobbio, passing shortly the famed Villa d'Este, which was built for Cardinal Gallio in 1589 and has since then passed through the hands of many notable owners, including Caroline, Princess of Wales. It became a hotel last century. It is famed for its formal parks, gardens and fountains and for the art treasures it houses. **Cernobbio** itself is a resort of distinction, as well as having a textile industry. From Cernobbio the road turns off along the Valle Breggia to **Chiasso**, a frontier town and one of Europe's busiest customs control posts for road traffic. From here the motorway encourages a swift return to Lugano (24km, 15 miles). But if time permits, or an overnight stay is contemplated in one of the towns in the Mendrisiotto, this tour could continue into the excursion through that district.

Porlezza

Tourists who prefer to use public transport can carry out the excursion just described on certain days during the summer season from Lugano. Details, which may vary according to season, are available from Postbus Services, Via San Balestra, Lugano, ☎ (091) 21 95 20.

The Grisons

When the time comes for the homeward journey some travellers enjoy retracing their steps, to see the ground traversed on the outward trip from the opposite angle; others seek to avoid this and return by an entirely different route. For those who have travelled into the Ticino by the Gotthard route, alternatives are available for the return north. Some may choose to reserve for this stage the exploration of the Blenio valley and the Lukmanier Pass route (described in the Ticino chapter) in reverse. Another interesting route which is not uncommonly adopted is to leave the Ticino by travelling west from Locarno by the Centovalli route, whether by road or rail, into Italy at Domodossola, and from there via the Simplon Pass route to Brig and the Rhône valley leading to Lake Geneva.

Less common, but very interesting in its variety, is to leave the

Ticino by travelling north-east and taking the chance of sampling the different landscape and atmosphere of the large neighbouring canton which English speakers usually call by its French name, the Grisons. (Although, in fact, French is not one of the mother tongues in that canton; these are German, Italian and the several dialects of Romansch, a language distinct from Italian yet descended from the vernacular Latin once spoken there when it was part of a Roman province. The canton's name in German is Graubünden, in Italian Grigioni and in Romansch Grishun.) Its mountainous nature and the isolation of its high valleys until comparatively modern times, give a clue both to the survival of the Romansch language in this region and to its historical isolation for many centuries. The Grisons was the eighteenth canton to come into the Swiss Confederation, in 1803.

In area it is the largest canton of all, but the most thinly populated, being predominantly mountainous. Paradoxically, although some of its individual villages and towns figure prominently among the names of well known and indeed fashionable Swiss resorts, such as St Moritz, Davos and Arosa, yet the great variety of landscape and atmosphere to be found in the canton as a whole is not so well known to the average English speaking traveller as are the areas of Central Switzerland, the Bernese Oberland or the Lake Geneva region. Two-thirds of its frontiers bound with Italy and Austria. Its alpine passes have been of great importance historically; yet its own economic resources have been poor until, in modern times, tourism (which accounts for 50 per cent of its income) and hydro-electric power generation made their contribution.

This route will be described in an extended form that will enable it to be used either as a 'round trip' excursion from the Ticino and returning there, or as a variant route for a 'homeward' return northwards and consequently broken off at an appropriate point.

The route from the Ticino again begins by way of Gandria, the Italian frontier, and San Mamete to Porlezza at the head of the lake. (Having passport formalities in mind, it should be noted that the route starts with an extensive and interesting passage through Italian territory). From Porlezza, instead of turning south round the lake shore, take the main road across the isthmus to Lake Como, 12km (7^1/$_2$ miles) away. The road passes the little glacial Lake Piano before rising over the watershed and then descending in curves (which offer a wide view over Lake Como and the surrounding mountains), through vineyards and orchards to **Menaggio**, a lively holiday and commercial centre. Many of its houses are decorated with popular fifteenth- and sixteenth-century wall painting themes. There soon follows a stretch of tunnelled road-galleries and a picturesque road with many rather breathtaking bends. In 7km (4 miles) is **Rezzonico** with a former castle on the right-hand side of the road, now a private residence but with one of the towers and part of the defensive wall surviving. The next stretch is sparsely inhabited, with only a few hamlets. The road then runs at a slight elevation above the lake giving a view to the towns ahead.

Dongo is one of the few industrial centres in the area — a survivor of a former tradition of working iron ore hereabout, although the ore mines have long been closed down. The town's name features in modern history books as the place where, in the public square on 28 April 1945, leading Fascists who escorted Benito Mussolini on his attempted flight to Switzerland were taken and summarily shot.

Gravedona, 3km (2 miles) further on, commonly rated as the most attractive place on the north arm of Como, is a historic old town. Its fifteenth- and sixteenth-century goldsmiths had an international reputation. Today it has paper and textile industries. From Gravedona the road runs round the head of the lake past the small village of **Sorico**, last place on the north shore of the lake. (It is perhaps worth observing that, at this top end of Lake Como, there are a fair number of seasonal camp sites.)

As the road crosses the mountain torrent of Sorico there is a good view of a fine waterfall on the left. The road then runs a short distance upstream of the river Mera, flowing into the lake from the north, swings then to the right and crosses the river. Disregarding the road leading ahead, half-right, for the entrance to the Valtellina, take the left fork which links with the Italian National Road No 36 leading north to Chiavenna. This road, running alongside the railway line, passes along the eastern shore of the Lake of Mezzola, formed by the Mera river here, and shortly reaches the small town of **Novate Mezzola**. Here, on the bank of the river near large granite quarries, stands a little church of great antiquity, going back to the eleventh to twelfth centuries and with frescoes that probably date from the eleventh. By this point the valley is more than 2km (just over a mile) wide and from now on is generally known as the Chiavenna plain; it is farmed largely in pasturage and in maize, with some fish-farming. The view ahead is of the Pizzo Stella (3,163m, 10,375ft) which dominates the right-angled junction of the Bregaglia valley (down which the river Mera runs east-west) with the San Giacomo valley (in which it runs north-south). At Cassiano the road swings round the spurs of Pizzo di Prata (2,727m, 8,945ft). Thereafter the valley is more narrow and stark, shut in by rocks and scrub. To the right is the village of Prata Camportàccio and a hydro-electric station. About 23km (14 miles) from the head of Lake Como is **Chiavenna**, a town of around 5,000 inhabitants, lying on the banks of the river Mera at the junction of the valleys, and overhung by precipitous mountains. It is a commercial and industrial centre (producing cotton goods, skis, and food products) but also a tourist centre. Some derive its name from the Latin *clavis*, a key, with allusion to its strategic position commanding the Splügen, Septimer, Maloja and Julier alpine passes; there is certainly evidence that it was a Roman post of some importance. During the sixteenth to eighteenth centuries it was subject to the Grisons, later in the dominion of France and of Austria, and finally united to Italy in 1859. Its significance is reflected in some handsome seventeenth-century patrician residences, an impressive old quarter to the town, and the handsome parish church of St Lorenzo, of Romanesque origin, the baptistry of which possesses a twelfth-century monolithic font sculptured with primitive but expressive figures in half-relief.

It is worth observing that the neighbourhood of Chiavenna is noted for the prevalence of *grotti* — those local gastronomic and social places of resort which owe their origin to natural cellar-caves which store wines, cheese and sausage at a proper temperature (see Ticino chapter).

It is possible, however, to bypass Chiavenna, crossing (left) the river Mera to its north bank and taking the road for St Moritz, Italian National Road No 38 (which becomes N3 after the Italian-Swiss frontier.) The valley in which the road runs is known as the Bregaglia valley as far as the Maloja Pass, (after which it is called the Upper Engadin valley). The Bregaglia (or Bregell to the German speaking Swiss) lies almost entirely in Switzerland; its inhabitants are largely of Italian stock and protestant religion, speaking a Lombard dialect with some Romansch. Drained by the river Mera, its landscape has picturesque variety — chestnut trees at low level, meadows and coniferous forests on the heights, surrounded by high mountains with short glaciers in the high valley-junctions.

Such is the valley into which the road starts to climb from Chiavenna. On the valley floor vines and chestnut trees flourish, overlooked by bare but elegant peaks. Within a few kilometres, just before Borgonovo village, there is an attractive waterfall with two branches on the left, while on the right lies the massive landslip — now covered with chestnut woods — which in 1618 fell from Monte Conto after a deluge of rain and entirely buried the village of Piuro, killing 1,200 people.

Bregaglia valley

Running in the valley floor among chestnut groves and vine-yards, the road, after 7.5km (4¹/₂ miles) enters the last Italian village, **Villa di Chiavenna**. At this point the river opens into an artificial lake feeding two power stations. (The treasure of the parish church here is a processional cross of chased silver made by Venetian silver-smiths in 1671.) Almost 3km (2 miles) further on is the frontier and customs post, at the beginning of the village of Castasegna. At the next village, Spino, a side road goes off to the left which makes a worthwhile detour. It leads, after 3.5km (2 miles) of climbing through turns, to **Soglio**, nearly 300m (984ft) higher, a particularly picturesque village situated on a level terrace amid woodlands of fir and larch with a spectacular panorama back over the main valley to the granite peaks appearing over the glacier in the Bondasca valley, away to the south of the main valley. Rising above the compact outlines of the tightly grouped village houses in Soglio are a number of distinguished mansions of the sixteenth and seventeenth centu-ries built by members of the powerful Salis family. One of these mansions is now a hotel.

The main valley road shortly crosses to the south bank of the river Mera and reaches the village of **Promontogno** in its sheltered site at the mouth of the Val Bondasca. Soon a gallery takes the road under

Soglio

a crag on which is perched the church of Our Lady (Chiesa di Nossa Donna) abandoned in the mid-sixteenth century and restored in the mid-nineteenth; and the tower of Castelmur where there was once a Roman post and where excavations have revealed remains of bath-houses and living quarters. After passing through coniferous woodland the road reaches the upper part of the Bregaglia, fairly level pastureland. Piz Duan (3,131m, 10,270ft) towers on the left. Soon **Stampa** village is reached, a holiday resort which enjoys stupendous panoramic views of the jagged peaks to the south. In a former patrician mansion is a very informative museum devoted to Bregaglia ways of life.

Swiss geographers tell us that there is a spot on a ridge between two of these peaks in the Stampa district at a height of just over 2,700m (8,856ft) above sea level that is the roof-ridge of Europe; if rain drops fall there, it is a matter of chance whether they finally finish up in the North Sea, the Mediterranean or the Black Sea — depending on whether they roll north-west into the catchment of the Rhine, or south into a torrent that will carry them to Lake Como and the river Po, or downhill north-east into a stream that will join the river Inn and ultimately the Danube.

After Stampa there is a straight stretch with impressive views of Piz Bacun (3,244m, 10,640ft). Then **Vicosoprano** is reached, main place of the valley, holiday and excursions centre, with a sixteenth-century town house. Another straight stretch of road follows and then comes a series of climbing turns onto level, green pastureland. By the time **Casaccia** is reached the road is nearly 457m (1,500ft) above sea level; this village is situated below the ruins of the Castle of Turatsch and at the mouth of the Marozzo valley from which the river Mera flows. Next to be noted on the left are the picturesque ruins of the pilgrimage church of St Gaudentius, which was destroyed in the troubled early eighteenth century.

At Casaccia the mule-track road over the Septimer Pass (2,310m, 7,577ft) to Bivio goes off to the left. This track goes up through the woods, zigzagging an ascent into the Marozzo valley and ultimately (after approximately 4 hours walking) reaches the Septimer Pass, which was used by the Romans and still shows traces of the paved road in places.

Back on the road, Maloja now comes into sight with, directly ahead, the Castello del Belvedere on the brink of the precipice. The road starts up in the valley of the Orlegna torrent, but meeting the obstacle of a cliff-like step in the valley floor has to surmount this in a sequence of thirteen steep hairpin bends cut into the face. (Half way up these hairpins a path goes off to the gorge and waterfall of the Orlegna.) At 5km (3 miles) beyond Casaccia — and 360m (1,181ft) higher — is the pass itself, where suddenly the horizon levels to reveal the great tableland valley of the Upper Engadin. The 'En' of Engadin is the Romansch form of the name of the river Inn, whose long and beautiful valley, running south-west to north-east forms the key natural route through the Grisons to Austria.

Immediately beyond the pass is **Maloja**, summer resort and winter sport centre; houses and hotels line the road between the pass and the nearby lake. A walk of 15 minutes takes one to the Castello del Belvedere from which there is a splendid view back down the Val Bregaglia.

Septimer Pass Excursion Walk

The road built over the Septimer Pass in the fourteenth century is thought to have been one of the first alpine pass roads able to take vehicles. It is now only a mule track of minor importance, but in the medieval period it was much used as, in combination with the Muretto Pass to the south, it linked Chur with the Valtellina region (now Italian) which was then subject to Chur dominion.

Leave Maloja by the side road from the English church leading to the hamlet of Pila, to find the start of a footpath that climbs up alongside the first course of the river Inn to its source at Lake Lunghin (2,484m, 8,148ft) at the foot of Piz Lunghin (the triple watershed referred to previously is near here). Skirting the south of the lake the route continues up to Lunghin Pass (2,645m, 8,676ft) and then descends slightly to Septimer Pass at 2,310m (7,577ft). The walking time to this point is about $3^1/_2$ hours. At the pass turn south to traverse the Marozzo valley and reach Casaccia in $2^1/_2$ hours. There is a postbus service back to Maloja if required (Line No 940. 80).

From Maloja the road descends fairly imperceptibly in the Upper Engadin valley, which opens and levels out as far as St Moritz in an attractive landscape of forests, lakes and meadows framed by lofty and shapely mountain peaks. It crosses the river Inn (coming in left from Lake Lunghin) and skirts the left bank of Lake Sils. At the end of the 5km (3 mile) long lake is one of the villages which make up Sils, winter sports and summer resort on the alluvial plain. The road follows the Inn, which next flows into Lake Silvaplana (3km, 2 miles, long), dominated to the south by snow capped Piz Corvatsch (3,451m, 11,319ft). The well known resort of **Silvaplana** is situated on the isthmus separating the lake of the same name from the Lake of Champfer, just where the road from the Julier Pass coming from the north joins the road from Maloja. And on the opposite side of Silvaplana lake at the village of **Surlej** is the lower station of the Corvatsch cablecar line which serves the north-east slope of Piz Corvatsch (with Fuorcla Surlej its first station). The road now skirts the left bank of the smaller Lake of Champfer, divided into two basins by a pine-clad peninsula, and reaches Champfer, at the mouth of the Suvretta valley. Here the road forks. The main branch, left, leads direct to St Moritz village (St Moritz Dorf) while the right-hand branch slopes down towards the narrows of the river Inn, passing St Moritz Bad, winter sports and spa resort, beside its little lake.

St Moritz earns mention here as the destination of a Swiss postbus route from Locarno and Lugano which enables visitors without private transport to undertake in public transport most of this tour from the Ticino to the Upper Engadin. (For information ☎ Locarno: 093 33 61 15; Lugano: 091 21 95 20; St Moritz: 082 3 30 72.)

From Silvaplana Northward via Julier Pass

Road No 3 is the first section of the road to Chur, the cantonal capital of the Grisons, and is usually kept open all year round. It climbs steeply from Silvaplana in zigzags that give grand views to the south over the Bernina range and over the Engadin lakes, reaching first the Julier mountain refuge hut and then the Julier Pass (Passo del Giulio) (2,284m, 7,492ft) in its splendid alpine setting between Piz Lagrev to the south and Piz Julier to the north. The pass was used in Roman times and there are traces still of its paving, and the stumps of two Roman columns stand by the roadside.

The zigzag descent on the far side of the pass leads through a rather austere valley to Bivio, the village whose name hints at its one-time function as a staging-post at the fork where the Septimer Pass track goes off to Casaccia. From Bivio the road descends the valley, passes the artificial lake of Marmorera and continues to descend in 'steps' the Oberhalbstein valley, past **Tinizong** with its baroque church of St Blasius to the main town of the valley, **Savognin**, which shows many features of a typical modern winter sports centre, although the older parts include no less than three seventeenth-century churches worth visiting. A seasonal exhibition marks the town's associations with the nineteenth-century painter of Lombardy and the Grisons, G. Segantini. After passing some small villages there is a rapid descent to Tiefencastel, in its key position at the junction of the Albula and Giulia streams and the corresponding pass roads.

This is the point at which those travellers who have followed this excursion as part of a return homeward will probably wish to continue their journey northward to Chur and on to Zürich or some further destination.

Those doing the 'round trip' back to the Ticino will turn west from Tiefencastel. Crossing to the north side of the Albula, turn left above Mistail. The road has to negotiate the spectacularly wild Schin Gorge

The Schin gorge

Tiefencastel, at the head of the Schin gorge

(Schinschlucht) of the Albula. This it does with a series of tunnels into the south face of the gorge. The road gives a glimpse of Baldenstein Castle below, bypasses Sils-im-Domleschg, runs east of the small market-village of Thusis and joins the N13 motorway coming south from Chur along the Hinter-rhein valley.

The motorway, heading south through the tunnel and up the west bank of the Hinterrhein through an area of land reclaimed from the river flats, now enters the Via Mala, a notorious gorge of limestone cliffs, 500m (1,640ft) high. From it the motorway emerges into the open valley of Schons lying between Piz Beverin (2,998m, 9,833ft) to the west and Piz Curvèr (2,972m, 9,748ft) to the east. Halfway along the Schons valley lies the village of **Zillis** which justifies making an exit from the motorway for a visit. It has the remarkable Reformed church of St Martin which possesses the rarest wholly painted ceiling of the twelfth century, in the form of 153 painted panels attached to the roof beams. Nearby, in the village, there is also an ethnographic museum in a sixteenth-century peasant house, exhibiting tools, textiles, furniture, agricultural equipment etc.

Five kilometres (3 miles) from Zillis is **Andeer**, the main village of the district, nowadays a climatic resort. Here the motorway can be rejoined. (Some features are more readily seen from the old road, others from the new.) Soon comes the Roffla ravine with its Rhine cataract, which is better seen from the old road. The N13, shortly after passing through a tunnel, has an exit road to the Val Ferrera, which is the lovely high valley of the Averser-rhein; this scantily frequented road, after a 27km (17 mile) course in a south-easterly direction, ends at **Juf**, deemed to be the highest hamlet in Europe which is occupied all year round, at 2,133m (6,996ft).

The main road swings south-west to enter the Rheinwald valley, skirts a small reservoir and reaches the village of Splügen. Here the left-hand fork is for the Splügen Pass leading south to Chiavenna in Italy. The N13, however, here heads west, giving a distant view of the Rheinwaldhorn on the Grisons-Ticino border. Eleven kilometres (7 miles) on from Splügen the N13 enters the San Bernardino tunnel (6.6km, 4 miles, long, opened in 1967) which pierces the massif below the historic pass of the same name. (The pass honours the name of the fourteenth- to fifteenth-century preacher; it was formerly called the 'Bird Pass' (Passo Uccello) after a nearby mountain, Piz Uccello. Since the tunnel was completed the Chur-Bernardino motorway has been considered the fastest route from south Germany to northern Italy.)

Both motorway and old road have access to the village of **San Bernardino**, lying as it does beyond the tunnel. From this point onward the sweeping curves and viaducts of the motorway offer better views than the old road, including a fine view to the left of the hilltop Castello di Misox (or Mesocco) which gives its name to this valley, Val Mesolcina. At about this point too, the change of climate and vegetation from an alpine to a southern character becomes marked with the appearance of vines and mulberries. **Mesocco**, the principal place of the Val Mesolcina, is well worth a visit, although

The San Bernardino tunnel

the general appearance of the village has suffered from the motor-way constructions. The now ruined Castello di Misox, on its commanding crag above the river Moesa, was a medieval fortified place of refuge for the local population. It was extended in the twelfth century by the Counts Sax, the local magnates, and is an impressive reminder of this valley's history. The castle's outer works also take in, at the bottom of the crag, the twelfth-century church of St Maria al Castello which, with its well preserved fifteenth-century interior paintings, ranks among the most precious art treasures of the Grisons. It is easy to forget that this Mesolcina valley — which looks to the Ticino, and is Italian in language and Catholic in religion — belongs to the Grisons.

The valley exhibits some attractive waterfalls. There is a good view soon, on the right, of a particularly fine one, the Buffalora Cascade. With every passing kilometre the outlines of the villages, their Romanesque bell-towers and their other stonework are more and more evocative of the Ticino, the cantonal boundary of which is ultimately crossed shortly before the site of the Battle of Arbedo. At the next crossroads the left-hand turn leads into the suburbs of Bellinzona; the right-hand bends back north to the Gotthard; straight ahead leads shortly into the motorway N2 for Lugano.

Further Information

— Tours over the Ticino Borders —

Museums and Other Places of Interest

Gandria
Cantine di Gandria
Customs Museum
Accessible by lake-boat.
Open: April to September daily
2.30-5.30pm.
☎ 091/23 98 43

Mesocco
Church of St Maria al Castello
Wall paintings
Ask in village for keys, or
☎ 092/94 12 14 for information.

Stampa
Ciasa Granda
Val Bregaglia Museum

Open: June to mid-October daily
2-5pm.
☎ 082/4 12 92
Natural history of the valley; crafts; domestic and agricultural implements.

Zillis
Schams Valley Museum
Open: July and August daily 10am-12noon and 2-5pm; September, Sundays only.

Tourist Information Office

Grisons Cantonal Office:

Verkehrsverein Graubuenden
Alexanderstrasse 24
CH-7001 Chur
☎ 081/22 13 60

Index

ACCOMMODATION AND EATING OUT

As pioneers of catering for tourists for more than 150 years the Swiss have become known not only as highly experienced in hotel-keeping and hotel management, but also as exporters of these skills to other countries. Even so, although Switzerland can boast many examples of world-famous hotels in the international class, it is the well run family-owned hotel that is still very characteristic of Switzerland today. The kind of hotel accommodation likely to be sought by the majority of readers of this book will be a small-town inn or hotel-café-restaurant (as they often comprehensively proclaim themselves), family run, that caters for the local inhabitants having an evening meal out, a Sunday lunch or a weekly evening meeting of some local club; and where the foreign visitor can have the inestimable privilege of seeing a little of the life of the people.

Thanks to the 150 years of catering for visitors, Swiss hotel cooking is fairly international because they have exported much of it to others. The dishes they do most often and best are likely to be made from what they are best at rearing — veal and pork. With their agricultural economy based on dairy production, they also tend to favour dishes with a cheese content.

Accommodation

The Swiss Hotel Association publishes a yearly guide of 2,616 hotels and pensions which are members of the Association. The guide shows the rates addresses, telephone/telex/telefax numbers, opening dates and amenities of the various hotels. The guide is available from Swiss National Tourist Offices (SNTO).

The SNTO does not make hotel reservations. Visitors are advised to book direct with the hotel, through a travel agent or hotel representative. Advance reservations at peak times are advisable; in holiday resorts generally from July to early September, over Christmas and New Year and February to mid-March. In towns more especially during important trade fairs or other large events. Those not wishing to make advance reservations may obtain advice on arrival at local tourist offices, during business hours. Some main railway stations and airports have hotel reservation facilities.

Useful addresses to contact for accommodation in Switzerland are:

Schweizer Hotelier-Verein (SHV)   Schweizer Alpenclub (SAC)
(Swiss Hotel Association)   (Swiss Alpine Club)
Monbijoustrasse 130   Helvetiaplatz 4
3001 Berne   3005 Berne
☎ 031-50 71 11   ☎ 031-43 36 11

Currency and Credit Cards

Visitors can purchase foreign currencies, in the form of traveller's cheques or foreign bank notes, from their bank. Swiss Bankers Traveller's Cheques (in Swiss francs) are accepted in Switzerland at their face value and without deductions.

Traveller's cheques in sterling or other foreign currencies are cashed in Switzerland by banks or by official exchange offices at airports and principal railway stations, at the current rate of exchange, less commission.

The use of credit cards such as Eurocard/Mastercard, Visa, American Express and Diner's can be useful to supplement cash and travellers cheques. It should be remembered that in rural areas the use of credit cards may be infrequent or even non-existent. Eurocheques backed by the cheque guarantee card are widely accepted in Switzerland including the withdrawal of cash at banks.

The famous Swiss Franc, a symbol of neutrality and stability, is printed in notes of 10, 20, 50, 100, 500 and 1000 Swiss Francs together with $\frac{1}{2}$, 1, 2 and 5 Franc coins. There are also three coins representing less than $\frac{1}{2}$ Franc: 5, 10 and 20 Centimes.

Telephone Services

To telephone Switzerland, the international code to add is from USA 011 41, Canada 011 41, UK 010 41, Australia 0011 41. When making an international call remember to delete the first number from the area code when dialling.

Tipping

Tips are automatically included on all hotel and restaurant bills, as well as on most taxi fares. It is neither necessary nor expected to leave an extra tip.

Tourist Information Offices

The main Swiss National Tourist Offices are:

UK   **USA**
(SNTO) and Swiss Federal   SNTO
  Railways   Swiss Center
Swiss Centre, Swiss Court   608 Fifth Avenue
London W1V 8EE   New York City
☎ 071 734 1921   NY 10020
Open: 9am-5pm Monday to Friday.   ☎ 212/757 5944

Canada
SNTO
154 University Avenue
Suite 610
Toronto
Ontario M5H 3Y
☎ 416 971 9734

Local Regional Tourist Offices
It may well be worth contacting local regional tourist boards for accommodation and other details. Some countries are better organised than others, but regional offices are more likely to be used to such requests. Tourist offices are listed in the Further Information section at the end of each chapter.

Accommodation and Eating Out

❋❋❋ Expensive
❋❋   Moderate
❋   Inexpensive

Chapter 1 •
The North: From The Aare To The Rhine Falls

Accommodation

Aarau
Hotel Aarauerhof ❋❋❋
☎ 064/24 55 27
98 beds. All year.

Baden
Hotel Ochsen ❋❋
Badstrasse
☎ 056/22 52 51
50 beds. Part of a complex of hotels in the spa precinct. Rates include full board.

Brugg
Hotel Rotes Haus ❋
☎ 056/41 14 79
40 beds. All year.

Neuhausen
By Schaffhausen
Hotel Bellevue ❋❋
Above Rheinfall
Bahnhofstrasse
☎ 053/22 21 21

50 beds. All year. Terrace overlooking the Rhinefalls. Well-favoured restaurant.

Olten
Hotel Olten ❋❋
☎ 062/26 26 30
63 beds. All year.

Rapperswil
Hotel Schwanen ❋❋❋
12 Seequai
☎ 055/21 91 81
31 beds. All year. Centrally sited; historic and comfortably modernised.

Rheinfelden
Hotel Schiff am Rhein ❋❋
☎ 061/87 60 87
80 beds. All year. Quiet surroundings.

Schaffhausen
Hotel Kronenhof ❋❋
7 Kirchhofplatz
☎ 053/25 66 31
54 beds. All year.

Stein am Rhein
Hotel Adler ❋❋
Rathausplatz
☎ 054/42 61 61
42 beds. All year. At heart of Old Town, comfortably modernised interior and picturesque exterior.

Eating Out

Additional to those indicated under Acommodation entries listed above.

Olten
Bahnhofbuffet Restaurant ❀❀
Am Bahnhof 062/26 54 54
Open: until 11.30pm. Three dining-rooms. Swiss and international cuisine.

Rapperswil
Hotel Eden Restaurant ❀❀
☎ 055/27 12 21
Open: 12noon-2.30pm; 5-10.30pm. Weekly closure, Monday. High quality food in the Old Town area. Gastronomic and fish dishes.

Schaffhausen
Restaurant Gerberstube ❀❀
8 Bachstrasse
☎ 053/25 21 55
Open: 12noon-2pm, 6.30-10pm. Weekly closure, Monday. Specialises in Italian dishes.

Stein am Rhein
Restaurant Sonne ❀❀❀
127 Rathausplatz
☎ 054/41 21 28
Open: 12noon-2pm, 6-9.30pm. Weekly closure, Thursday. Fine food and fine wines at heart of town.

Chapter 2 •
The North: Around the Bodensee

Accommodation

Appenzell
Romantik Hotel Säntis ❀❀
☎ 071/87 87 22
60 beds. All year. Good restaurant; local fish dishes.

Hotel Appenzell ❀❀
Landsgemeindeplatz
☎ 071/87 42 11
31 beds. Pleasant modern hotel on town's historic square. Moderate rates. Has restaurant and café.

Arbon
Hotel Rotes Kreuz ❀❀
3 Hafenstrasse
☎ 071/46 19 14

30 beds. All year. Open situation near lake. Good value simple rooms. Restaurant offers good regional specialities.

Heiden
Hotel Krone ❀❀
☎ 071/91 11 27
50 beds. February-December.

Kreuzlingen
Hotel Bahnhof Post ❀❀
☎ 072/72 79 72
60 beds. All year. Inexpensive for its class. Restaurant with regional specialities.

Kreuzlingen-Bottighofen
Hotel Schlössli ❀❀
☎ 072/75 12 75
21 beds. February-December. In developing lake-resort adjacent Kreuzlingen.

Romanshorn
Hotel Parkhotel Inseli ❀❀❀
☎ 071/63 53 53
76 beds. All year. Sited in own grounds, peaceful. Rates moderate for this standard.

Hotel Seehotel Schweizerhaus ❀❀
☎ 071/63 42 94
26 beds. All year. Quiet lakeside position.

Rorschach
Hotel Parkhotel Waldau ❀❀❀
Seebleichestrasse
☎ 071/43 01 80
70 beds. Noted restaurant (indoor and outdoor). Has many recreational facilities.

Hotel Anker ❀❀
☎ 071/41 42 43
71 beds. All year. Facing marina.

Schwägalp (Urnäsch)
Hotel Schwägalp ❀❀
☎ 071/58 16 03
54 beds. All year.

St Gallen
Hotel Walhalla ❀❀❀
Bahnhofplatz
☎ 071/22 29 22
80 beds. All year. Conveniently situated, modernised hotel with two good restaurants.

Hotel Dom (Garni) ❀❀
22 Webergasse
☎ 071/23 20 44
59 beds. All year. No restaurant. Breakfast only.

Trogen
Hotel Krone ❋
☎ 071/94 13 04
17 beds. March-January. Simple, homely.

Unterwasser
Hotel Säntis ❋❋❋
☎ 074/5 28 11
64 beds. All year. Half-board included in reasonable rates. Popular with families.

Wildhaus
Hotel Hirschen ❋❋
☎ 074/5 22 52
130 beds. All year. Snack-bar and restaurant; many other facilities. Half-board included in rates.

Eating Out

Additional to those indicated under Accommodation entries listed above.

Appenzell
Restaurant Säntis ❋❋
At Hotel Säntis
☎ 071/87 87 22
Open: 11.30am-2pm, 6.30-10pm. Variety of menus including regional dishes; popular fixed price and *à la carte* meals.

Rorschach
Restaurant Bahnhofbuffet ❋❋
Bahnhofplatz
☎ 071/41 60 25
Lakeside terrace. Lake fish dishes.

St Gallen
Restaurant Bahnhof buffet SBB ❋❋
2 Bahnhofplatz
☎ 071/22 56 61
Open: until 11pm. Regional and international modern cuisine.

Restaurant Kongresshaus Schützengraben ❋❋
38 St Jakobstrasse
☎ 071/24 71 71
Open: until 11.30pm. Large establishment. Fondue speciality.

Chapter 3 •
Zürich

Accommodation

Rapperswil
Hotel Freihof ❋
Hauptplatz
☎ 055/27 12 79

33 beds. All year. Picturesque building with modernised interior. Good value accommodation.

Winterthur
Hotel Garten-Hotel ❋❋❋
4 Stadthausstrasse
☎ 052/71 71
90 beds. All year. Ideally situated hotel, central yet within the city park. Good restaurant too.

Hotel Krone ❋❋
49 Marktgasse
☎ 052/23 25 21
66 beds. Long established, popular. Reopens August 1993 after renovations. Situated centrally in Old Town.

Zürich
Hotel Schweizerhof ❋❋❋
7 Bahnhofplatz
☎ 01/211 86 40
150 beds. All year. Opposite main station. Mainly single rooms. Traditional grand hotel modernised. Convenient.

Hotel Ascot ❋❋❋
9 Tessinerplatz
☎ 01/201 18 00
120 beds. All year. Stylishly renovated in recent time. Also good restaurant.

Hotel Ambassador ❋❋❋
6 Falkenstrasse
01/261 76 00
70 beds. All year. Reasonable for its category. Near lake.

Hotel Glockenhof ❋❋❋
31 Sihlstrasse
☎ 01/211 56 50
166 beds. All year. Rates moderate for category and central situation convenient for tourists.

Hotel Seidenhof ❋❋
9 Sihlstrasse
☎ 01/211 65 44
142 beds. All year. Well situated and well-run by the Zürich Frauenverein (Women's League) as an alcohol-free establishment.

Hotel Bristol (Garni) ❋❋
34 Stampfenbachstrasse
☎ 01/261 84 00
100 beds. All year. Moderate rates for its category. Breakfast only catered for.

Hotel Krone-Limmatquai ❋
88 Limmatquai
40 beds. All year. Good value on this
central riverside site.

Zürich-Erlenbach
Hotel Erlibacherhof ❋
83 Seestrasse
☎ 01/910 55 22
Country inn. 34 beds. All year. Residential village along Lake Zürich. Inn
recommended for comfort and typical
regional cuisine.

Eating Out

Additional to those indicated under
Accommodation entries listed above.

Zürich
Restaurant Agnes Amberg ❋❋❋
5 Hottingerstrasse
☎ 01/251 26 26
Open: until 12.30am excluding Saturday
and Monday. Weekly closure, Sunday.
Zürich's temple of *haute cuisine*.

Restaurant Fischstube Zürichhorn ❋❋
160 Bellerivestrasse
☎ 01/422 25 20
Open: 12noon-2pm, 6-11pm. On
lakeside. First-class quality. Fish specialities, including lobster.

Restaurant Bahnhofbuffet ❋❋
Hauptbahnhof
☎ 01/211 15 10
Open: until 11.30pm. Comprises group
of restaurants beneath same roof and
suits a variety of purses and tastes.

Restaurant Le Dezaley ❋❋
7-9 Römergasse
☎ 01/251 61 29
Open: 9am-2.30pm, 5pm-12midnight.
Weekly closure, Sunday. Haunt of
French-speaking Swiss; French-Swiss
atmosphere; Vaud dishes and great
variety Vaud wines.

Restaurant Bierhalle Kropf ❋
16 In Gassen
☎ 01/221 18 05
Open: 11.30am-1.45pm, 5.45-9.45pm.
Weekly closure, Sunday. Not far from
Paradeplatz and Bahnhofstrasse.
Attracts wide range of guests. Reliable
cooking.

Restaurant Hilti Vegi ❋❋
28 Sihlstrasse
☎ 01/221 38 70
Open: 6.30-9pm. All imaginable vegetar-
ian dishes of season.

Chapter 4 •
Central Switzerland

Accommodation

Altdorf
Hotel Goldener Schlüssel ❋❋
9 Schützenstrasse
☎ 044/2 10 02
50 beds. With inexpensive restaurant. In
heart of town.

Amsteg
Hotel Stern und Post ❋❋
Gotthardstrasse
☎ 044/6 44 40
40 beds. Former post-house. Good
atmosphere and cuisine.

Brunnen
Hotel Seehotel Waldstaetterseehof ❋❋❋
Waldstaetterquai
☎ 043/33 11 33
160 beds. Grand style, own lakeside
grounds; many facilities.

Hotel Bellevue au Lac ❋❋
2 Axenstrasse
☎ 043/31 13 18
90 beds. Lakeside site, well-renovated,
has *Kursaal* (Casino) nightlife.

Hotel Ochsen ❋
Ochsen-platz
☎ 043/31 11 59
17 beds. Historic inn, hospitable, well-
run. Restaurant with good Swiss traditional fare.

Flüelen
Hotel Flüelerhof-Grill Rustico ❋❋
38 Axenstrasse
☎ 044/2 11 49
50 beds. Splendid outlook. Modern,
comfortable.

Gersau
Hotel Müller ❋❋❋
☎ 041/84 19 19
60 beds. Recently modernised. Splendid
outlook.

Luzern
Hotel Schweizerhof ❀❀❀
3 Schweizerhofplatz
☎ 041/50 22 11
214 beds. Elegant, traditional old-style.

Hotel Monopol and Metropole ❀❀❀
1 Pilatusstrasse
☎ 041/23 08 66
183 beds. Hotel restaurant.

Hotel Flora ❀❀❀
5 Seidenhofstrasse
☎ 041/24 44 44
40 beds. Modern style, central. Good
restaurant.

Hotel des Alpes ❀❀
5 Rathausquai
☎ 041/51 58 25
90 beds. Quiet situation; café-restaurant
on riverside terrace.

Tourist-Hotel ❀
12 St Karliquai
☎ 041/51 24 74
100 beds. Not far from station.

Schwyz
Hotel Wysses Rössli ❀❀❀
3 Hauptplatz
☎ 043/21 19 22
45 beds. Traditional, central situation.

Seelisberg
Hotel Bellevue ❀❀
☎ 043/31 16 46
75 beds. Spectacular site, quiet, own
grounds.

Vitznau
Hotel Seehotel Vitznauerhof ❀❀❀
Hauptstrasse
☎ 041/83 13 15
90 beds. Lakeside, on own property.

Weggis
Hotel Rössli ❀❀
2 Aegeri-strasse
☎ 041/93 11 06
30 beds. Peaceful site centrally on
lakeside road.

Eating Out

Additional to those indicated under
Accommodation entries, listed above.

Gersau
Cafe Mueller & Gero Restaurant ❀❀❀
At Hotel Mueller
☎ 041/84 19 19
Open: 11am-2pm, 5.30-9.30pm. Very
fine cuisine.

Luzern
Arbalete (Hotel Monopole) ❀❀❀
1 Pilatusstrasse
☎ 041/23 08 66
Open: 6pm-12.30am. Elegant.

Kunst- u. Kongress-Haus Restaurants ❀
Am Bahnhof
☎ 041/23 18 16
Open: 12noon-2.30pm and 6.30-11pm.
At large convention centre beside main
station; three restaurants in complex.

Chapter 5 •
Bernese Mittelland

Accommodation

Bern
Hotel Schweizerhof ❀❀❀
11 Bahnhofplatz
☎ 031/22 45 01
157 beds. Facing main station. Grand
comfort, service, in elegant surroundings. For restaurant see under
Schultheissenstube.

Hotel Hospiz zur Heimat ❀
50 Gerechtigkeitsgasse
☎ 031/22 04 36
70 beds. Perfect location for sightseeing
in Old Town, and good value.

Burgdorf
Hotel Touring Bernerhof ❀
Am Bahnhof
☎ 034/22 16 52
55 beds. Modern. At station yet reasonably quiet. Restaurants.

Entlebuch
Hotel Drei Könige ❀
☎ 041/72 12 27
24 beds. Recommended for comfort and
typical regional cuisine.

Giswil
Hotel Krone ❊❊
☎ 041/68 24 24
130 beds. Good value.

Gunten am Thunersee
Hotel Hirschen-am-See ❊❊❊
☎ 033/51 22 44
110 beds. March to October. Own grounds on lakeside adjacent lakesteamer jetty. Good cuisine.

Heiligenschwendi
Hotel Niesenblick ❊❊
☎ 033/43 27 27
25 beds. In sheltered situation in rolling foothills above Lake Thun.

Langnau im Emmental
Hotel Hirschen ❊
☎ 035/2 15 17
36 beds. Recommended for comfort and typical regional cuisine.

Merligen am Thunersee
Hotel Beatus Merligen ❊❊❊
☎ 033/51 21 21
125 beds. Own lido-beach, caters for water-sports etc.

Murten
Hotel Schiff ❊❊
☎ 037/71 27 01
30 beds. Quiet situation on lake. Comfortable. Good restaurant.

Sigriswil
Hotel Adler ❊❊
☎ 033/51 24 81
45 beds. Set on sun-terrace with splendid outlook over Lake Thun to Oberland mountains.

Thun
Hotel Freienhof ❊❊❊
3 Freienhofgasse
☎ 033/21 55 11
98 beds. Quiet location on Aare riverbank, yet central.

Hotel Elite ❊❊❊
1 Bernstrasse
☎ 033/23 28 23
72 beds. Modern, central near castle.

Trubschachen im Emmental
Hotel Hirschen ❊
☎ 035/6 51 15

10 beds. Recommended for comfort and typical regional cuisine.

Worb
Hotel Gasthof zum Löwen ❊❊
3 Enggisteinstrasse
☎ 031/83 23 03
60 beds. Handsome traditional inn building. Has good rustic yet stylish restaurant.

Eating Out

Additional to those indicated under Accommodation entries listed above.

Bern
Schultheissenstube ❊❊❊
At Hotel Schweizerhof
11 Bahnhofplatz
☎ 031/22 45 01
Open: 12noon-2pm and 6.30pm-12midnight. Weekly closure, Sunday. One of Switzerland's leading restaurants.

Goldener Schlüssel ❊❊
72 Rathausgasse
☎ 031/22 02 16
Open: 11.30am-2pm, 6.00-10.30pm. Weekly closure, Friday and Saturday evenings. Good value in typical traditional Swiss fare.

Gfeller am Bärenplatz ❊
21 Barenplatz
☎ 031/22 69 44
Open: 10.30am-8pm. A favourite for generous lunches and afternoon teas.

Thun
Bahnhofbuffet ❊❊
3 Seestrasse
☎ 033/23 22 23
Open: until 11.30pm. At station, facing lakeship quays. Fish specialities.

Chapter 6 •
Bernese Oberland

Accommodation

Adelboden
Hotel Beau-Site ❊❊❊
3715 Adelboden
☎ 033 732222

Brienz am See
Hotel Rothorn Kulm ❊
☎ 036 511221 (summer) 511232 (winter)

Grindelwald
Hotel Hirschen ❀❀
3818 Grindelwald
☎ 036 532777

Gstaad
Hotel Gstadderhof ❀❀
3780 Gstaad
☎ 030 83344

Interlaken
Victoria-Jungfrau Grand Hotel ❀❀❀
Höheweg
3800 Interlaken
☎ 036 271111

Kandersteg
Hotel Alpina ❀
☎ 033 751246

Lauenen
Hotel Alpenland ❀❀
3782 Lauenen
☎ 030 53434

Lenk
Hotel Rössli ❀
3775 Lenk
☎ 033 811225

Meiringen
Park-Hotel Sauvage ❀❀❀
3860 Meiringen
☎ 036 714141

Mürren
Hotel Jungfrau und Lodge ❀❀❀
3825 Mürren
☎ 036 552824

Wengen
Hotel Eiger ❀❀
3823 Wengen
☎ 036 551131

Wilderswil
Hotel Alpenblick ❀❀
3812 Wilderswil
☎ 036 220707

Eating Out

Adelboden
Alder Sporthotel ❀❀❀
3715 Adelboden ☎ 033 734141

Brienz am See
Bellevue ❀❀
Kienholz
3855 Brienz am See
☎ 036 511413

Diemtigtal
Hotel Rössli ❀❀
3753 Diemtigtal
☎ 033 811225

Grindelwald
Oberland ❀❀
3818 Grindelwald
☎ 036 531019

Au Rendez Vous/Le Mignon ❀❀
Haupstrasse
3818 Grindelwald
☎ 036 531181

Gstaad
Rialto ❀❀
3780 Gstaad
☎ 030 43474

Interlaken
Schuh ❀❀
Höheweg, 56
3800 Interlaken
☎ 036 229441

Burestube ❀❀❀
Höheweg, 57a
3800 Interlaken
☎ 036 226512

Meiringen
Mägisalp ❀
3860 Meiringen
☎ 036 712916

Mürren
Piz Gloria ❀
Schilthorn
3825 Mürren
☎ 036 552141
Restaurant at the top of the Schilthorn cableway 3,000m (10,000ft) above sea level, revolves to offer mountain view.

Chapter 7 •
The Valais

Accommodation

Arolla
Hotel du Pigne d'Arolla ❀❀
1986 Arolla
☎ 027 831165

Leukerbad
Hotel Bad Maison-Blanche ❀❀
3954 Leukerbad
☎ 027 621161

Martigny
Hotel de la Poste ❀❀
8 Rue de la Poste
1920 Martigny
☎ 026 221444

Münster
Hotel Diana ❀
☎ 028 731818

Saas Fee
Hotel Sasserhof ❀❀❀
3906 Sass Fee
☎ 028 573551

Sierre
Hotel Atlantic ❀❀
3960 Sierre
☎ 027 552535

Sion
Hotel Ibis ❀
Avenue Grand Champsec
1950 Sion
☎ 027 331191

Verbier
Hotel Verluisant ❀❀❀
1936 Verbier
☎ 026 316303

Visp
Hotel Mont-Cervin ❀❀
3930 Visp
☎ 028 463491

Vouvry
Hotel Edirol ❀
1896 Vouvry
☎ 025 811416

Zermatt
Grand Hotel Zermatterhof ❀❀❀
3920 Zermatt
☎ 028 463491

Zinal
Hotel Les Bouquetins ❀❀
3961 Zinal
☎ 027 652509

Eating Out

Brig
Schlosskeller ❀❀❀
3900 Brig ☎ 028 233352

Fiesch
Rustica ❀❀
3984 Fiesch
☎ 028 711635

Martigny
Lion D'Or ❀
Avenue Grand-St-Bernard 1
1920 Martigny
☎ 027 418243

Münster
Spycher ❀❀
3985 Münster
☎ 028 731777

St Maurice
Le Mazot ❀❀
1890 St Maurice
☎ 025 652157

Sierre
Piscine de Guillamo ❀
3960 Sierre
☎ 027 559775

Sion
La Croix Fédérale ❀❀❀
1950 Sion
☎ 027 221621

Stalden
Arvenstubli-Höhlgassli ❀❀
3922 Stalden
☎ 028 521256

Ulrichen
Walser ❀❀
3988 Ulrichen
☎ 028 732122

Verbier
Grange ❀❀❀
1936 Verbier
☎ 026 316431

Vouvry
Porte-du-Scex ❀❀
1896 Vouvry ☎ 025 812203

Chapter 8 •
Ticino

Accommodation

Bellinzona
Hotel Unione ❀❀
☎ 092/25 55 75
67 beds. In own grounds. Good restaurant.

Biasca
Hotel Al Giardinetto ❀❀
☎ 092/72 17 71
54 beds. Hospitable hotel. Very good and correspondingly priced restaurant.

Faido
Hotel Faido ❁
☎ 094/38 15 55
30 beds. All year.

Gandria
By Lugano
Hotel Moosmann ❁❁
☎ 091/51 72 61
55 beds. March to November. Spectacular outlook.

Gordola
Hotel La Rotonda ❁❁
☎ 093/67 36 35
35 beds. All year. Hotel garni. All rooms with facilities.

Intragna
Hotel Antico ❁
093/31 03 33
50 beds. All year.

Locarno
Hotel Muralto ❁❁❁
8 Piazza Stazione
☎ 093/33 01 81
146 beds. All year. Good central position on lake with fine views. Reasonably priced considering facilities.

Hotel Dell'Angelo ❁❁
1 Piazza Grande
☎ 093/31 81 75
100 beds. All year. Good value considering its facilities and central site.

Lugano
Hotel Bellevue au Lac ❁❁❁
10 Riva Caccia ☎ 091/54 33 33
120 beds. April to October. Central site on lakeside promenade road. Swimming pool and sun-terrace. Good cuisine.

Lugano-Paradiso
Hotel Meister ❁❁
11 Via San Salvatore
☎ 091/54 14 12
130 beds. March to November. Superior family hotel. Swimming pool in grounds. Well-equipped rooms.

Morcote
Hotel Olivella au Lac ❁❁❁
☎ 091/69 10 01
140 beds. March to December. Luxurious hotel, lakeside situation, water sports etc. Expensive. Restaurant reputed one of the best in Switzerland.

Olivone (Val Blenio)
Hotel Olivone e Posta ❁
☎ 092/70 13 66
46 beds. All year.

Piora
Hotel Lago Ritom ❁
☎ 094/38 16 16
24 beds.

Ponte Tresa
Hotel Del Pesce ❁❁
☎ 091/71 11 46
44 beds. Lakeside situation. Water sports.

Quinto-Altanca
Hotel Genziano ❁
☎ 094/38 16 16
14 beds.

Vira Gambarogno
Hotel Touring Bellavista ❁❁
☎ 093/61 11 16
110 beds. March to November. Splendid views of Lake Maggiore.

Eating Out

Additional to those indicated under accommodation entries listed above.

Faido
Albergo Pedrinis ❁❁
Piazza Fontana
☎ 094/38 12 41
Open: 11.30am-2.30pm and 6.30-10pm. Fine cuisine includes regional dishes.

Gandria/Lugano
Locanda Gandriese ❁❁
☎ 091/51 41 81
Open: 12noon-2pm and 6-10pm. Has lakeside terrace. Popular for regional dishes.

Locarno
Restaurant Saleggi ❁❁
38 Via Angelo Nessi
☎ 093/31 41 71
Open: until 12midnight. Local Ticinese cuisine.

Lugano
Locanda del Boschetto ❁❁
8 Via Boschetto
☎ 091/54 24 93
Open: 12noon-2pm and 7-10pm. Weekly closure, Monday. Good value for simple dishes of top quality.

Restaurant Monte Ceneri ❁
44 Via Nassa
☎ 091/23 33 40
Open: 11.30am-2pm and 7.30-10pm.
Family-run, popular for inexpensive
fixed-price meals.

Chapter 9 •
Over the Ticino Borders

Accommodation

Agno
Hotel La Perla ❁❁❁
Via Pestariso
☎ 091/59 39 21
238 beds. All year.

Maloja
Hotel Maloja Kulm ❁❁
☎ 082/4 31 05
43 beds. Open: May to October and
December to April. Spectacularly sited
historic hotel at pass-summit. Half-
board included in reasonable room rates.

Mendrisio
Hotel Milano ❁❁
☎ 091/46 57 41
55 beds. Open-air pool.

Ponte Tresa
Hotel Del Pesce ❁❁
Via Cantonale
☎ 091/71 11 46
44 beds. All year.

San Bernardino Villaggio
Hotel Brocco e Posta ❁❁❁
☎ 092/94 11 05
60 beds. Open: June to October, December to April. Half-board inclusive in
room rates.

Sils-Maria
Hotel Maria ❁❁
☎ 082/4 53 17
65 beds. Half-board included in room
price. Moderate. Hotel has sailing school
and ice-rink.

Silvaplana
Hotel Sonne ❁❁
☎ 082/4 81 52
80 beds. Half-board inclusive in room-price.

Splügen
Hotel Posthotel Bodenhaus ❁❁
☎ 081/62 11 21
51 beds. Open: May to October, December to April. Sun terrace, restaurant.

Thusis
Hotel Splügen ❁❁
081/81 41 51
60 beds. All year.

Tiefencastel
Hotel Albula ❁❁
☎ 081/71 11 21
85 beds. Open: December to October.

Eating Out

Additional to those indicated under
accommodation entries listed above.

Sils-Maria
Restaurant Waldhaus ❁❁
Restaurant of de-luxe Hotel Waldhaus
☎ 082/4 53 31
Open: 12noon-2.15pm and 7-9.30pm.
Highly regarded menus. Fixed-price
meals not expensive considering stand-
ards of establishment.

Silvaplana
Restaurant Rustica ❁❁
Chesa Munterots
☎ 082/4 81 66
Open: until 11pm. Closed Monday.
Local cuisine. Private parking.

A Note To The Reader

The accommodation and eating out lists in this book are based upon
the authors' own experiences and therefore may contain an element of
subjective opinion. The contents of this book are believed correct at the
time of publication but details given may change. We welcome any
information to ensure accuracy in this guide book and to help keep it
up-to-date.
Please write to The Editor, Moorland Publishing Co Ltd,
Moor Farm Road, Airfield Estate, Ashbourne, Derbyshire,
DE6 1HD, England.

 American and Canadian readers
please write to The Editor,
The Globe Pequot Press,
6 Business Park Road,
PO Box 833, Old Saybrook,
Connecticut 06475, USA.

MPC

Discover a New World
with
Off The Beaten Track Travel Guides

Austria
Explore the quiet valleys of Bregenzerwald in the west to
Carinthia and Burgenland in the east. From picturesque
villages in the Tannheimertal to the castles north of
Klagenfurt, including Burg Hochosterwitz. This dramatic
castle with its many gates stands on a 450ft high limestone
cliff and was built to withstand the Turkish army by the
man who brought the original Spanish horses to Austria.

Britain
Yes, there are places off the beaten track in even the more
populated areas of Britain. Even in the heavily visited
national parks there are beautiful places you could easily
miss — areas well known to locals but not visitors. This book
guides you to such regions to make your visit memorable.

Greece
Brimming with suggested excursions that range from
climbing Mitikas, the highest peak of Mount Olympus, the
abode of Zeus, to Monemvassia, a fortified medieval town
with extensive ruins of a former castle. This book enables
you to mix a restful holiday in the sun with the fascinating
culture and countryside or rural Greece.

Italy
Beyond the artistic wealth of Rome or Florence and the hill
towns of Tuscany lie many fascinating areas of this ancient
country just waiting to be discovered. From medieval towns
such as Ceriana in the Armea valley to quiet and
spectacular areas of the Italian Lakes and the Dolomites
further to the east. At the southern end of the country, the
book explores Calabria, the 'toe' of Italy as well as Sicily,
opening up a whole 'new' area.

Germany

Visit the little market town of Windorf on the north bank of the Danube (with its nature reserve) or the picturesque upper Danube Valley, which even most German's never visit! Or go further north to the Taubertal. Downstream of famous Rothenburg with its medieval castle walls are red sandstone-built villages to explore with such gems as the carved altar in Creglingen church, the finest work by Tilman Riemenschneider — the Master Carver of the Middle Ages. This book includes five areas in the former East Germany.

Portugal

Most visitors to Portugal head to the Algarve and its famous beaches, but even the eastern Algarve is relatively quiet compared to the more popular western area. However, the book also covers the attractive areas of northern Portugal where only the more discerning independent travellers may be found enjoying the delights of this lovely country.

Scandinavia

Covers Norway, Denmark, Sweden and Finland. There is so much to see in these countries that it is all too easy to concentrate on the main tourist areas. That would mean missing so many memorable places that are well worth visiting. For instance, there are still about sixty Viking churches that survive in Norway. Alternatively many private castles and even palaces in Denmark open their gardens to visitors. Here is your guide to ensure that you enjoy the Scandinavian experience to the full.

Spain

From the unique landscape of the Ebrodelta in Catalonia to the majestic Picos d'Europa in the north, the reader is presented with numerous things to see and exciting things to do. With the mix of cultures and climates, there are many possibilities for an endearing holiday for the independent traveller.

Switzerland

Switzerland offers much more than the high mountains and deep valleys with which it is traditionally associated. This book covers lesser known areas of the high mountains — with suggested walks in some cases. It also covers Ticino, the Swiss Lakeland area near to the Italian Lakes and tours over the border into the latter. In the north, the book covers the lesser known areas between Zurich and the Rhine Falls, plus the Lake Constance area, with its lovely little towns like Rorschach, on the edge of the lake.

Forthcoming:

Northern France
Southern France

Touring the ancient fishing port of Guethary, hiking in the Pyrennees and visiting the old archway in Vaucoulers (through which Joan of Arc led her troops), are just a few of the many opportunities these two books present.

Scotland

Heather-clad mountains, baronian castles and magnificent coastal scenery, all combined with a rich historical heritage, combine to make this an ideal 'off the beaten track' destination.

Ireland

Ireland not only has a dramatic coastline, quiet fishing harbours and unspoilt rural villages, but also the natural friendliness of its easy-going people. *Off the Beaten Track Ireland* will lead you to a memorable holiday in a country where the pace of life is more relaxing and definitely not hectic.

TRAVEL GUIDE LIST

Airline/Ferry details ....
....
....
....
....

Telephone No. ....

Tickets arrived ☐

Travel insurance ordered ☐

Car hire details ....
....
....

Visas arrived ☐

Passport ☐

Currency ☐

Travellers cheques ☐

Eurocheques ☐

Accommodation address ....
....
....
....

Telephone No. ....

Booking confirmed ☐

Maps required ....
....
....

DAILY ITINERARY

Date ....

Places visited

.. . .
.. . .
.. . .
.. . .
.. . .
.. . .

Accommodation ....
....
....
Telephone No. ....

Booking confirmed ☐

Notes:

DAILY ITINERARY

Date ....

Places visited

....
....
....
....
....
....

Accommodation ....

....

....

Telephone No. ....

Booking confirmed ☐

Notes: